Politeness Across Cultures

Also by Francesca Bargiela-Chiappini

THE HANDBOOK OF BUSINESS DISCOURSE (editor, 2009)

FACE, COMMUNICATION AND SOCIAL INTERACTION (co-editor with Michael Haugh, 2009)

BUSINESS DISCOURSE (with Catherine Nickerson and Brigitte Planken, 2007)

ASIAN BUSINESS DISCOURSE(S) (co-editor with Maurizio Gotti, 2005)

WRITING BUSINESS: GENRES, MEDIA AND DISCOURSES (co-editor with Catherine Nickerson, 1999)

THE LANGUAGES OF BUSINESS: AN INTERNATIONAL PERSPECTIVE (co-editor with Sandra J. Harris, 1997)

MANAGING LANGUAGE: THE DISCOURSE OF CORPORATE MEETINGS (with Sandra J. Harris, 1997)

Also by Dániel Z. Kádár

POLITENESS IN CHINA AND JAPAN (with Michael Haugh, forthcoming)

CHINESE DISCOURSE AND INTERACTION (co-editor with Yuling Pan, 2011)

POLITENESS IN EAST ASIA (co-editor with Sara Mills, 2011)

UNDERSTANDING HISTORICAL (IM)POLITENESS (co-editor with Marcel Bax, 2011)

POLITENESS IN HISTORICAL AND CONTEMPORARY CHINESE (with Yuling Pan, 2010)

HISTORICAL CHINESE LETTER WRITING (2010)

HISTORICAL (IM)POLITENESS (co-editor with Jonathan Culpeper, 2010)

MODEL LETTERS IN LATE IMPERIAL CHINA: 60 SELECTED EPISTLES FROM 'LETTERS OF SNOW SWAN RETREAT' (2009)

IT'S THE DRAGON'S TURN: CHINESE INSTITUTIONAL DISCOURSES (co-editor with Hao Sun, 2008)

TERMS OF (IM)POLITENESS: A STUDY OF THE COMMUNICATIONAL PROPERTIES OF TRADITIONAL CHINESE (IM)POLITE TERMS OF ADDRESS (2007)

Politeness Across Cultures

Edited by

Francesca Bargiela-Chiappini
Honorary Associate Professor, University of Warwick, UK

and

Dániel Z. Kádár
Research Fellow, Hungarian Academy of Sciences
Associate Professor, Asia University, Taiwan

palgrave
macmillan

First published 2011 by
PALGRAVE MACMILLAN

Palgrave Macmillan in the UK is an imprint of Macmillan Publishers Limited, registered in England, company number 785998, of Houndmills, Basingstoke, Hampshire RG21 6XS.

Palgrave Macmillan in the US is a division of St Martin's Press LLC, 175 Fifth Avenue, New York, NY 10010.

Palgrave Macmillan is the global academic imprint of the above companies and has companies and representatives throughout the world.

Palgrave® and Macmillan® are registered trademarks in the United States, the United Kingdom, Europe and other countries.

ISBN: 978–0–230–23648–6 hardback

This book is printed on paper suitable for recycling and made from fully managed and sustained forest sources. Logging, pulping and manufacturing processes are expected to conform to the environmental regulations of the country of origin.

A catalogue record for this book is available from the British Library.

A catalog record for this book is available from the Library of Congress.

10 9 8 7 6 5 4 3 2 1
20 19 18 17 16 15 14 13 12 11

Printed and bound in Great Britain by
CPI Antony Rowe, Chippenham and Eastbourne

Contents

Acknowledgements vii

Foreword by Chris Christie ix

Notes on Contributors xi

1 Introduction: Politeness Research In and Across Cultures 1
Dániel Z. Kádár and Francesca Bargiela-Chiappini

Part I: Face in Interaction

2 Some Issues with the Concept of Face: When, What, How and How Much? 17
Jim O'Driscoll

3 On the Concept of Face and Politeness 42
Maria Sifianou

Part II: Im/politeness in Intracultural Interaction

4 Im/politeness, Rapport Management and Workplace Culture: Truckers Performing Masculinities on Canadian Ice-Roads 61
Louise Mullany

5 Why Are Israeli Children Better at Settling Disputes Than Israeli Politicians? 85
Zohar Kampf and Shoshana Blum-Kulka

6 Korean Honorifics and 'Revealed', 'Ignored' and 'Suppressed' Aspects of Korean Culture and Politeness 106
Lucien Brown

7 Modern Chinese Politeness Revisited 128
Yueguo Gu

8 Modes of Address Between Female Staff in Georgian Professional Discourse: Medical and Academic Contexts 149
Manana Rusieshvili

Part III: Im/politeness and Face: Intercultural and Crosscultural Perspectives

9 Indirectness in Zimbabwean English: A Study of Intercultural Communication in the UK 171
Karen Grainger

10 On Im/politeness Behind the Iron Curtain 194
Eva Ogiermann and Małgorzata Suszczyńska

11 Conflict, Culture and Face 216
Yasuhisa Watanabe

12 Cultural Variability in Face Interpretation and Management 237
Ewa Bogdanowska-Jakubowska

Epilogue by Sandra Harris 258

Index of Names 267

Index of Subjects 272

Acknowledgements

We would like to express our gratitude to the following colleagues who generously acted as reviewers: Kate Beeching, Ronald Carter, Chris Christie, Jonathan Culpeper, Bethan Davies, Holly Didi-Ogren, Sandra Harris, Michael Haugh, Thomas Holtgraves, Kathryn M. Howard, Noriko Inagaki, Alan H. Kim, Kenneth Kong, Miriam Locher, Leyla Marti, Andrew Merrison, Sara Mills, Shigeko Okamoto, Annick Paternoster and Şükriye Ruhi. We are particularly grateful to Chris Christie and Sandra Harris for agreeing to write the Preface and the Epilogue, respectively.

We would also like to thank Priyanka Gibbons and her colleagues at Palgrave Macmillan for their support in completing this project.

Acknowledgements

Foreword

In recent years there has been an urgent need for a volume that focuses on politeness phenomena across cultures that goes beyond the more heavily studied European languages but that, in doing so, also critically engages with the theoretical developments in politeness research that have proliferated during this time. Although the postmodern turn, in particular, has acted as a corrective to the flattening out and sometimes erasure of key aspects of cultural difference in some of the projects that adopted earlier models of politeness, recent theoretical developments have presented other problems for research in the field, such as difficulties in adequately operationalising some of the analytical concepts new frameworks have made available. Indeed, there has been a danger of a new, sometimes insufficiently questioned, orthodoxy overtaking politeness research that has had the potential to close down rather than open up the scope of politeness scholarship. The richness of the data and the analysis presented in this volume is therefore particularly welcome because it offers an evidence-based body of work that is used by the contributors in this volume – or else has the potential to be used in future scholarship – to direct important questions at these newer paradigms. As such, the volume provides both the grounds and the impetus for the current debates to move on so that new and previously unconsidered questions can be asked about what is meant by the terms 'culture', 'face' and 'politeness' and what is the relationship between them.

In particular, many of the chapters in this volume prepare the ground for a more informed engagement with the debates about first and second order notions of politeness and of face that have been generated by the recent politeness frameworks. These are key issues for any engagement with interactions across cultures: if there is not some sense that related phenomena are being addressed within and across a cultural divide, the comparisons or contrasts that scholarship brings into view can have no relevance. While evaluations of the relative merits and validity of etic and emic accounts of politeness phenomena are still being played out in the literature, for politeness research to take place at all it is necessary to be able to use the abstract term 'politeness' as though writer and reader were able to assign a meaningful concept to that term. At some level, then, a tacit acceptance of a second order notion of politeness is a necessary precondition of any politeness research, and in particular of politeness research that engages with cultural difference. This may actually mean that research into politeness across cultures, in resting on such a precarious axiom, is itself a precarious enterprise. However, the extent to which the authors in this volume are able to articulate a case for seeing, in the specific cultural contexts they are addressing and in other contexts, a sufficient correspondence between conceptualisations of behaviour and how that behaviour is evaluated indicates that there are solid grounds for accepting such a precondition. And the pay-off for accepting it is that the studies here are able to bring into view a wealth of ways of understanding culture-specific perceptions and behaviours that do not underplay variation in either the cultures under discussion or the conceptualisations of face and politeness they are engaging with.

The editors of this volume, in bringing together chapters that foreground heterogeneity in the conceptualisation and realisation of face and politeness and a willingness to engage with all of the attendant issues that this raises, offer a very welcome addition to existing politeness scholarship, and a gift to future scholarship in the field.

Chris Christie
Loughborough University

Notes on Contributors

Francesca Bargiela-Chiappini is co-editor of the *Journal of Politeness Research*. Her recent publications include an edited volume (2009) and a special journal issue on 'Face' (2010), both with Michael Haugh. She is Honorary Assistant Professor in the Centre for Applied Linguistics at the University of Warwick.

Shoshana Blum-Kulka is Professor Emerita in the Department of Communication and School of Education at The Hebrew University of Jerusalem. Her research interests include media discourse, political discourse, cross-cultural pragmatics, pragmatic development in first and second languages and family discourse.

Ewa Bogdanowska-Jakubowska is Assistant Professor in the Institute of English at the University of Silesia in Katowice. Her main research interests are sociolinguistics, crosscultural communication and politeness theory. She is author of the book *Cross-Cultural Dimensions of Politeness in the Case of Polish and English* (1999) and of several papers on politeness and face.

Lucien Brown is Research Fellow in the Centre of Korean Studies at the School of Oriental and African Studies, London. His research interests include language acquisition, sociopragmatics and politeness in Korean. He is particularly interested in exploring the contextual use of Korean honorifics by both native and non-native speakers.

Chris Christie of Loughborough University is a founder member of the Linguistic Politeness Research Group and was editor-in-chief of the *Journal of Politeness Research* from 2005 to 2010. She has published on politeness, gender and pragmatics.

Karen Grainger obtained her PhD in 1993 from the University of Wales and is currently Senior Lecturer in Communication at Sheffield Hallam University. She researches and publishes in the areas of interaction in health care settings, intercultural pragmatics, politeness theory, computer-mediated interaction and educational sociolinguistics. She is co-editor of the *Journal of Politeness Research*.

Yueguo Gu, MA, PhD (Lancaster), is Research Professor and Head of the Contemporary Linguistics Department at the Chinese Academy of

Social Sciences. His research interests include pragmatics, discourse analysis, corpus linguistics, rhetoric and online education. He is the holder of a special professorship at the University of Nottingham and Academic Advisor for The Hong Kong Polytechnic University. His personal website can be found at www.multimodal.cn.

Sandra Harris is Professor Emeritus at Nottingham Trent University. She has a long-standing interest in institutional discourse, particularly in the courtroom. She has contributed a large number of articles and chapters to international journals and edited collections. Her current research interest is in linguistic im/politeness, especially in institutional and political contexts, and she is one of the original editors of the *Journal of Politeness Research.*

Dániel Z. Kádár is Research Fellow at the Research Institute for Linguistics of the Hungarian Academy of Sciences and Associate Professor at Asia University, Taiwan. His main fields of interest include linguistic politeness, sociopragmatics and the sociocultural development of politeness in the East Asian region. His recent publications include *Politeness in East Asia* (with Sara Mills, 2010) and *Politeness in Historical and Contemporary Chinese* (with Yuling Pan, 2010), as well as papers in journals of international standing.

Zohar Kampf is Lecturer in the Department of Communication and Journalism at the Hebrew University of Jerusalem. His main research interest is the linkage between language, media and politics. He has published articles in leading journals in the areas of discourse analysis, political communication, visual culture and journalism.

Louise Mullany is Associate Professor of Sociolinguistics in the School of English Studies, University of Nottingham. Her research focuses on sociolinguistic and pragmatic approaches to discourse in institutional and professional contexts. Recent publications include *Gendered Discourse in the Professional Workplace* (2007) and the co-authored *Introducing English Language* (with Peter Stockwell, 2010).

Jim O'Driscoll, BA (Cambridge 1974), MA (Essex 1986), PhD (Ghent 1999), has several research interests concerning language-in-situated-use. His publications on the concept of face have appeared in *Journal of Pragmatics, Multilingua, Journal of Politeness Research and Intercultural Pragmatics*. He is also the author of *Britain: for Learners of English.*

Eva Ogiermann is Lecturer in Intercultural Communication at the University of Surrey. Her main research interests are pragmatics, sociolinguistics, politeness theories, language and gender, and conversation analysis. Most of her work takes a contrastive approach and centres on the question of the culture-specificity of language use.

Manana Rusieshvili is Full Professor and Head of the English Department and Coordinator of Western Philology at Tbilisi State University and President of the English Teachers' Association of Georgia. She has published more than forty works in Georgian, English and Russian, among which are one monograph and several textbooks for English students.

Maria Sifianou is Professor at the University of Athens. Her publications include *Politeness Phenomena in England and Greece* (1999), *Discourse Analysis* (2001) and a number of articles. She has co-edited *Themes in Greek Linguistics* (1994, with Irene Philippaki-Warburton, Katerina Nicokidis) and *Linguistic Politeness across Boundaries* (2001, with Arin Bayraktaroğlu), among other books. Her main research interests include politeness phenomena and discourse analysis.

Małgorzata Suszczyńska teaches sociopragmatics and conversational analysis at the University of Szeged, Hungary. Her main research interests are linguistic im/politeness and gender and cross and intercultural pragmatics. She has done research on apology and remedial work in Hungarian, also in comparison with Polish and English.

Yasuhisa Watanabe is Lecturer in Japanese at the University of Melbourne. His research interests include face and politeness, business communication, second language acquisition and CALL. His current projects involve the study of face and politeness in Japanese multiparty business communication and face of language learners in online discussion fora.

1
Introduction: Politeness Research In and Across Cultures

Dániel Z. Kádár and Francesca Bargiela-Chiappini

This volume includes essays on face and politeness in a wide range of cultures. While previous monographs on politeness have tended to concentrate on one or sometimes two languages, the present volume utilises data drawn from as many as nine languages, including some 'key languages' in politeness research such as English and Japanese, as well as some lesser-studied languages, such as Georgian.

Before introducing the goals, methodology and contents of this collection, we will briefly discuss ways in which 'culture' is represented in contemporary politeness studies, in comparision with its theorisation in other fields (Lévi-Strauss 1955, Hodder 1982). This selective retrospective will place the present volume in the context of current debates on politeness.

1. Introduction: politeness research and culture

Many would argue that politeness research is an independent field in communication studies. Since the 1970s and the seminal publications by Robin T. Lakoff (1973, 1977) research on linguistic politeness has been of interest to many scholars in fields such as pragmatics, sociolinguistics, psycholinguistics, language philosophy and discourse analysis. During the past four decades, hundreds of papers and dozens of monographs have been published on both politeness and impoliteness (cf. Watts 2003). Now politeness research has its own dedicated journal (*Journal of Politeness Research*, Berlin: Mouton de Gruyter) and there are annual conferences devoted to both politeness and impoliteness, while the Linguistic Politeness Research Group (LPRG) has a list of over 200 members worldwide.[1]

One could rightly ask why politeness is so intriguing to many scholars investigating human communication: politeness is arguably an important aspect of human interaction, but is a topic that is rarely mentioned in debates on metapragmatics in contemporary societies – although there are cases when politeness does make the headlines.[2] More precisely, as noted by Mills and Kádár (2011), if politeness is discussed at all outside academia, it is most often referred to as a phenomenon in decline across modern societies. Thus, politeness cannot compete with, for instance, popular interest in graffiti discourse (Adams and Winter 1997); mainstream debates on academic politeness research seem to have failed to capture the imagination and to resonate with the everyday experience of the proverbial man or woman in the street.

A possible explanation for this state of affairs is that politeness – along with humour, impoliteness and a few other unique aspects of human interaction designated as interactional 'principles' by Geoffrey Leech (1983) – is among the most abstract aspects of communication. As ethologists argue, animals can convey complex messages such as the location of a tree in the case of bees (Endler 1993). The phenomenon of politeness, however, is *uniquely* human: animals can communicate aggression, submission or friendliness, but they cannot communicate politeness, simply because it is an abstract message related to the other or the *alter*, and not to the *ego* (Bax 2010, 2011). And, because politeness is part of the common behavioural heritage of humanity, it is *culturally* as diverse as the human race is: since its earliest studies, politeness has been discussed as a 'culture-specific phenomenon'.

In Lakoff's research (cited above) – the first influential work devoted to this issue and inspired by Grice's 'Cooperative Principle' (Grice 1975) – politeness appears as a phenomenon by means of which *cultures* can be categorised, or vice versa, which can be categorised according to cultures. Lakoff claimed that politeness serves to avoid conflict, which legitimises the flouting of the maxims of the Cooperative Principle, that is, the ways in which people are assumed to convey information logically in communication – though according to Lakoff politeness can also be generated without conflicting with the Cooperative Principle. Whenever a speaker flouts the norms of cooperation in a context that necessitates politeness, the interlocutor will infer that the speaker has done so due to politeness considerations. There are three rules for conflict avoidance: (1) distance, (2) deference and (3) camaraderie. *Cultures* can be categorised depending on which of the rules are more prominent, for example, British culture gives prominence to 'distance', Japanese culture prefers 'deference', while Australian culture is often described as based on 'camaraderie'.

Robin Lakoff is also remembered for describing the workings of politeness beyond a particular language; in other words, hers is the first universal politeness framework or politeness theory in the strict sense of the word. Lakoff's was soon followed by another very influential theoretical contribution and now a classic of politeness: through their work, Penelope Brown and Stephen Levinson (1978, 1987) shaped the development of the field for at least two decades. Following Lakoff, Brown and Levinson also defined politeness in terms of conflict avoidance based on the Cooperative Principle, but they approached the issue of universality differently: they elaborated different concepts by means of which politeness can be described *across cultures*. Predictably, it was not long before their framework was subjected to criticism: non-Western scholars – most importantly Ide (1989), Gu (1990) and Nwoye (1992) – argued, based on data from their respective cultures, that Brown and Levinson's framework could not account for many *culture-specific* manifestations of linguistic politeness.

In summary, due to its pervasiveness in human communication politeness continues to be a topic of interest to many researchers in a range of disciplines; not only that, its situated nature has implicated politeness research with culture, often as a defining analytical dimension. It is thus not surprising that the publication of Gino Eelen's *A Critique of Politeness Theories* (2001) should stir much debate and open a new chapter in politeness studies. In his illuminating discussion of the weaknesses of the then-dominating approaches to politeness, Eelen argued that politeness researchers needed to abandon the notion of 'culture' because it is too vague. As Eelen (2001: 173) notes:

> [...] in the practice of reasoning and exemplifying, the notion of "culture" tends to become rather blurred. [...] A notion that can simultaneously denote any group of people based on any (combination of) characteristic(s) loses its operational value.

Eelen's critique was justified: until the publication of his monograph many politeness researchers had treated 'culture' as a normative concept, talking about the proper 'rules' of politeness in British, Japanese, Chinese etc. culture. Some researchers such as Richard Watts (e.g. Watts 1989) had taken a relatively cautious stance on this question, while many others (in particular those who had criticised Brown and Levinson for their culture-specific data) regarded culture – even if implicitly – as a normative concept. This is now a rather difficult stance to defend as the concept of 'culture' has been subjected to intensive critique in the humanities and social sciences and it has therefore been stripped of much of its original essentialist character (see Bargiela-Chiappini 2009 for an appraisal of ongoing debates). Eelen's problematisation of 'culture' has proved to be influential: post-2000 frameworks of linguistic politeness tend to treat culture more critically.

Contemporary analytical frameworks are the product of a discursive theorisation of linguistic politeness; they are also widely referred to as 'postmodern', although this designation can be problematic (cf. Kádár 2010, 2011). While this development in politeness research can be attributed to Eelen (2001) it was soon embraced by other influential thinkers in the field such as Mills (2003), Watts (2003), Locher (2004), Terkourafi (2005), Locher and Watts (2008) and Bousfield (2008) and continues to be reflected in collections such as Bousfield and Locher (2007) and Kádár and Mills (2011). In fact, intimations of discursive approaches can already be found in Watts (1989) but it was not until the 2000s that these approaches began to gain momentum. While discursive (or postmodern) researchers use diverse methodologies and terminologies, they share some basic concepts which differentiate their work from other approaches to politeness. Firstly, the 'discursive school', as its name makes evident, analyses politeness as a phenomenon traceable in longer fragments of authentic interactions. This is in contrast with previous research inspired by Brown and Levinson, which was predominantly based on brief examples, often constructed by the researchers.

Secondly, within longer discourse fragments, discursive researchers focus not only on the speaker's production of certain utterances but also on the hearer's evaluation of these utterances. As Eelen notes, "in everyday practice im/politeness occurs not so much when the speaker produces behaviour but rather when the hearer evaluates that behaviour" (Eelen 2001: 109).

Thirdly, the discursive perspective is careful to differentiate between interactants' and researcher's interpretations of politeness, labelling the former 'first-order' politeness and the latter 'second-order' politeness. As discursive scholars argue, researchers are inevitably influenced by their own experience and stereotypical knowledge when analysing politeness, therefore excluding the researcher's evaluation from the analysis is certainly an aim in this type of approach. Researchers' influence on the analysis is also problematic whenever they consciously or unconsciously enforce their own understanding of 'politeness' over 'lay' interpretations by common language users, thus leading to the exclusion of potentially insightful contributions.

In order to promote a more comprehensive and sophisticated interpretation of situated politeness, researchers need to focus on lay interpretations (of politeness) by exploring hearer's and speaker's evaluations in longer fragments of discourse and furthering second-order politeness understanding.

As the discussion thus far suggests, in discursive approaches to politeness 'culture' *as a normative concept* plays a far lesser role than in earlier analytical frameworks. Since many discursive theorists focus on interactions within diverse contexts, 'culture' has now been put in its proper place, as it were. Culture now tends to be regarded as a micro-level concept, according to which interactants make their own (or their community's) culture relevant in interaction. In other words, culture no longer occurs as a higher-order governing concept but it becomes activated and diffused in interaction and may also help us interpret personal behavioural features of the interactants. Discursive researchers do not deny the importance of the notion of culture but apply it with due qualifications. As Mills and Kádár (2011) argue:

> the relationship between culture and politeness can in fact be studied but should be approached with some caution. We believe that it is possible to critically study politeness in [...cultural] settings, provided that one refrains from generalising statements based on the language practices of certain dominant groups or stereotypes of those groups. In other words, the dominant politeness norms of these areas can be faithfully represented as long as it is not claimed that they are absolute norms, and as long as other "norms" are discussed in relation to them.

For the discursive researcher culture is a dynamic and complex set of values which become visible in interaction as they influence the interactants' behaviour. Culture is also subject to ideological challenges and changes and, therefore, it is in continuous flux.

While the re-interpretation of the notion of 'culture' brought politeness research closer to other disciplines such as cultural anthropology, culture remains a problematic concept in the field for one other reason: so far, few 'cultures' have been studied from a discursive perspective. In fact, most of the discursive studies use English data, apart from a few exceptions such as Geyer (2007), Kerbrat-Orecchioni (2006) and Mills and Kádár (2011). The aim of the present collection of essays is to partly fill a gap in the literature by showcasing analyses of lesser studied languages and communities.

2. Objectives and structure of the volume

2.1. Objectives

The present volume aims to contribute to the field of politeness research, intercultural and crosscultural communication, cultural studies, cultural anthropology and cultural psychology by providing a selection of newly commissioned essays on 'culturally situated' politeness practices. The tradition of crosscultural studies of politeness includes a small number of titles: Hayashi and Minami's (1974) *Sekai no keigo* 世界の敬語 (*Politeness in Various Languages*), Lakoff and Ide's (2006) *Broadening the Horizon of Linguistic Politeness*, Hickey and Stewart's (2005) *Politeness in Europe* and Kádár and Mills' (2011) *Politeness in East Asia*. As far as we are aware, these four volumes are the only book-length publications to overview politeness in a range of cultures.

An innovative feature of the present volume is the inclusion of discursive analyses of politeness and face in a range of diverse cultures. The cultural breadth in Hayashi and Minami (1974) is noteworthy but their analytical approach now appears both dated and prescriptive. Many of the essays in Lakoff and Ide (2006) do not reflect recent developments in linguistic politeness research. Hickey and Stewart (2005) focus on politeness in European cultures and therefore their scope is limited to 'western' cultures. Finally, Kádár and Mills' (2011) is the only collection to apply a discursive approach to politeness in a range of cultures but focuses exclusively on the East Asian region.

The essays in this volume are quite diverse in their qualitative approaches to linguistic politeness. Some authors (e.g. Grainger and Mullany) apply a discursive approach, while others (e.g. Gu) propose an approach to politeness that combines discursive theory with a phenomenological epistemology. Others yet (e.g. Ogiermann and Suszczyńska) take a more descriptive (historical) approach to politeness. The first two essays do not explore linguistic politeness per se but concentrate on face, which some would consider the most important social-psychological factor *behind* polite behaviour. The contributors acknowledge the importance of 'culture' in their treatment of politeness behaviour as a (culture-)situated activity, but avoid engaging with 'culture' as a higher-order normative concept.

Importantly, the present volume was not conceived as a handbook of politeness across cultures. Such a project would require a book series. The essays in this volume have been commissioned to include analyses of politeness in both widely studied 'cultures' such as Japanese (Watanabe), Chinese (Gu), British (Grainger, O'Driscoll), Israeli (Kampf and Blum-Kulka) and Greek (Sifianou), and in less-researched cultures such as Korean (Brown), Canadian (Mullany), Polish and Hungarian (Bogdanowska-Jakubowska, Ogiermann and Suszczyńska) and Georgian (Rusieshvili). It is hoped that by providing essays on varied and distant cultural environments, the reader will gain some new insights into the *complexity* and *diversity* of politeness phenomena.

Finally, the book analyses the interaction between culture and politeness by focusing on: (1) face and politeness, (2) politeness in intracultural contexts and (3) politeness in intercultural contexts and crosscultural perspectives. The rationale behind this tripartite structure is discussed in the next section.

2.2. Structure

This volume aims to contribute to the theorisation of politeness by providing a multi-dimensional analysis of the culture-politeness interface.

The chapters in Part I approach the cultural variation of politeness from the theoretical vantage point of face, which is arguably a basic anthropological construct in the study of politeness across, as well as within, cultures. The opening chapter (O'Driscoll) reviews the concept of face, while the second contribution (Sifianou) studies the connection between face and polite behaviour as exemplified in the Greek language and culture.

Against this background, Part II introduces the reader to politeness phenomena in intracultural contexts. While comprehensiveness is beyond the scope of a single volume, the editors have selected chapters *representative* of cultures that are likely to appeal to both seasoned politeness scholars and newcomers to the field. Thus, the essays in this section overview aspects of intracultural 'polite behaviour' in a varied selection of languages and cultural communities. They include: an exploration of the communication norms of a Community of Practice (Wenger 1998) from the perspective of gender and politeness (Mullany); a comparison of communicative norms and practices in two very different groups in Israel (Kampf and Blum-Kulka); a critical examination of the complexity of seemingly uniform (grammatically encoded) sociopragmatic phenomena such as honorifics in Korean (Brown); a reinterpretation of politeness in Chinese (Gu); and an investigation of differences in discursive practices in two professional contexts in an under-studied language, Georgian (Rusieshvili).

Finally, the chapters in Part III offer insights from intercultural and crosscultural perspectives on politeness and face. The first chapter (Grainger) looks at politeness strategies of Zimbabwean speakers of

English in Britain while Ogiermann and Suszczyńska compare politeness in Poland and Hungary from a longitudinal perspective. The last two chapters examine the relevance of face in situated interactions: Watanabe analyses facework in an intercultural encounter in Australia while Bogdanowska-Jakubowska compares face in American and Polish situations.

In the Epilogue, Sandra Harris shares her reflections on the contribution made by the collection and suggests avenues for future research.

3. Chapter contents

In this section we briefly overview the volume contents. In the opening chapter Jim O'Driscoll revisits the concept of face, thus providing a theoretical framing for some of the discussions in the volume. Face is known as a pivotal socio-psychological factor behind politeness behaviour: self-esteem and acknowledgement of the other's self-esteem is a basic rationale for 'wrapping up' messages in a polite way. The etic concept of face derives from a Chinese emic notion recovered by Goffman (1955/1967); following a period of relative neglect, since the 1970s face has become a topic of singular importance within politeness studies. One of the reasons for this development could be that face is interpreted differently across cultures and the cultural variability of this socio-psychological construct manifests itself also in the (crosscultural) diversity of politeness at behavioural level. O'Driscoll reinterprets the notion of face by delving into its theoretical complexity; therefore his contribution has important implications for future empirical studies: seeing face as 'make-up', to use the author's metaphor, that is, a 'put on' and ephemeral phenomenon, warns us against accepting uncritically culture-based stereotypes of face.

Maria Sifianou's study blends face research and politeness research by first exploring the conceptualisation of face and then considering the relationship of face to politeness. Sifianou's discussion works well as a 'bridge' between theoretical politeness research and culture-situated data analysis in that the author explores metaphorical expressions of face in the Greek language. Just as in O'Driscoll's work, Sifianou's approach to face is discursive, and thus goes some way towards deconstructing static views of face, politeness and culture. The discursive elaboration of the interactants' faces becomes politeness behaviour when the interactants maintain and modify each other's face. As the author argues:

> individuals enter interactions already possessing some kind of face, modification of which may or may not become relevant or salient in the specific encounter. It becomes relevant when speakers' and addressees' evaluations indicate a mismatch which may trigger change. However, any change may be either temporary or may have long-term repercussions reflecting poorly on the individual and/or the group s/he belongs to. (p. 55)

The first chapter in Part II by Louise Mullany represents intracultural politeness research in the strictest sense of the word, as it explores the politeness phenomenon in a monocultural 'Community of Practice'. By focusing on data extracted from the documentary series *Ice Road Truckers*, Mullany analyses Canadian male intergroup communication patterns: notably, the truckers exhibit discursive practices which are not necessarily unique to them but certainly go against 'norms' dominant in other communities within the same 'culture', that is, Canada. For example, swearing "is commonplace and can perform hegemonic masculinity, functioning as a device to establish and maintain solidarity/collegiality, often in conjunction with banter, as well as functioning as a face-attacking impoliteness device used to contest, challenge and threaten" (p. 80). Mullany's study zooms into the specifics of an under-studied work 'culture', but also theorises gender, language and politeness from a critical discursive perspective, which avoids the use of essentialist notions (cf. Mills 2003 and Mills 2011).

In their chapter, Zohar Kampf and Shoshana Blum-Kulka present an engaging discussion of intracultural discursive practices between two very different communities, thus also implicitly contesting the notion of 'culture' as normative and homogenous. Kampf and Blum-Kulka compare – not without a certain irony – the dispute resolution practices of two Israeli groups, namely, young children and politicians. As their analysis shows, Israeli children use politeness in a considerably more skilful way than politicians do because "children use highly sophisticated strategies to pre-empt, mitigate and resolve conflictual situations" (p. 86); a characteristic that does not seem to apply to the (adult) political representatives of the population. Interestingly, the differences between children and politicians do not only reside in *practices* proper, but facework in the two groups requires different theorisation – a finding that has important implications for intracultural research on face.

In the next chapter, Lucien Brown examines the relationship between Korean honorifics and culture, a valuable undertaking considering that Korean is under-represented in politeness research in spite of its extremely complex honorific system (Kim 2011). Besides the choice of topic, Brown's approach is particularly innovative because the author "sets out to disentangle the ideologies that surround honorifics from their actual patterns of usage and to reconsider the place of honorifics within notions of Korean culture and politeness" (p. 107). In so doing, Brown echoes a recent trend in Japanese politeness research (e.g. Pizziconi 2003; Cook 2008) which aims to deconstruct nationalistic stereotypes of honorifics. Extending our discussion on culture, Brown's analysis convincingly applies Walker's (2000) tripartite framework of 'revealed culture', 'suppressed culture' and 'ignored culture', with intriguing results.

Yueguo Gu is arguably the 'father' of modern research of Chinese politeness: his 1990 paper was the first socio-pragmatic study of Chinese politeness and remains one of the most influential contributions to the field. The originality of the author's essay written for the current volume lies not only in the re-examination of Gu (1990) in light of recent developments in the field, but also, and especially, in an original conceptualisation of the politeness phenomenon that supersedes cultural considerations. By applying a phenomenological approach, Gu represents verbal and non-verbal politeness as a 'lived experience' and deconstructs – and re-constructs – Chinese discursive practices in a multi-dimensional framework. This approach alerts us to the potential benefits of a multi-modal analytical approach to 'polite behaviour'.

Manana Rusieshvili examines politeness practices in a culture which some, including many western politeness scholars, may think of as 'exotic'. While Georgia is a culture with ancient roots, little research has been carried out on the pragmatic features of Georgian communication, not to mention 'polite behaviour'. Rusieshvili's work is doubly interesting because it explores the intracultural diversity of politeness in professional and institutional settings. Such contexts are usually understood as governed by norms and conventions that bind both institutional members and lay individuals.

Part III opens with Karen Grainger's chapter, which examines indirectness in Zimbabwean English. A noteworthy characteristic of this essay is that it explores intercultural issues in a *monolingual* setting, hence showing how the use of a *lingua franca* does not imply shared cultural values. As Grainger shows, conventional intercultural differences, theorised according to Brown and Levinson (1987), fade into irrelevance when crosscultural encounters are approached from a discursive perspective. This may result in the neglect of cultural differences but these are suddenly less salient when examined in authentic interactions. The chapter contributes new insight to a discursive understanding of politeness by showing that "*both* first-order and second-order politeness are simultaneously relevant and valuable" (p. 188). In recent years a debate has been raging in politeness research circles as to whether analysts should focus on 'lay' (first-order) or scholarly (second-order) interpretations of politeness: through persuasive and convincing argumentation, Grainger offers a possible answer.

Eva Ogiermann and Małgorzata Suszczyńska approach politeness from an original historico-pragmatic perspective ('original' with the exception of Culpeper and Kádár's [2010] volume, which also takes such an approach to politeness). The chapter is a warning against the dangers of describing 'politeness in x culture' as independent of history. The authors proceed to discuss the large-scale changes in politeness practices that took place during and after the Communist dictatorships in Hungary and Poland; changes that caused large-scale differences in intracultural politeness behaviour in the communities studied here. And yet, and here comes Ogiermann and Suszczyńska's distinctive contribution to crosscultural research, in spite of the shared recent history, Polish and Hungarian cultures cannot be treated in the same way, as language politics influenced them differently. The authors persuasively conclude that the "broader socio-political context redefines cultural values and has a deep impact on politeness-related concepts and behaviour" (p. 213); their analysis also shows that complex relations between 'polite behaviour' and 'culture' can generate quite distinct practices in neighbouring communities sharing apparently very similar historical circumstances.

Yasuhisa Watanabe's chapter returns to the role of face; this time in intercultural conflict management. The chapter concentrates on two aspects of face in interaction thus far neglected by politeness research, "namely the strategies that the interlocutors can adopt to enhance their face in interaction and the need to include third parties in the analysis of face in a multi-party interaction" (p. 234). The author's latter point, that is, the involvement of side-parties in behavioural analysis, is particularly intriguing: Watanabe persuasively demonstrates that the "perspectives of the side-participants can also explain why one chooses to enhance and/or sacrifice one's face in order to save that of another interlocutor" (p. 234). Besides its theoretical contribution, the value of Watanabe's study resides also in its methodology and data: it combines ethnographic methods with conversation analysis to examine a Japanese-English bilingual meeting video-recorded in a Japanese company based in Australia.

Poland features again in the concluding chapter by Ewa Bogdanowska-Jakubowska, which introduces a new cultural concept of face and tests it in a crosscultural comparison of Polish and American data. Her model is constructed (and analysed) at multiple (social and individual) levels. As the author argues, "dimensions of face [...] are culture-general. What makes particular emic concepts of face different from one another is the content of face which depends on the cultural context (social organisation, social norms, moral rules and a hierarchy of social values)" (p. 243). In other words, culture-specific elements of face can be captured if researchers focus on the contents of emic face conceptualisations, which themselves may also be subject to critique and disagreement.

Notes

1. More information can be found at http://research.shu.ac.uk/politeness.
2. Cf. 'They Speak Their Minds and Mind Their Manners' feature in www.newsobserver.com/2010/04/05/421900/they-speak-their-minds-and-mind.html.

References

Adams, K.L., and Winter, A. (1997) 'Gang Graffiti as a Discourse Genre', *Journal of Sociolinguistics*, 1/3, pp. 337–360.

Bargiela-Chiappini, F. (2009) 'Facing the Future: Some Reflections', in F. Bargiela-Chiappini and M. Haugh (eds), *Face, Communication and Social Interaction*, London, Equinox, pp. 307–326.

Bax, M. (2010) 'Epistolary Presentation Rituals: Face-Work, Politeness, and Ritual Display in Early Modern Dutch Letter-Writing', in J. Culpeper and D.Z. Kádár (eds), *Historical (Im)politness*, Berne, Peter Lang, pp. 37–85.

Bax, M. (2011) 'An Evolutionary Take on (Im)politeness: Three Broad Developments in the Marking Out of Socio-Proxemic Space', in M. Bax and D.Z. Kádár (eds), *Understanding Historical (Im)politeness*, Double Special Issue of *Journal of Historical Pragmatics*.

Bousfield, D. (2008) *Impoliteness in Interaction*, Amsterdam and Philadelphia, John Benjamins.

Bousfield, D., and Locher, M.A. (eds) (2007) *Impoliteness in Language: Studies in Interplay with Power in Theory and Practice*, Berlin and New York, Mouton de Gruyter.

Brown, P., and Levinson, S.C. (1978) 'Universals in Language Usage: Politeness Phenomena', in E.N. Goody (ed.), *Questions and Politeness*, Cambridge, Cambridge University Press, pp. 56–311.

Brown, P., and Levinson, S.C. (1987) *Politeness: Some Universals in Language Usage*, Cambridge, Cambridge University Press.

Cook, H. (2008) *Socializing Indentities through Speech Styles: Learners of Japanese as a Foreign Language*, Clevedon, Multilingual Matters.

Culpeper, J., and Kádár, D.Z. (eds) (2010) *Historical (Im)politeness*, Berne, Peter Lang.

Eelen, G. (2001) *A Critique of Politeness Theories*, Manchester and Northampton, St. Jerome Publishing.

Endler, J.A. (1993) 'Some General Comments on the Evolution and Design of Animal Communication Systems', *Philosophical Transactions of the Royal Society*, 340, pp. 215–225.

Geyer, N. (2007) *Discourse and Politeness: Ambivalence in Japanese Face*, London and New York, Continuum.

Goffman, E. (1967 [1955]) 'On Face-Work', in E. Goffman (ed.), *Interaction Ritual: Essays on Face-to-Face Behavior*, Harmondsworth, Penguin, pp. 5–45. (Originally in *Psychiatry: Journal for the Study of Interpersonal Processes*, 18/3, pp. 213–231.)

Grice, P. (1975) 'Logic and Conversation', in P. Cole and J. Morgan (eds), *Syntax and Semantics, 3: Speech Acts*, New York, Academic Press, pp. 41–58.

Gu, Y. (1990) 'Politeness Phenomena in Modern Chinese', *Journal of Pragmatics*, 14/22, pp. 237–257.

Hayashi, S. 林四郎, and Mianmi F. 南不二男 (eds) (1974) *Sekai no keigo* 世界の敬語 [*Politeness in Various Languages*], Tokyo, Meiji Shoin.

Hickey, L., and Stewart, M. (2005) *Politeness in Europe*, Clevedon, Multilingual Matters.

Hodder, I. (1982) *Symbols in Action: Ethnoarchaeological Studies of Material Culture*, Cambridge, Cambridge University Press.

Ide, S. (1989) 'Formal Forms and Discernment: Two Neglected Aspects of Universals of Linguistic Politeness', *Multilingua*, 8/2–3, pp. 223–248.

Kádár, D.Z. (2010) 'Reflections on the Critical Turn: A Research Report', available at: http://research.shu.ac.uk/politeness/meetingdec09.html.

Kádár, D.Z. (2011) 'Postscript', in Linguistic Politeness Research Group (ed.), *Politeness Now!* Berlin and New York, Mouton de Gruyter.

Kádár, D.Z., and Mills, S. (eds) (2011) *Politeness in East Asia*, Cambridge, Cambridge University Press.

Kerbrat-Orecchioni, C. (2006) 'Politeness in Small Shops in France', *Journal of Politeness Research*, 2/1, pp. 79–103.

Kim, A.H. (2011) 'Politeness in Korea', in Kádár and Mills (2011).

Lakoff, R.T. (1973) 'The Logic of Politeness; Or, Minding Your P's and Q's', in C. Corum, T. Smith-Stark and A. Weiser (eds), *Papers from the Ninth Regional Meeting of the Chicago Linguistic Society*, Chicago, Chicago Linguistic Society, pp. 292–305.

Lakoff, R.T. (1977) 'What You Can Do with Words: Politeness, Pragmatics, and Performatives', in A. Rogers, B. Wall and J.P. Murphy (eds), *Proceedings of the Texas Conference on Performatives, Presuppositions, and Implicatures*, Arlington, Center of Applied Linguistics, pp. 79–105.

Lakoff, R.T., and Ide, S. (eds) (2006) *Broadening the Horizon of Linguistic Politeness*, Amsterdam and Philadelphia, John Benjamins.

Leech, G. (1983) *Principles of Pragmatics*, London and New York, Longman.

Lévi-Strauss, C. (1955) *Tristes Tropiques* (trans. D. Weightmann and J. Weightmann), New York, Atheneum Press.
Locher, M.A. (2004) *Power and Politeness in Action*, Berlin and New York, Mouton de Gruyter.
Locher, M.A., and Watts, R.J. (2008) 'Relational Work and Impoliteness: Negotiating Norms of Linguistic Behaviour', in D. Bousfield and M.A. Locher (eds), *Impoliteness in Language*, Berlin, Mouton de Gruyter, pp. 77–99.
Mills, S. (2003) *Gender and Politeness*, Cambridge, Cambridge University Press.
Mills, S. (2011) 'Discursive Approaches to Politeness and Impoliteness', in Linguistic Politeness Research Group (ed.), *Politeness Now!* Berlin and New York, Mouton de Gruyter.
Mills, S., and Kádár, D.Z. (2011) 'Politeness and Culture', in Kádár and Mills (2011).
Nwoye, O.G. (1992) 'Linguistic Politeness and Socio-Cultural Variations of the Notion of Face', *Journal of Pragmatics*, 18/4, pp. 309–328.
Pizziconi, B. (2003) 'Re-Examining Politeness, Face, and the Japanese Language', *Journal of Pragmatics*, 35/10–11, pp. 1471–1506.
Terkourafi, M. (2005) 'Beyond the Micro-Level in Politeness Research', *Journal of Politeness Research*, 1/2, pp. 237–263.
Walker, G. (2000) 'Performed Culture: Learning to Participate in Another Culture', in R. Lambert and E. Shohamy (eds), *Language Policy and Pedagogy: Essays in Honor of Richard Lambert*, Amsterdam and Philadelphia, John Benjamins, pp. 221–236.
Watts, R.J. (1989) 'Relevance and Relational Work: Linguistic Politeness as Polite Behaviour', *Multilingua*, 8/2–3, pp. 131–166.
Watts, R.J. (2003) *Politeness*, Cambridge, Cambridge University Press.
Wenger, E. (1998) *Communities of Practice: Learning, Meaning, and Identity*, Cambridge, Cambridge University Press.

Part I: Face in Interaction

2
Some Issues with the Concept of Face: When, What, How and How Much?

Jim O'Driscoll

1. Introduction

As this volume and numerous other works demonstrate, the concept of face has proved enormously stimulating to scholars of the interpersonal aspects of communication. Its appeal seems to lie in the possibilities it offers for examining instantiation both of the macro concept of identity and also of personal concerns such as self-esteem, self-image and reputation – things which in themselves have nothing to do with interaction – within interaction.

This chapter is a wide-ranging, though patchy, discussion of the concept and our use of it. Because the concept was introduced into sociopragmatics by Goffman (1967 [1955]: 5), it is not possible to conduct such a discussion without quoting his original definition. Here it is:

(1) The positive social value
(2) a person effectively claims for himself
(3) by the line others assume he has taken
(4) during a particular contact

I have represented it this way so that in the following text I can refer to its various elements as line numbers.

To start with this quote risks the inference that what follows is a kind of biblical exegesis. And indeed, so powerful and alluring is Goffman's exposition that there is a danger that discussion on this matter can be reduced to mere argumentation about 'what Goffman really meant'. This chapter may appear at times to fall into this trap. But I hope it becomes clear that the reason for its exegetical tendencies is simply that Goffman's work can provide an avenue into further exploration of the concept. We scholars are, of course, unbound by any religiose affiliations and are free to suggest any modification to Goffman's concept that we deem useful (and I hope this will become clear too).

However, there are limits to what can be accomplished in just one paper. This chapter begins (Section 2 below) by painting a picture of what, in my view, makes face distinctly face (i.e. not just a buzzword for some other phenomenon). But it is not principally concerned with the precise nature of the concept. It only briefly engages with Arundale's (2009) objections to Goffman's concept and his alternative conceptualisation. (See Section 8 below. For greater engagement, see Jakubowska, this volume.) It is chiefly concerned with the operationalisation of the concept in studies of interpersonal communication, with special reference to crosscultural and intercultural studies.

To foreground face, and at the same time to omit the words 'politeness' and 'culture' in the title of a chapter which appears in a volume entitled *Politeness Across Cultures*, requires some explanation. The succinct explanation is that this chapter focuses on the 'across' part of this volume's title. And face, it is argued, is an ideal concept for engaging with the crosscultural and intercultural precisely because it does *not* implicate specific cultures (see Section 4) or construals of politeness which are inevitably culture-specific (see Section 3). Having thus argued for the value of the concept of face, the remaining sections of this chapter raise a series of problematical issues connected with it. These are framed as questions, to which I offer answers which are extremely sketchy but nevertheless often forthright. The main intention is to suggest an agenda for future discussion.

2. The 'reality' of face: its reciprocality

Imagine a podium event. It could be a paper being presented at a conference, a theatre play, a speaker at a political rally or just a teacher doing upfront chalk-and-talk in a teenage classroom. Now imagine that something very untoward happens which distracts attention from the main business, something which utterly destroys, albeit only momentarily, the credibility of the major actor. The conference presenter lets off a very loud fart, the actor forgets his/her lines in mid speech, the political speaker's false teeth come shooting out of his/her mouth or the teacher displays sudden and extreme incontinence. As a result, the victim is visibly and greatly discomfited. S/he suffers extreme embarrassment. S/he is, as the English saying goes, covered in confusion.

On the page, incidents of this kind come across as laughable. In real life they come across very differently. Typically, all those present experience the same sense of horror as the victim. They feel embarrassed *for* him/her. They too will be visibly discomfited. Moreover, the extent of their discomfiture, while not as great, will be in direct proportion to that of the victim. The more the latter is humiliated, with no relieving humour or subsequent new focus of attention on the horizon, the greater it will be; the more s/he is able to demonstrate poise (Goffman 1967: 8–9) – either by successfully appearing to ignore the incident entirely and just 'moving on' or by passing it off through jocularity or some other incorporation into his/her performance – the less it will be. Moreover, the other participants will eagerly cooperate in any such repair work. (If this is a joke, for instance, they will laugh loudly.)

A couple of factors could affect the precise degree of this remarkable demonstration of fellow-feeling. When participants' sense of commitment to the occasion is great, we may expect the fellow feeling to be a little greater. (In the conference scenario above, for instance, participants are there of their own willing accord, so that they assume some personal responsibility for the proceedings.) When it is small, they may share less in the discomfiture of the main performer (as with pupils in a classroom, who are forced to be present). Similarly, interpersonal affect might play a role. Participants who personally like and identify with the victim may feel greater discomfiture than those who are in some way hostile (the pupils in the classroom, perhaps). In this latter case, they might even feel pleased at the victim's misfortune.

However, a moment's reflection allows us to realise that these factors seem to have only a minimal influence on the reactions of participants. Typically, even someone who has no commitment to the occasion and personally dislikes the victim will nevertheless be visibly discomfited. If s/he is pleased, s/he is *secretly* pleased – and for later but not for now. S/he may pass a sniggering remark to an adjacent participant, but this is not so much an attempt to further discomfit the victim as it is a response to his/her *own* discomfiture.

The origin of this demonstrable fellow feeling, then, cannot be found solely in interpersonal affect or in any other particularity of the situation. It seems to be built into us as interactants. We are affectively implicated in the affective adventures of others merely by being in their presence. It is in this reciprocal nature – whereby damage to one person's face leads to the damage of everybody's face – and the repair of that face simultaneously involves the repair of all faces – that the phenomenon of face may be described as 'real'. It cannot be reduced to the outward show of inner feelings (as Brown and Levinson's 1987 [1978] conception of 'face as wants' tends towards).

The examples I have conjured up above to illustrate this point are all extreme and – mercifully – rare. In an attempt to emphasise this distinction between face and feelings concerning relationships, I now examine a trifling example. It occurred during a conference presentation which I gave some years ago. I began by apologising for the fact that my talk was going to be essentially the same one I had given at the conference of the same organisation the previous year. Anxious that no participants should be irritated by finding themselves listening to the same old stuff they had heard at that time, I assured any such people that they should feel free to get up and leave immediately and that if they did so I would not find it the least bit rude. At this point, one member of the audience, who had indeed been present at my talk the previous year, interjected with 'What makes you think we remember it?'

Through more-or-less conventional implicature, it could be inferred from this utterance that she herself did not remember the details of my talk the previous year and that probably any others in her position did not do so either, leading to the further inference that there was no need for me to apologise for the repetitive content of the upcoming talk.

In addition, still further inferences could be drawn. These concern the perlocutionary intent of the utterance. One, via a selfdeprecating allusion to the speaker's powers of memory, was of reassurance that what I was about to say would be of interest. But the alternative, via an implicature that my talk the previous year had been singularly unmemorable, was of criticism that I am the kind of speaker who gives boring presentations. The interjector was (and is) a personal friend and occasional collaborator of mine. I was (and remain) perfectly confident that her intention was supportive. Consequently, I did not feel 'personally' attacked by her remark and my feelings suffered no damage whatsoever. However, aware of the possible latter interpretation, and aware that others were aware of it (a small ripple of laughter passed through the section of the audience who heard the remark), my face *was* attacked. In English-language parlance, I was momentarily 'put out' and had to exercise a little poise in order to deflect the attack. Given the circumstances, this was easy to do. But to further emphasise the point that face and interpersonal affect are different, let us imagine that my interjector had actually had malign intent. Although this might have made it slightly more difficult for me to overcome the face-attack, it still would have been possible for me to do so. I still could have behaved *as if* the intention of the remark was supportive. In this case, my face would have remained intact, even though my feelings would have been severely damaged.

In further support of the 'reality' of face, I now argue that it cannot be equated to the management of personal reputation either. It may be argued that the reason for the mutual embarrassment in the extreme examples above, and the failure of any who are personally antipathetic to the victim to take advantage of his/her vulnerability, is that participants have their own faces to protect and therefore have to manage the impression of themselves given off to all others present. After all, few people wish to be thought of as heartless or cruel. There is, of course, much truth in this view. However, face as fellow-interactant-feeling seems to be more deeply ingrained than such instrumental considerations. We also do not wish to look heartless or cruel to *ourselves*, as in Goffman's (1967: 10) example of a person being "trapped by considerateness" into buying something they really do not want, even when there is no one else around to witness the salesperson's defacement if we do not buy. Indeed, it is so pervasive that precisely the same empathetic reaction as above can often occur when we are not even present. For instance, when watching a TV sitcom whose humour lies in awkward social situations, we sometimes find ourselves squirming, perhaps momentarily shielding our eyes from the screen or covering our ears even while we laugh. Our reactions, in other words, are those of extreme social discomfiture, despite the fact that we ourselves have no role in the social occasion. We behave as if our faces are at stake when our reputations cannot be. (This matter of face effects, even when the faces affected are nowhere near the action, raises analytical problems which I deal with in Section 5 below.)[1]

This section has argued in support of the use of the face-concept by attempting to show its conceptual and analytical independence from related aspects of (inter)personhood. However, its frequent use in scholarship over the past two decades, its success as a term which is sometimes bandied about rather loosely, carries its own dangers. The rest of this chapter discusses the issues which have emerged thereby.

3. What is the relation of face to im/politeness?

For historical reasons – mainly the fact that most of us were first drawn into the study of face and politeness via Brown and Levinson (1987) – these two attributes are routinely yoked together like some famous double act. (Indeed, a googlefight search returns as many entries for the hyphenated 'face-and-politeness' as it does for the unhyphenated version.) So I begin by stating the obvious. Face and politeness are not the same thing. They *cannot* be, simply because one is a trait of interact*ants* while the other is a trait of interact*ion*. One is something interactants have; the other something they do.

In Brown and Levinson – and commonly thereafter – the former is appealed to as an explanation for the latter. This is a perfectly feasible claim. However, the causal relationship between the two, especially when it is taken for granted, can mask a number of nuances. Arguably, face is not the only explanation for politeness (or, for that matter, impoliteness – see Culpeper, forthcoming) and politeness is quite definitely not the only aspect of behaviour which face can explain. Goffman's original exposition (1967) of facework amounts to some 12,000 words but contains only four instances of the lexeme 'polite(ness)', none of which attempts to define the lexeme or its relation to face.[2]

Moreover, to uphold the claim that people's faces cause them to be polite, it is necessary to assume either that politeness, when it occurs, is objectively identifiable ('Look, here is an instance of politeness') or that face is as salient a concept to interactants as politeness ('I am polite for reasons of face'). Neither assumption seems warranted. The former entails the adoption of a 'second-order approach' to politeness (Watts et al. 1992), which has come under increasing fire in the past decade or so by those (e.g. Eelen 2001; Watts 2003; Mills 2003, 2005) who advocate and practice a 'first-order approach' ('politeness1', as it has come to be called) which focuses on subjective participant evaluations of what is and is not considered polite. Given the fact that the lexeme 'polite(ness)' is value-laden, that comparable (but not synonymous) lexemes exist in all cultures and that all these lexemes are salient to language users, there is much to be said for this approach.

The salience of the term 'face' as characterised above, on the other hand, appears to be very crossculturally limited. Moreover, even where comparable lexemes *are* salient, they do not appear to capture quite the same phenomenon as that sketched above (see below). The term 'facework' is even less salient. For this reason, it seems to me that in contrast to politeness, face lends itself more naturally to a second-order approach. Because Brown and Levinson take such an approach and because a conception of face is the lynchpin of their model, it is probably more helpful to view their model as a theory of facework rather than of politeness (Watts 2003; Locher and Watts 2005).

Thus face and politeness are distinct both substantively and methodologically. Clearly, there *is* a relation, but it is one of mutual hyponymy, not a causal one. Which is the hyponym and which the superordinate term is a matter of perspective. Seen from the inside, this chapter places face in the superordinate position; that is, politeness is regarded as a (possible) aspect of facework. This relationship follows from the conception of politeness as culture-specific (as above) and face as pan-cultural (see immediately below). Seen from the outside, on the other hand, this chapter can be seen as a discussion of one very important component of politeness, so that politeness is in the superordinate position and face in the hyponymic one.

4. Face across cultures

As suggested by my comments so far, the face that I am discussing in this chapter is a 'second-order notion' – a term that can be used by scholars from all over the world to denote the same concept whatever their origin or the specifics of their empirical application of it. This chapter is not about the English lexeme 'face' or roughly equivalent lexemes in particular languages. It makes occasional reference to diverging culture-specific instantiations but it is not principally concerned with these. The focus is on the use of a universal parameter – a lens through which the divergences may be compared and better understood. Following Terkourafi (2007), I call this 'face2'.

This is not to deny the value of studies of emic, culture-specific constructs instantiated by such lexemes (see, for example, Koutlaki 2002; Ruhi and Işik-Güler 2007; Lim 2009; Ruhi 2009; Ukosakul 2009; Sifianou, this volume). As argued by Haugh (2009: 11–14) (and demonstrated by these studies), these can enrich our understanding of actual instances of interaction. But I take it as axiomatic that comparisons across cultures are more valid when we have a concept which is in itself culture-neutral; that is, what Terkourafi (2007) has termed a 'methodological abstraction' (see O'Driscoll 1996 for further argument to this effect). Such a concept also has the advantage that is does not require an essentialist conception of culture or of the extent of the influence of this or that culture on a person's interactive behaviour. In keeping with the argument expounded in the introduction to this volume, cultural norms are seen as just one possible contribution to this behaviour, the weight of which can vary from situation to situation (see Section 9 below).

It might be argued that, in order to avoid confusion between first-order and second-order perspectives on face, a term should be found for the latter which is transparently exclusively technical (i.e. not salient in any culture). The fact that the English lexeme 'face' and its equivalents in other languages play a role, albeit usually a minor one, in everyday usage might therefore make it an unsuitable candidate. However, quite apart from the difficulty of persuading all researchers to recognise and adopt such a term, employing one which has reflexes in everyday usage actually has an advantage. It helps us to guard against our research straying too far from everyday experience. It can also suggest nuances and conceptualisations that we might otherwise miss (I offer one such example below). I therefore think it advisable to stay with the term 'face' for the second-order notion. When the possibility of confusion with the first-order notion arises it is only necessary to specify 'face2'.

5. When *can* face be relevant?

This is a question about the range of communicative behaviour to which the concept might be applied. As the English-language lexeme suggests, face and facework prototypically pertain to face-to-face interaction. It is, after all, only when people are visibly in each other's presence that the kinds of face effects discussed in Section 2 above can occur. It is also fairly clear that it was this kind of interaction which Goffman had in mind in his exposition of the concept; notwithstanding his remark, two-thirds of the way through his exposition, that "most of what has been said so far applies to encounters of both an immediate and mediated kind", all his exemplification assumes face-to-face encounters and anyway it is "during direct personal contact" that "the significance of face becomes especially clear" (Goffman 1967: 33).[3]

This conception of face – as operational in face-to-face interaction – leads to one deduction and one problem. The deduction is that people do not have faces in the way that they have legs or bicycles. People have the latter whether or not they are walking or pedalling. But people have faces only when they are interacting. Face is "constructed discursively with other [interactants]" and is thus "attributed in each individual instance of interaction" (Locher and Watts 2005: 12). Such a limitation is, of course, implicit in line 4 of Goffman's definition and in his oft-quoted statement that a person's face is "on loan to him from society" (Goffman 1967: 10).[4]

This limitation to interaction does not, of course, mean that we interactants enter each encounter with entirely blank faces. We carry around with us the building blocks of face construction (see below) outside interaction, all of which have their own histories. As a result, a person's face in the present encounter usually has a connection with his/her face in previous encounters (especially those with the same interlocutors), with the non-interactive background to the present encounter and indeed his/her more general non-interactive experience, so that a full exploration of the nature of his/her face in the present encounter may often need to take these factors into account. (See Haugh 2009: 11–12 and Spencer-Oatey 2009: 137–138, 151–152 for calls to this effect; see Sifianou in this volume for a considered argument.) These elements and factors all have some sort of bearing on face.

Nevertheless, I would argue that these building blocks get assembled, albeit in a microsecond, only in interaction (see Terkourafi 2005: 248–249; also Goffman 1967: 7–8). It seems to me that this restriction on the potential relevance of face is a necessary one. Without it, it becomes difficult to separate the concept of face from that of self-image (i.e. the set of ideas which a person has about him/herself and would like other people to have), or reputation (i.e. the image that other people have of this person when they happen to call him/her to mind) or identity (i.e. images that other people have when calling this *type* of person to mind). It may be argued that face can still be a useful term for the aggregate of these characterisations about a person. However, Section 2 above has indicated that in interaction things can happen which none of these terms nor their aggregate can capture. Without this limitation, we lose sight of the immediacy of face as illustrated above.

But it is the insistence of face as a feature manifest in face-to-face interaction which raises a problem. Despite the above considerations, the concept of face is now frequently, and convincingly, used in studies of interpersonal aspects of communication between people who cannot see each other's faces at the time. Examples include studies of telephone communication (e.g. Sifianou 1989; Economidou-Kogetsidis 2005; Marquez-Reiter 2005, 2009), radio-talk (e.g. Ferenčík 2007), conventional written communication (e.g. many of the contributions in Culpeper and Kádár 2010), e-mail encounters (Davies et al. 2007; Merrison et al. in prep.) and other kinds of computer-mediated communication (e.g. Pizziconi 2007) and even published scientific articles, where, therefore, most readers are unidentified and potentially unrestricted (Myers 1989; Koutsantoni 2004).

In these types of communication, the interdependent and situated characteristics of face noted above seem to be missing. What the producer says or writes may be extremely hurtful or pleasing to one or more receivers. It may present the producer in a very unflattering light or divulge information which is damaging to the reputation of one or more of the receivers. But in all such cases, I would argue that participants' faces remain untouched *at the time* because there are no faces on the scene.

This lack of face engagement is even more obvious in written communication, when production and reception of messages are dislocated not only in space but also in time (so that it becomes problematical to pinpoint exactly when the 'interaction' – if that is what it is – is going on). In these cases, the producer is not present to witness the reception of a message and so receivers do not have to manage their reception of it (and the producer, aware of this, does not have to take such immediate reception into account when composing it – hence the ubiquitous modern tendency to ill-judged e-mail messages which turn out to cause offence).

It may be thought at this point that I am confusing the purportedly second-order concept which is the focus of this paper with a very literal denotation of the English lexeme (therefore first-order) 'face'. And certainly even in a rather impersonal form of dislocated communication such as this paper, I am performing self-presentation. Indeed, I am taking a lot of care to present myself as the possessor of relevant positive attributes, as someone whose arguments are interesting, well-expressed and convincing. Both my self-image and reputation are at stake. But my face is not (at least not right now – see below). It has taken me about an hour to compose this paragraph. Were I to take even a quarter of that time to make the same points in a face-to-face encounter, my claim to two of the above positive attributes would be shot to pieces. And if at this point you throw up your hands in a gesture of irritation, sneer and shout 'rubbish', it does not touch my face because I do not know you are doing it. If you then proceed to broadcast this negative opinion to relevant colleagues, including me, I will feel downcast, deflated and perhaps hurt. And if you express this opinion convincingly, my self-confidence will take a severe dent. But until I meet you and/or these colleagues, there are no face effects.

In addition, there is actually only a narrow bandwidth of my self-image and reputation at stake right now. Face presents an image of the whole person. In face-to-face interaction,

> on the basis of a few known attributes, [a person] is given the responsibility of possessing a vast number of others. His coparticipants are not likely to be conscious of the character of many of these attributes until he acts perceptibly in such a way as to discredit his possession of them. (Goffman 1967: 7)

In the present circumstances I do not have this responsibility. I am wearing an old dressing gown, I am unshaven and I have just picked my nose. But you are not here to perceive any of this.

Given these observations, we need to ask how face can be relevant to dislocated communication. In what sense(s) can it be valid to refer to face, as so many studies have done, when analysing instances of this kind of communication? I have two answers. The first is to advance the face-to-face encounter as our human prototype for communication, with which, therefore, we habitually frame *all* kinds of communication and which therefore influences our behaviour even in dislocated communication. (Some such metaphorical extension seems to be going on in our reactions to sitcom situations noted above.) Notwithstanding the conceptual distinction argued above between face and feelings of self-worth, it is undeniable that the two are closely related. In most cases, damage or enhancement of our faces tends to lead to damage or enhancement to our sense of self-worth (Goffman 1967: 6). Now, because these kinds of feelings are operative regardless of the mode of communication, it is quite possible that we habitually behave with an eye to our faces in all modes; that we project them onto page, or screen or into the mouthpiece.

In support of the feasibility of this view, we may note that until the advent of telecommunications and mass literacy – both very recent indeed in the sweep of human history – face-to-face was the only direct means of linguistic communication available to the vast majority of people. Perhaps, therefore, we humans are hard-wired for face-to-face interaction and thus carry over its features into all kinds of communication. Certainly, when talking on the phone, we tend to use many of the same facial expressions and physical gestures as when we are physically present to our interlocutors. Moreover, it is only through the assumption that dislocated communication is felt almost as immediately as face-to-face interaction that we can make sense of recent concerns in the media about 'cyber bullying'.

However, there is a limit to this answer. It remains easier to lie over the phone than it is face-to-face (and this is just one reason why so many have misgivings about the prospect of video phones). And other kinds of dislocated communication do not exhibit those physical symbols of the face-to-face mode. Moreover, the face-to-face-as-prototype answer is based on an explanation of our communicative behaviour but says nothing about face effects. An additional defence of studies employing the concept of face in the analysis of dislocated communication is therefore required. It lies in 'the future'; that is, in the mutual awareness of participants that there is at least a possibility – however remote – that they will meet face-to-face at some time hence. The result of this possibility is that while such communicants do not have faces at the time, what transpires is likely to have consequences for their future faces. Aware of this, participants in dislocated communication take these into account and face becomes salient. The more likely future face-to-face contact, the more salient face will be.

The point remains, however, that no acts performed in writing can be directly face-damaging or face-enhancing for the simple reason that (I repeat) there are no faces involved. They can be face-threatening only in the sense that they may impact on future face-to-face contact. (See Goffman 1967: 7–8 and O'Driscoll 2007a: 240–242 for similar presentations of future face consequences.) In the study of dislocated communication, therefore, it is more meaningful to employ face in the analysis of the producer's language and his/her intentions than it is to employ it in any estimation of actual face effects.

6. When and how much is face *actually* relevant?

This is a question of the explanatory value of the concept of face for the analyst when s/he considers instances of interaction. Just as I have argued the people do not strictly have faces when they are not interacting face-to-face, so for the same reason people *always* have faces when they are. By definition, therefore, face is always *potentially* relevant in any such interaction. It is always 'immanent' (Tracy 1992).

However, it is plain that sometimes it matters an awful lot and sometimes it matters hardly at all. There have been arguments that some interactive behaviour is better explained by other means. For instance, there are situations when desire for clarity and/or attention to the impersonal task at hand is all-consuming. Some of those put forward by Brown and Levinson (1987: 94–98) to explain 'bald on record' utterances fall into this category. And certainly a recurrent thread of this chapter is that it is wise not to try to make face do too much analytical work. This is a point made by Spencer-Oatey (2009), who offers examples of other interactional goals being pursued regardless (even in spite of) face.

Another kind of argument is to advance culture-specific values as impacting on the amount of salience accorded face (and therefore on its explanatory value). Hill et al.'s (1986) much-followed notion of 'discernment', which purportedly takes precedence over face in Japanese society, is one such example. Another (apparently contradictory) example is the view that 'the east' values face over objective truth while 'the west' does the opposite (see, for example, Goffman 1967: 17n.). However, whether such values can in themselves affect the amount of importance given to face is doubtful (see O'Driscoll 2007b: 470 and 2010: 274–275 for arguments against the discernment view). It is in the nature of face as conceived in this chapter that it is not dependent on such values. At the same time, however, it is consistent with this conception to expect the significance of face to vary crossculturally – not in the general sense of overall interactional ethos implied above but rather with respect to specific types of situation.

One observable divergence concerns how comparable encounters are framed. The notions of occasion (Goffman 1963: 18–21), activity type (Levinson 1992 [1979]) and speech event (Hymes 1972) are all broadly similar in that they allow for subjectively and culturally influenced responses to the question: what sort of thing is going on here? Divergent answers to this question will produce frames which bring face more or less to the fore. For example, my personal experience and observation suggests that default behaviour in certain kinds of podium event in Belgian culture (such as public PhD defences, the introducing of guest speakers to an audience or political debates on TV) highlight face by addressing the main actors directly as 'you', much more than they do in British culture, which downplays the significance of face by avoiding 'you' in such situations. (See O'Driscoll 2007b: 483–484 for a similar example.)

Another attested divergence is in the face-significance attached to particular speech acts. For example, Thomas (1983) and Smith (1985) offer examples in which a westerner objects to the expectation that they should proffer an apology on the grounds that this is a personal admission of fault which therefore impacts negatively on their faces, whereas we are told that in the cultural milieu it is a mere formality and carries no such face damage.

Other aspects of variability in face-salience are culture-neutral. One such aspect which may be tentatively advanced as applying in all cultures pertains to participant relationships. Following Wolfson (1988), who observed what she called the 'bulge' in address forms and other aspects of interpersonal behaviour, it can be suggested that face is always likely to be more salient in interaction with people who are neither strangers nor intimates than with people who are. Additional variables suggested by O'Driscoll (2007a: 252–253) are numbers of participants and relative predictability of the encounter; all else being equal, the greater this number and the less expected the encounter, the more face will be at stake.

7. Lexico-grammatical considerations

Lurking behind attempts to answer the questions asked in other sections of this chapter – and potentially befuddling discussion of them – are a number of lexico-grammatical issues. In order to facilitate discussion on the face concept and its application to the study in instances of interaction, I suggest we need to be clear each time we use the term about the following:

7.1. Positive attribute versus existential attribute

In other words, are we using the term to denote a desideratum of interactants or to denote something which they have anyway but which can vary in quality? The most common expression in everyday modern English containing the lexeme is probably 'lose face', which indicates the former. Other expressions used in the scholarly literature such as 'give face', 'gain face' and 'claim face' similarly present face as a value-laden term, denoting a trait of which people can be divested, or have more or less of, during interaction. Other collocations, on the other hand (e.g. damage face, enhance face, boost face), tend to present face as something mutable but ineradicable (i.e. existential attribute). Still others (e.g. threaten face) could be interpreted as of either type.

Goffman himself allows for both interpretations. He distinguishes early on in his essay (Goffman 1967: 8) between a state of being 'out of face' (i.e. face-as-positive-attribute) and that of being in the 'wrong face' (i.e. existential attribute). Immediately thereafter, however (Goffman 1967: 8–9), he describes either state as possibly leading to being 'shame-faced' (the state portrayed in Section 2 above) and proceeds to remark that in modern English 'lose face' can apparently refer to any three of these states and 'save face' to any actions taken to repair or avoid any of the three. Subsequently, he makes no explicit distinction between the results of being 'out of face' or in the 'wrong face' (i.e. they are nearly always mentioned together). In other words, Goffman is not much help in this matter.

I do not wish to suggest that we as scholars must arrive at a decision as to which conception of face we should follow. I only wish to enjoin us, for the sake of avoiding possible misinterpretation, to be clear about which of these two senses of face we mean whenever we use the term. As indicated above, my own preference is for face-as-existential-attribute, as something whose quality can be threatened in interaction but whose existence cannot. From this viewpoint, collocations such as losing face, gaining face or giving face refer only metaphorically to the dispossession, repossession or acquisition of face and are understood to denote various kinds of change in the quality of face (in the same way that in English, talk of a person 'losing his/her reputation' is understood to mean a change from a *good* reputation to a *bad* reputation). However, it may be that there is room for the face-as-positive-attribute conception as well, in the sense that some kinds of people in some kinds of situation, for example very young children among adults, are often presumed not to have any kind of face at all.

7.2. Temporal perspective

It is possible to analyse a moment of interaction from a before-perspective or an after-perspective. If we take the former, we are focused on producer intentions and so will naturally refer to face-wants, face-threats and efforts to avoid such threats or mitigate their potential effects (as in Brown and Levinson's scheme). But if we take the latter perspective, we are focused on receivers and actual effects. This is what the discursive approach mentioned above does. In such cases, it makes more sense to talk about face-damage (rather than threat) and repair work (rather than mitigation). Phrases such as face-saving and face-attack can refer to either perspective; that is, as attempt or as achievement.

7.3. Mass versus count noun

In other words, are we using the term to denote face the phenomenon of interaction or its myriad instantiations in interactants at any one time? The distinction to be made here is similar to that between (uncountable) language as a biological human phenomenon and (countable) languages as social creations. So far, as indicated in the section headings above, the discussion has been centred on various aspects of face-the-phenomenon and it has been suggested that face is an existentially inevitable trait of interactants (by virtue of them entering into interaction). But included in the discussion have been references to people's faces (plural) on the assumption that the precise nature of the face of any one person in any one instance of interaction can vary and be distinct from that of other interactants and that in other instances of interaction. The section headings below refer to faces (plural) because they address questions of how this variation and distinctness may be described.

The effort in Sections 9 and 10 below is to discuss the construction and composition of individual faces in instances of interaction. In the course of this effort, reference is sometimes made to crosscultural variation in the conceptualisation of face-the-phenomenon, but it needs to be stressed that this kind of variation, being a first-order matter, is not the focus of the discussion. Rather, the attempt is to explore variation from a face2 perspective, in which, therefore, the variability arises not from divergent conceptualisations but from varying proportions of the suggested universally available building blocks (Section 9) of face and different degrees of salience of various possible aspects of face (to which crossculturally divergent values are just one contributory factor). But before that, it is necessary to raise one more very basic question.

8. To whom or what do faces pertain?

In the discussion so far, it has been assumed that faces belong to interacting individuals. In reaction to the individualist (usually qualified as 'western', sometimes characterised as 'self-obsessed') orientation that they perceive as thereby implied, some researchers have questioned this assumption. Two alternatives have been offered. One is the notion of group face (e.g. Nwoye 1992; De Kadt 1998), introduced to account for the fact that many cultures subscribe to a collectivist orientation to identity, so that the 'self' with which face is connected may better be described as pertaining to a relevant social group. Goffman hints at this possibility when, immediately following his definition of face, he adds the face is "an image [of self] that others may share, as when a person makes a good showing for his profession or religion by making a good showing for himself". And indeed, as Sifianou demonstrates in this volume, one does not have to be a 'collectivist' to feel the face effects of the actions of others who are not present.

The notion of group face is not a refutation of the conception of face as residing with the individual, but simply an argument that it does not entirely do so. The second alternative, however, attempts a blanket refutation. It regards Goffman's conception as peculiarly western (e.g. Bargiela-Chiappini 2003: 1463) and therefore unsuited as a culture-neutral one (i.e. face2). As an alternative, Arundale (2006, 2009) proposes 'face-constituting theory', in which "face is not an individual possession" (Arundale 2009: 38) but rather "a relational phenomenon [which] arises in the dialectic interplay between what is individual and what is social" (Arundale 2009: 43).

In its emphasis on face achieved *within* interaction, as an effect rather than a cause of moves in interaction, and therefore in continual flux *during* interaction, Arundale's view reflects the picture painted in the second section above and is in accord with the argument in Section 5 above that face exists only in interaction. However, I cannot myself see any inconsistency in accepting this view but nevertheless locating faces (plural) firmly as pertaining to *individual* interactants. This is not to deny their interdependence or their mutability. It is just that I find it difficult to see how, practically and meaningfully, we could find a way to describe the nature or quality of 'the face' (singular) of a plurality of interactants. Nor is it to deny the existence of collectivist or even holistic (Lim 2009) orientations in some cultures, resulting in interactional behaviour that is intimately concerned with the self-image(s) of the group(s) which an interactant is taken to represent. But I would regard this orientation simply as affecting the balance of ingredients contributing to a (singular) person's face (see below).

I *do*, conversely, see a problem with the notion of group face, stemming from the simple observation that it is very rare indeed for two or more whole groups (that is, *all* their members) to participate in the same encounter. And yet if face exists only in interaction, such a condition would be necessary for 'group face' to have meaning.[5] Without it, the term 'face' extends beyond interaction, so that 'face' and 'reputation' or 'self-image' become essentially synonymous.

This issue is not closed. But having nailed my colours to the mast in this respect, I assume in the remaining sections below that faces belong to individuals.

9. What are faces made *from*?

This is a question about the elements contributing to an interactant's face at any one time; about the inputs to that face. I propose that all of the following building blocks can contribute, though in varying proportions.

9.1. Personal wants regarding self-image

The face-as-wants approach is Brown and Levinson's truncation of Goffman's definition. It ignores lines 3 and 4 and arguably downplays the 'effectively' in line 2 as well (see O'Driscoll 2007b: 467–468). Nevertheless, it is clear that how we would *like* to be seen by others has an effect on how we *will* be seen because it influences our behaviour. In some respects, we have clear conscious choices in this matter. We can, for example, pick and choose what clothes to wear because we know that our decision will effect the faces we will later be given. In other respects, there is little, if any, consciousness involved and our interactive behaviour is simply a reflection of our own self-images and/or a compulsion to behave in a certain manner. But neither a lack of self-awareness nor the undoubted influence of social norms, sometimes very strong, are in themselves refutations of the contribution of personal wants (O'Driscoll 2010: 274–275). Likewise, the fact that there are severe methodological problems in estimating how such unobservable phenomena actually play out in interaction (Arundale 2006: 199) is no excuse for denying their existence.

9.2. Ascribed characteristics

I have in mind here the usual social identity variables such as age, gender, ethnicity, occupation and geographical provenance, as well as evident physical characteristics. Clearly, if I find myself identified by others in interaction as a large, elderly, male British/Irish academic from London, certain behavioural expectations are conferred upon me which can be difficult to wriggle out of. They constitute part of the 'line' I am assumed to be taking. I have suggested above (Section 8) that this ingredient will make a larger contribution for members of collectivist cultures than it would for members of more individualistic ones.

9.3. Personal reputation

Even people we have never met before have often heard about us, so that frequently we enter into interaction with our own histories having already arrived. As a result, with all except complete strangers, the line which we are assumed to be taking, in addition to the typological characteristics above, involves personal ones such as early riser, friendly, honest, untidy and so on. It is this contributor to face2 which seems to be emphasised, albeit with a significant admixture of ascribed characteristics, in lexemes approximating to the English 'face' (i.e. face1) in some East-Asian cultures. (See, for example, Lim and Choi 1996 for Korean culture; Gao 2009 for Chinese; and Ukosakul 2009 for Thai.)

9.4. Interpersonal history

This contributor applies to all but only those encounters between people who have had dealings on previous occasions. If they have met on many occasions and have 'a relationship', they will have developed certain habits of interaction which emphasise certain aspects of their faces. But even if they met just once before, a particularly memorable encounter will have its effects the next time they meet. (Hadfield and Hahn's covenant face – see Section 10 below – derived with reference to Korean culture, adds this element to the construal of face1 mentioned in the previous paragraph. See Sifianou in this volume for a fuller account of this contributor.)

9.5. Culture

It is well known that cultural background involves certain values and norms of behaviour in interaction which induce certain habits and expectations among interactants. It is divergences between those of one culture and those of another, of course, which have been appealed to in innumerable studies of interaction across cultures and cross-cultural comparisons. Sometimes these divergences pertain directly to interaction, such as the historical Chinese norm of self-denigration and other-elevation (see, for example, Kádár 2010). In Section 6 above, it was suggested that divergent conceptions of speech acts and activity types can affect the degree of salience of face. But these can also, of course, affect which aspects of face are presumed to be important (see O'Driscoll 2007b: 475–477 for a simple example). And sometimes the divergences also involve values not directly pertaining to interaction themselves but nevertheless having a crucial affect upon it (see Ting-Toomey 2009: 236–242 for a recent example).

9.6. Situation

Here, I have in mind all those elements listed in Hymes' (1972) famous SPEAKING mnemonic. I have left this contributor until last because I suspect it is the most important. This follows from the conception of face as co-constructed within interaction. Indeed it might be thought that, if face only exists in interaction and interactants' faces emerge as their joint accomplishment (Arundale 2006), the *unfolding* situation encompasses *all* that contributes to them. However, as Haugh (2009: 5–12) reminds, face is not only co-constituted *in* interaction but also constitutive *of* it. All situations of interaction are subject to historical influences. The other contributors listed in this section are, in effect, an attempt to itemise these.

The crucial role of situation, I suggest, lies in the fact that it influences strongly the relative weights accorded to the other ingredients. In Goffman's words:

> During a contact of a particular type, an interactant…can expect to be sustained in a particular face…Given his attributes and the conventionalized nature of the encounter, he will find a small choice of lines will be open to him and a small choice of faces will be waiting for him. (Goffman 1967: 7)

Different elements of situation thrust different building blocks to the fore or consign them to the background. For example, if the ascribed identities of participants differ in salient ways, the salient characteristic(s) can become a major contributor to faces. (See O'Driscoll 2001 for an example concerning ethnolinguistic identity.) Conversely, if two people with a long and strong interpersonal history find themselves interacting among several others who are not privy to that history, this factor will become a much less important contributor to their faces than if they were alone together.

But in truth I suspect that *all* these building blocks can affect each other, which is why the construction of faces is such a complicated matter. Arguably, one might regard situation as the origin and all the others as derivatives. Or perhaps one might encapsulate all of them in a combination of situation and culture. At any rate, the relative weight to be accorded situation and culture in the construction of faces is a topic that needs more research.

10. What are faces made *of*?

What are the facets of faces? How do we actually talk about a person's face in interaction?

Can we identify an X, Y, Z, N face at any one time? Goffman's exposition is entirely lacking in any specification of the (cross-situational relatively permanent) constituents of face; that is, the 'social attributes' in terms of which, according to him, face is 'delineated' (Goffman 1967: 5). This absence is perhaps inevitable given his definition of face as radically situationally contingent (line 4), as this could be taken to imply that the total configuration of constituents will be somewhat different in every single instance of interaction.

However, the scary possibility that there are as many faces as there are encounter-times-participants has not deterred researchers from attempting to identify specific types and/or instantiations of face. The most well-known attempt is that of Brown and Levinson (1987), who posit just two types: positive and negative. Notwithstanding the widespread crosscultural criticism of both the applicability of these facets (in particular the latter) and their conceptualisation, they have proved remarkably durable in scholarship. A number of recent works have advanced what are effectively revised conceptions of them. Arundale (2006) and Terkourafi (2007) see them (albeit under different labels and radically different etiologies) as universal abstract concepts from which all visible actual faces in particular cultures and situations can ultimately be derived. O'Driscoll (2007b), on the other hand, sees them as comprising just one dimension of face which is constant across cultures and situations (though with greatly varying degrees of salience). Bravo (2008) suggests something in between these poles.

The implication of the one-dimensional view of positive and negative is that there are other facets to faces. This position has been argued on the grounds that Brown and Levinson's positive and negative are both too grossly defined and just do not cover enough grounds to capture the range of face concerns (e.g. Tracy and Baratz 1994: 290–291). And indeed, other kinds of face have been proposed. Some are straightforward additions to positive and negative, designed to account for phenomena which these facets seem unable to encompass (e.g. Lim and Bowers' 1991 competence face; O'Driscoll's 1996 culture-specific face; Hadfield and Hahn's 2007 covenant face). Other suggestions are more sweeping. They include the purportedly universally available inventory offered by Ting-Toomey (2005; see also 2009: 240), the list of culture-specific elements outlined by Mao (1994) and the series of face dimensions along each of which there can be certain 'settings' (Spencer-Oatey 2005).

While there is not necessarily any value in attempting to establish an agreed list of types of face, more research in this field into how we can principally go about describing the nature of faces at any one moment would be valuable.

11. Final word

As warned at the start, this chapter is very far from comprehensive. A number of worthwhile issues have *not* been discussed (for example, the issue of exactly how faces change during interaction and that of self-face versus other-face). To finish, here is a very tentative, and somewhat whimsical, suggestion. To capture the notion of faces being constructed from several elements (their composite nature), the relation between the elements and the construction, the mutability of faces and the fact that face is essentially a surface phenomenon (and thus different from self-image, self-esteem and other inner feelings of self-worth), I would like to advance the cosmetic metaphor of 'face make-up' as a way of describing a person's face at any one time. A person can choose what to put on (the personal-wants element), from what is generally acceptable (the culture element), what is more particularly expected for his/her kind of person (the ascribed characteristic element) and what is actually available at the time (the situation element). Note also that there are lingering after-effects of make-up (it does not come off so easily – the personal reputation and interpersonal history elements).

This metaphor probably gives too much emphasis to pre-interactive decision-making for it to have much value. We would have to see people as applying make-up to each other during interaction – in this cosmetic universe, people get together and routinely apply make-up *to each other*. But the notion of make-up is at least a way of emphasising that a person's face is a *composite*.

Notes

1. For anybody seeking evidence for the basic affective cooperativeness of interactants, I suggest that face effects such as those portrayed here would be the place to look – much more so than in Grice's (1975) misleadingly named Cooperative Principle, which is really about intelligibility, not affect.
2. The instances can be found in the following places: Goffman (1967: 14, 16, 28, 35).
3. Indeed, Goffmans conception of interaction itself is based around mutual physical presence. This approach is clear not only from the fact that nearly all his examples in all of his works assume such presence. It is also entailed, it seems to me, in his argument (e.g. Goffman 1964: 135–156 and 1981: 141–143) that talk should be studied not as 'conversation' but rather as just one aspect – albeit often a very important one – of encounters between people. (This is because when we analyse other kinds of encounter such as telephone or e-mail communication, the non-linguistic aspects tend to be crowded out and all we are left with is talk.)
4. This remark has sometimes been interpreted to mean that face is actually a property of society rather than the individual. I cannot see the value of this interpretation. I believe it stems from a lexico-grammatical confusion – see Sections 7.3 and 8 below.
5. Of course, if face is allowed to exist outside interaction as well as inside it, the notion of group face becomes much more feasible. See Sifianou's chapter in this volume.

References

Arundale, R.B. (2006) 'Face as Relational and Interactional: A Communication Framework for Research on Face, Facework, and Politeness', *Journal of Politeness Research*, 2/2, pp. 193–216.

Arundale, R.B. (2009) 'Face as Emergent in Interpersonal Communication: An Alternative to Goffman', in Bargiela-Chiappini and Haugh (2009), pp. 33–54.

Bargiela-Chiappini, F. (2003) 'Face and Politeness: New (Insights) for Old (Concepts)', *Journal of Pragmatics*, 35/10–11, pp. 1453–1469.

Bargiela-Chiappini, F., and Haugh, M. (eds) (2009) *Face, Communication and Social Interaction*, London, Equinox.

Bravo, D. (2008) '(Im)politeness in Spanish-Speaking Socio-Cultural Context: Introduction', *Pragmatics*, 18, pp. 563–576.

Brown, P., and Levinson, S.C. (1987 [1978]) *Politeness: Some Universals in Language Usage*, Cambridge, Cambridge University Press, pp. 56–289. (Main body of which first published in E. Goody (ed.), *Questions and Politeness*, Cambridge, Cambridge University Press.)

Culpeper, J. (forthcoming) *Impoliteness: Using Language to Cause Offence*, Cambridge, Cambridge University Press.

Culpeper, J., and Kádár, D.Z. (eds) (2010) *Historical (Im)politeness*, Berne, Peter Lang.

Davies, B.L., Merrison, A.J., and Goddard, A. (2007) 'Institutional Apologies in UK Higher Education: Getting Back into the Black Before Going into the Red', *Journal of Politeness Research*, 3/1, pp. 39–63.

De Kadt, E. (1998) 'The Concept of Face and Its Applicability to the Zulu Language', *Journal of Pragmatics*, 29, pp. 173–191.

Economidou-Kogetsidis, M. (2005) '"Yes, Tell Me Please, What Time Is the Midday Flight from Athens Arriving?": Telephone Service Encounter and Politeness', *Intercultural Pragmatics*, 2/3, pp. 253–273.

Eelen, G. (2001) *A Critique of Politeness Theories*, Manchester, St. Jerome.

Ferenčík, M. (2007) 'Exercising Politeness: Membership Categorization in a Radio Phone-in Programme', *Pragmatics*, 17/3, pp. 351–370.

Gao, G. (2009) 'Face and Self in Chinese Communication', in Bargiela-Chiappini and Haugh (2009), pp. 175–191.

Goffman, E. (1963) *Behavior in Public Places: Notes on the Social Organization of Gatherings*, New York, The Free Press.

Goffman, E. (1964) 'The Neglected Situation', *American Anthropologist*, 66/6, Part II (Special Issue), pp. 133–136.

Goffman, E. (1967 [1955]) 'On Face-Work', in E. Goffman (collection), *Interaction Ritual: Essays on Face-to-Face Behavior*, Harmondsworth, Penguin, pp. 5–45. (Originally in *Psychiatry: Journal for the Study of Interpersonal Processes*, 18/3, pp. 213–231.)

Goffman, E. (1981) *Forms of Talk*, Oxford, Blackwell.

Grice, H.P. (1975) 'Logic and Conversation', in P. Cole and J.L. Morgan (eds), *Speech Acts, Syntax and Semantics, Vol. III: Speech Acts*, New York, Academic Press, pp. 41–58.

Hadfield, H., and Hahn, J.-W. (2007) *Concepts of Face and Korean Apologies*, unpublished manuscript, accessed on 7 January 2010 from: http://www2.hawaii.edu/~hunterh/Docs/FaceAndKoreanApologies.pdf.

Haugh, M. (2009) 'Face and Interaction', in Bargiela-Chiappini and Haugh (2009), pp. 1–30.

Hill, B., Ide, S., Ikuta, S., Kawasaki, A., and Ogino, T. (1986) 'Universals of Linguistic Politeness: Quantitative Evidence from Japanese and American English', *Journal of Pragmatics*, 10, pp. 347–371.

Hymes, D. (1972) 'Models of the Interaction of Language and Social Life', in J. Gumperz and D. Hymes (eds), *Directions in Sociolinguistics: The Ethnography of Communication*, New York, Holt, Rinehart & Winston, pp. 38–71.

Kádár, D.Z. (2010) 'Exploring the Historical Chinese Polite Denigration/Elevation Phenomenon', in Culpeper and Kádár (2010), pp. 119–145.

Koutlaki, S. (2002) Offers and Expressions of Thanks As Face-Enhancing Acts: Tae'rof in Persian', *Journal of Pragmatics*, 34/2, pp. 1733–1756.

Koutsantoni, D. (2004) 'Certainty across Cultures: A Comparison of the Degree of Certainty Expressed by Greek and English Speaking Scientific Authors', *Intercultural Pragmatics*, 2/2, pp. 121–149.

Levinson, S.C. (1992 [1979]) 'Activity Types and Language', in P. Drew and J. Heritage (eds), *Talk at Work*, Cambridge, Cambridge University Press, pp. 66–100. (Originally in *Linguistics*, 17, pp. 365–399.)
Lim, T.-S. (2009) 'Face in the Holistic and Relativistic Society', in Bargiela-Chiappini and Haugh (2009), pp. 250–268.
Lim, T.-S., and Bowers, J.W. (1991) 'Facework: Solidarity, Approbation, and Tact', *Human Communication Research*, 17/3, pp. 415–450.
Lim, T.-S., and Choi, S.H. (1996) 'Interpersonal Relationships in Korea', in W.B. Gudykunst, S. Ting-Toomey and T. Nishida (eds), *Communication in Personal Relationships across Cultures*, Thousand Oaks, Sage, pp. 122–136.
Locher, M.A., and Watts, R.J. (2005) 'Politeness Theory and Relational Work', *Journal of Politeness Research*, 1/1, pp. 9–33.
Mao, L.M. (1994) 'Beyond Politeness Theory: "Face" Revisited and Renewed', *Journal of Pragmatics*, 21, pp. 451–486.
Marquez-Reiter, R. (2005) 'Complaint Calls to a Caregiver Service Company: The Case of Desahogo', *Intercultural Pragmatics*, 2/4, pp. 481–514.
Marquez-Reiter, R. (2009) 'How to Get Rid of a Telemarketing Agent? Facework Strategies in an Intercultural Service Call', in Bargiela-Chiappini and Haugh (2009), pp. 55–77.
Merrison, A., Haugh, M., Davies, B.L., and Wilson, J.J. (in preparation) 'Getting Stuff Done: Comparing "E-Mail Requests" from Students in Higher Education in Britain and Australia', *Journal of Pragmatics*, Special Issue on 'Im/politeness across Englishes'.
Mills, S. (2003) *Gender and Politeness*, Cambridge, Cambridge University Press.
Mills, S. (2005) 'Gender and Impoliteness', *Journal of Politeness Research*, 1/2, pp. 263–280.
Myers, G. (1989) 'The Pragmatics of Politeness in Scientific Articles', *Applied Linguistics*, 10, pp. 1–35.
Nwoye, O.G. (1992) 'Linguistic Politeness and Sociocultural Variation of the Notion of Face', *Journal of Pragmatics*, 18/4, pp. 309–328.
O'Driscoll, J. (1996) 'About Face: A Defence and Elaboration of Universal Dualism', *Journal of Pragmatics*, 25, pp. 1–32.
O'Driscoll, J. (2001) 'A Face Model of Language Choice', *Multilingua*, 20/3, pp. 245–268.
O'Driscoll, J. (2007a) 'What's in an FTA? Reflections on a Chance Meeting with Claudine', *Journal of Politeness Research*, 3/2, pp. 243–268.
O'Driscoll, J. (2007b) 'Brown & Levinson's Face: How It Can – and Can't – Help Us to Understand Interaction across Cultures', *Intercultural Pragmatics*, 4/4, pp. 463–492.
O'Driscoll, J. (2010) 'Epilogue', in Culpeper and Kádár (2010), pp. 267–289.
Pizziconi, B. (2007) 'Facework and Multiple Selves in Apologetic Metapragmatic Comments in Japanese', in W. Bublitz and A. Huebler (eds), *Metapragmatics in Use*, Amsterdam, John Benjamins, pp. 49–72.
Ruhi, Ş. (2009) 'Evoking Face in Self and Other Presentation in Turkish', in Bargiela-Chiappini and Haugh (2009), pp. 155–174.
Ruhi, Ş., and Iştk-Güler, H. (2007) 'Conceptualising Face and Relational Work in (Im)politeness: Revelations from Politeness Lexemes and Idioms in Turkish', *Journal of Pragmatics*, 39, pp. 681–711.
Sifianou, M. (1989) 'On the Telephone Again! Differences in Telephone Behaviour: England Versus Greece', *Language and Society*, 18, pp. 527–544.

Smith, L. (1985) 'EIL versus ESL/EFL: What's the Difference and What Difference Does the Difference Make?', *English Teaching Forum*, 23/4, pp. 2–6.
Spencer-Oatey, H. (2005) '(Im)politeness, Face and Perceptions of Rapport: Unpackaging Their Bases and Interrelationships', *Journal of Politeness Research*, 1/1, pp. 95–119.
Spencer-Oatey, H. (2009) 'Face, Identity and Interactional Goals', in Bargiela-Chiappini and Haugh (2009), pp. 137–154.
Terkourafi, M. (2005) 'Beyond the Micro-Level in Politeness Research', *Journal of Politeness Research*, 1/2, pp. 237–262.
Terkourafi, M. (2007) 'Toward a Universal Notion of Face for a Universal Notion of Cooperation', in I. Kecskés and L. Horn (eds), *Explorations in Pragmatics: Linguistic, Cognitive and Intercultural Aspects*, Mouton Series in Pragmatics 1, Berlin, Mouton de Gruyter, pp. 307–338.
Thomas, J. (1983) 'Cross-Cultural Pragmatic Failure', *Applied Linguistics*, 4/2, pp. 91–112.
Ting-Toomey, S. (2005) 'The Matrix of Face: An Updated Face Negotiation Theory', in W.B. Gudykunst (ed.), *Theorizing about Intercultural Communication*, London, Sage, pp. 71–92.
Ting-Toomey, S. (2009) 'Facework Collision in Intercultural Communication', in Bargiela-Chiappini and Haugh (2009), pp. 227–249.
Tracy, K. (1992) 'The Many Faces of Facework', in H. Giles and P. Robinson (eds), *Handbook of Language and Social Psychology*, Chichester, Wiley, pp. 209–226.
Tracy, K., and Baratz, S. (1994) 'The Case for Case Studies of Facework', in S. Ting-Toomey (ed.), *The Challenge of Facework*, Albany, State University of New York, pp. 287–305.
Ukosakul, M. (2009) 'The Significance of "Face" and Politeness in Social Interaction as Revealed through Thai "Face" Idioms', in Bargiela-Chiappini and Haugh (2009), pp. 289–305.
Watts, R.J. (2003) *Politeness*, Cambridge, Cambridge University Press.
Watts, R.J., Ide, S., and Ehlich, K. (1992) 'Introduction', in R.J. Watts, S. Ide and K. Ehlich (eds), *Politeness in Language: Studies in Its History, Theory and Practice*, Berlin and New York, Mouton de Gruyter, pp. 1–17.
Wolfson, N. (1988) 'The Bulge: A Theory of Speech Behavior and Social Distance', in J. Fine (ed.), *Second Language Discourse*, Norwood, Ablex, pp. 21–38.

3
On the Concept of Face and Politeness

Maria Sifianou

1. Introduction

Face is a notion that is intuitively meaningful to many people but one that is highly complex and hard to define. Broadly speaking, it can be seen as a positive social image akin to identity. In recent years, research and debate on the concept of 'face' have grown exponentially, so that Watts (2005: xxviii) is right in contending that it "has become an area of research in its own right". The concept of 'face' is assumed to have originated in Chinese (see, for example, Bargiela-Chiappini 2003: 1454) and although it has been brought to the attention of the west mainly through Goffman's (1972 [1955]) seminal essay 'On face-work', it is Brown and Levinson's (1978, 1987) theory of politeness which has popularised it.

The aim of this chapter is two-fold: first, to investigate the conceptualisation of 'face' through the exploration of related metaphorical expressions in Greek and secondly, to consider the relationship of face to politeness and, more specifically, to positive politeness. To this end, I follow an empirical first-order perspective and try to tease out lay people's understanding of the concept on the basis of 'face' expressions. It is argued that concerning its everyday use, it makes sense to talk about face both as an individual's possession (with group repercussions) and as a pre-existing (though not static) entity. This seems to be in accord with earlier approaches (e.g. Goffman 1972) but rather discordant with current theorising, which sees face as discursively co-constructed in interaction. There is no doubt that in social interaction there is negotiation of face, which, however, is based on the qualities assumed to be included in each other's face. In other words, what is argued here is that rather than being attributed anew in every interaction, interlocutors mostly maintain but may also modify each other's and their own face. Moreover, modification may be the result of more than one encounter.

2. Theoretical background

Brown and Levinson's (1978, 1987) theory of politeness has been extremely influential: based on speech act theory and Grice's theory of conversation, it has been extensively criticised for focusing on single acts rather than longer chunks of discourse. Its other source, Goffman's notion of 'face', has been identified as an essential component of interaction but in need of expansion and elaboration to include Goffman's broader conceptualisation.

For Goffman (1972: 319), "*face* may be defined as the positive social value a person effectively claims for himself by the line others assume he has taken during a particular interaction. Face is an image of self delineated in terms of approved social attributes – albeit an image that others may share". For Brown and Levinson (1978: 66), 'face' is "the public self-image that every member wants to claim for himself" consisting of two interrelated even though somewhat conflicting aspects: 'positive face' refers to the desire to be appreciated and approved of by at least some others and 'negative face' refers to the desire to be free from impositions.

Researchers exploring the issue of face mostly in non-western societies (see, for example, Matsumoto 1988; Gu 1990; Nwoye 1992; Mao 1994) were among the first to challenge Brown and Levinson's conceptualisation. They argue that the concept of 'face' is far broader than mere self-image with a positive and a negative aspect to it, since it involves social, moral and, in particular, group aspects. Subsequent research has paved the way for an increasing number of scholars (see, for example, Watts et al. 1992; Werkhofer 1992; Eelen 2001; Bargiela-Chiappini 2003; Watts 2003) to argue that Brown and Levinson's conceptualisation of face is too narrow and individualistic, focusing as it does on individuals' psychological wants and desires (but see O'Driscoll 1996, 2007). As a result, some (see, for example, Bargiela-Chiappini 2003; Watts 2003; Locher and Watts 2005) have espoused a return to the Goffmanian concept of face, since, as it has been argued, it provides a better basis for the social/interpersonal aspects of face. In contrast, Arundale (2005, 2006, 2009) rejects both Goffman's and Brown and Levinson's conceptualisations of face and offers an alternative relational and interactional approach to face, which he calls 'face constituting theory'. For him, face is conjointly co-constituted by interlocutors in interactions; that is, it is seen as an emergent property of situated relationships (Arundale 2005: 201, 202; see also Terkourafi 2009).

2.1. Brown and Levinson's and Goffman's concepts of 'face'

If one compares Brown and Levinson's (1978, 1987) definition of face to that of Goffman's (1972), it appears that the former is concerned with an individual whose face is the self-image that s/he projects, whereas Goffman is clearly concerned with the interaction of at least two interlocutors. This difference has sparked off a vast amount of criticism against Brown and Levinson for reinterpreting Goffman's notion in individualistic terms and ignoring its social aspects. However, a closer look at Brown and Levinson (see, for example, 1978: 65, 66) reveals that face, for them, is not merely an individual's "public self-image" but one that "consists in a set of wants satisfiable only by the actions (including expressions of wants) of others" and where "normally everyone's face depends on everyone else's being maintained". This understanding becomes even more articulate in the preface of their more recent book edition (1987: 13), where face is not a self-image claimed but rather one "attributed by interactants to one another".[1] Thus, the problem with Brown and Levinson's notion of face does not reside in its asocial nature. Despite criticism, it is fair to say that the dimension of interdependence of social beings is not absent from Brown and Levinson's conceptualisation of the notion. In this respect, it is not incongruent with Goffman's understanding of the discursive co-construction of face in social interactions. The difference is that, even though both Goffman (1972: 323) and Brown and Levinson (1987: 60) recognise that for an interaction to succeed both respect of self and consideration for the other are needed, Brown and Levinson have focused on other-face concerns through the mitigation of face-threatening acts (FTAs).[2] However, face is present throughout interactions and not only when face-threatening acts are likely to emerge (O'Driscoll 2007) as it is "diffusely located in the flow of events in the encounter" (Goffman 1972: 320). Brown and Levinson (1987: 233) attempt to account for this diffusion by suggesting the notion of 'face-threatening intention' (instead of FTAs), which covers conversational sequences made up of a number of turns. They therefore acknowledge their neglect of longer stretches of discourse, attributing it to the impact of speech act theory.

2.2. Longitudinal and group aspects of face

What seems to be missing from Brown and Levinson's account is the possibility that face involves issues not only within but also beyond the specific encounter (Ting-Toomey 2005: 73). This is acknowledged by Werkhofer (1992: 176) when he argues that face is not only connected to the narrow "here and now" but also "to processes that may go on over longer stretches of time". This understanding of face is related to Ho's (1994: 274) definition, for whom face is consistent over time and across situations. Interestingly, this rather neglected enduring aspect of face can also be found in Goffman's (1972: 320) work, who says that in order for someone to maintain face in the current situation s/he must have abstained from certain acts in the past that would be difficult to confront later (cf. O'Driscoll 1996: 6). This understanding does not necessarily contradict the discursive co-construction of face and its relational character but highlights the argument that what is co-constructed on the spot also draws from prior encounters and socio-cultural resources available to interlocutors. In order to act at any moment, interlocutors employ the socio-historical knowledge they possess and evaluate which aspects of their multifaceted face are relevant to the current situation.

Single interactions are not entirely autonomous events but have links to prior and future similar ones, as initial greetings and closing farewells clearly indicate (Goffman 1972: 343). In the cases in which interlocutors have relational histories, they expect to be granted a specific kind of face. In fact, it can be argued that no interlocutor enters an interaction 'faceless', expecting to co-construct face on the spot and because of its social and cognitive nature, it may actually be misleading to explore its interactional aspect only (Spencer-Oatey 2007: 648; see also Jakubowska and Watanabe, this volume). Interlocutors normally come to interaction with a 'face' encompassing qualities accumulated over time through self- and other-evaluation. This largely shared image is projected to and accorded by others, and will of course differ from situation to situation. In my understanding, this is what Goffman (1972: 322) calls 'social face', which "can be his [the person's] most personal possession and the center of his security and pleasure". It is thus reasonable to suggest that in social encounters between participants with ongoing relationships facework will be 'unmarked'. This means that interlocutors take for granted each other's face and sustain it through their actions.

However, the understanding of face as being on loan from society (Goffman 1972: 322) implies the possibility of change and, more specifically, of damage or loss of face in actual encounters, or in other words, of 'marked facework'. Damage or loss of face may result from either the individual's evaluation of their own behaviour as inappropriate or their concession that the other has correctly evaluated their behaviour as inappropriate. The same applies to their enhancement of face as a result of the speaker's concomitant agreement with the addressee's evaluation. However, any change may be either temporary, that is, pertaining only to the specific interaction, or may have further repercussions for the individual or the group s/he belongs to and may affect future interactions. Moreover, change may take several interactions to be established.

It is now widely accepted that claiming and attributing qualities does not necessarily involve two interacting individuals alone but may draw from and reflect on the groups an individual belongs to. Others may accord or withdraw one's face on the basis not only of an individual's conformity to social expectations but also on the actions performed by closely related others (see, for example, Ho 1994: 271). These closely related others may constitute any social group to which the individual belongs, such as their close and extended family, their work group, their neighbourhood or even their nationality group. Their actions may reflect favourably or unfavourably on the individual's face and vice versa. This understanding gives rise to the concept of 'group face' or 'corporate face' (see, for example, Goffman 1972: 344; Nwoye 1992: 315; Hirschon 2001: 23; Spencer-Oatey 2005: 106–107), which may even take priority over individual face, especially in cases of competition between groups (see also Terkourafi 2008: 319). The relative priority of group face depends obviously on the degree to which the individual identifies with a specific group, but the very existence of group face indicates that face cannot merely be a construct of just any current interaction.

In the relevant literature, the idea of group face has been advanced especially in relation to Japanese and Chinese cultures. For instance, it has been argued that Brown and Levinson's concept of face reflects western individualism, since in some Asian cultures it is the social group that one belongs to which is more important. Consequently, face must be seen as an open category whose components vary cross-culturally (see, for example, Matsumoto 1988; Ide 1989; Gu 1990; Mao 1994; Haugh 2007a; Jakubowska, this volume). Such objections are not restricted to East-Asian socio-cultural contexts. For instance, Nwoye (1992: 310) argues that in the egalitarian Igbo (Nigerian) society "concern for group interests rather than atomistic individualism is the expected norm". Similar concerns are raised in relation to the Turkish, Persian and Zulu cultures (Bayraktaroğlu 2000; Koutlaki 2002, 2009, de Kadt 1998: 176, respectively).

2.3. Positive and negative face

A common denominator in much research has been the culture-specificity and problematic nature of the concept of negative face (see, for example, O'Driscoll 1996, 2007). Particularly troublesome has been its close association with the notions of 'imposition' and 'threat'. Brown and Levinson (1987: 14) seem to endorse this concern, even though tentatively, when they say that "it perhaps reflects the bias of a culture obsessed with individual rights and wants". This is an important acknowledgement since it explains why 'negative face wants', a specific type of wants, have been elevated over 'positive face wants', which is a much broader construct; the former is explored in 80 pages and the latter in less than 30.

The conceptual breadth of positive face becomes obvious if we look more closely at Brown and Levinson's (1987: 62, 63) definition of positive face; that is, one's desire to have one's possessions, goals and achievements "ratified, understood, approved of, liked or admired". This leads to the suggestion that it is positive face which is closer to folk notions of face (O'Driscoll 1996: 6) and, as a result, it has been found less problematic than negative face in subsequent crosscultural research. This conceptual breadth of positive face led Lim and Bowers (1991) to suggest that it has two distinct dimensions: (1) the want to be included or 'fellowship face' and (2) the want to be respected for one's abilities or 'competence face'. Brown and Levinson's negative face is termed 'autonomy face'. Ting-Toomey (2005: 81) draws even finer distinctions between face content domains which include 'autonomy', 'inclusion', 'approval', 'reliability', 'competence' and 'moral face'. This same focus on the breadth of positive face motivates O'Driscoll (2007: 474) to advocate the confinement of the positive aspect to "pertain solely to connection and belonging". In this way, he preserves the positive/negative relationship by retaining the term 'positive' but restricting its content to the exact opposite of the negative; something akin to Lim and Bower's (1991) 'fellowship face'. Other significant aspects of face, such as general esteem, shame, pride, embarrassment, confidence and approval have also been identified. It is these aspects, as O'Driscoll (2007: 480, 481) contends, that bear considerable crosscultural and situational variation and may have little to do with the positive and the negative aspects.

Dissatisfied with the concepts of 'positive' and 'negative' face, in a recent paper Bravo (2008) expands on her earlier suggestion of 'affiliation' and 'autonomy' aspects of face. The former refers to being a member of a group and the latter to having one's own identity within a group (Bravo 2008: 566). According to Bravo, these notions are interdependent and can account for the interdependence of individuals in society. In order to uncover this interdependence through the discursive negotiation of face in interactions, alternatives such as 'rapport-management' (Spencer-Oatey 2000, 2005), 'relational work' (see, for example, Locher and Watts 2005; Locher 2006) and 'face constituting theory' (Arundale 1999, 2005, 2006) have been proposed. These terms are akin to 'face-work' but they are preferred to it, since in early politeness research 'face-work' was associated with the mitigation of face-threatening acts (see, for example, Goffman 1972: 324; Locher 2006: 250).

This widespread unease with the concept of face indicates not only its complexity but also the need to delve deeper into its contents or range of meanings. In other words, one needs to specify what Goffman's 'approved social attributes' really are and what Brown and Levinson's (1978: 66) "publicly relevant content of personality" is. These contents are not only culture-specific (see, for example, O'Driscoll 2007; Haugh 2007a; Bravo 2008; Terkourafi 2009) but will also vary in different situations within the same culture.

2.4. The content of face

The multitude of qualities that have been attributed to face give the impression of great variability. For Spencer-Oatey (2000: 12) face "is concerned with people's sense of worth, dignity and identity, and is associated with issues such as respect, honour, status, reputation and competence". In relation to Persian, Koutlaki (2002: 1742) sees 'pride' and 'honour' as its two basic components, including 'personality', 'character', 'self-respect' and 'social standing' but also 'esteem' and 'dignity'. For Ting-Toomey and Kurogi (1998: 190) the relevant notions are: "respect, honor, status, reputation, credibility, competence, family/network connection, loyalty, trust, relational indebtedness and obligation". In Thai, these are "dignity, self-esteem, prestige, reputation and pride" (Ukosakul 2005: 119). In broader terms, for Ting-Toomey (2005: 73), "the concept of face is about identity respect and other-identity consideration.... Face is tied to the emotional significance and estimated calculations that we attach to our own social self-worth and the social self-worth of others". Acts threatening these qualities of face may lead to feelings of embarrassment, shame and/or guilt, whereas acts enhancing them may lead to some kind of pride.

Bargiela-Chiappini (2009: 307) sums up the roots of face concerns "in values such as honour, shame and pride". Brown and Levinson (1987: 13) themselves see face as linked to cultural notions of "honour and virtue, shame and redemption" and, in relation to Greek, Hirschon

(2001: 20) views 'face' and 'honour' as conceptual equivalents. While these definitions initially appear to encompass a variety of different qualities of face, they are related in sharing a core concept of honour, which, however, is not restricted to Asian cultures (cf. Scollon and Scollon 1995: 34). Thus the concepts of face and facework are undoubtedly broader than that of politeness in its initial conceptualisation as avoidance or mitigation of face-threatening acts. Moreover, considering these definitions, it is noteworthy that while there seems little connection between 'face' and 'negative face' (one's want that his/her actions be unimpeded), one could discern a clearer link with the broad concept of 'positive face' (one's want that his/her wants be desirable).

3. The concept of 'face' in Greek

Collecting data for this project was a difficult task, as it appears that 'face' expressions occur mostly in informal settings and are rather infrequent. This does not mean that such expressions are out of use as detailed entries in contemporary dictionaries attest (see, for example, Kriaras 1995; Babiniotis 1998; Triandafyllidis 2003). The dataset for this study includes 78 instances collected from daily interactions, television, newspapers and popular magazines. However, most of my examples (about 120) come from the internet and corpora (Sketch Engine/GkWaC – www.sketchengine.co.uk). Interestingly, most of these instances are drawn from blogs (rather than more traditional written sources) where interlocutors use more informal varieties of language. This suggests that face expressions in Greek are restricted to informal uses of language. In relation to English there is disagreement, since for Ervin-Tripp et al. (1995: 48) such expressions are restricted to educated use, whereas they have been found to be in use among ordinary speakers in their daily interactions (Haugh and Hinze 2003: 1597).

In this section, I will consider examples from my data that appear to support my contention that face is not simply an image co-constructed in specific encounters. In Greek, at least, face is understood as an individual's property which may be modified in interaction, much like Goffman's (1972) and Brown and Levinson's (1978, 1987) conceptualisations.

The concept of face in Greek seems to be broader than that in English though not as rich as the one in East-Asian cultures, such as Japanese, Chinese and Korean (Haugh 2007a; Mao 1994; Ervin-Tripp et al. 1995). Similar to these languages, Greek has more than one term for 'face', and just like the Japanese (*kao, menboku* and *taimen*) and the

Chinese (*lian* and *mianzi*) lexical items, they differ in their range of meanings. In addition to *πρόσωπο* (*prósopo*), the general word for 'face', there is the more colloquial *μούτρα* (*mútra*). Even though the two can be used interchangeably in the sense of integrity (e.g. *Δεν έχω πρόσωπο/μούτρα να δω άνθρωπο* 'I don't have face to see anybody'), it is noteworthy that *μούτρα* has a wider collocational range and is more frequently used in related expressions.[3] This reinforces the suggestion made earlier in relation to the informal use of such expressions.[4] In addition, *μέτωπο* (*métopo*) and its informal variant *κούτελο* (*kútelo*) 'forehead' are also used in related expressions (e.g. *Θέλω/Έχω το μέτωπό/κούτελό μου καθαρό* 'I want/have my forehead clean') to express desire or possession of integrity. Here again the latter is the predominant lexeme in Greek. *Φάτσα* (*fátsa*, from the Italian *faccia*) is rarely used. All these terms can be used to refer to the physical part of the body but are also used metaphorically and reflect emotions and significant values for the construal of the social person (cf. Ruhi and Işık-Güler 2007 on *yüz* in Turkish, and Haugh 2007a on *kao* in Japanese). It is important to note here that all individuals are assumed to have face, irrespective of their status and achievements, unlike East-Asian cultures where status is an important component of face (Ho et al. 2004: 68). As Herzfeld (1980: 342) suggests, 'honour' can be found in conditions of extreme poverty.

Drawing on dictionary definitions and my collection of related expressions, it appears that face in Greek primarily involves the concepts of honour and dignity. As mentioned earlier, Hirschon (2001: 20) sees 'face' and 'honour' in Greek as conceptual equivalents and the latter as "a key notion for the interpretation of Greek social conduct and values". In Greek, there are no expressions which directly render either *save* or *lose face* but rather one either drops his/her face (*ρίχνει τα μούτρα του/της*) or one's face falls (*τα μούτρα του/της πέφτουν*). One may drop their face if other concerns are seen as more significant than concern for face. For instance, in the midst of the global financial crisis, in a recent newspaper article (*Vima*, Tuesday 1 July 2008) one reads that "the Prime Minister 'drops his face' and asks Brussels for help". Similarly, in a TV magazine agony column (*Tiletheatis*, No 1030: 90, January 2009), the writer describes his problems with his ex-wife, saying that whenever they had a dispute and she would not speak to him for long periods, he was always the one to 'drop his face' and to approach her in order to find a way out. More specifically, one drops one's face consciously after calculating the pros and cons of a prospective action, whereas one's face falls by accident if one or closely related others inadvertently violate social norms. For instance, parents' face may fall as a consequence of their children's misbehaviour. In such cases, people may say *μου 'πεσαν τα μούτρα* 'my face fell', which is a situation-specific expression used to evaluate the result of somebody admitting a mistake or wrongdoing or the result of breaking some social convention. Interestingly, this is an evaluative judgement that can be made by an individual in relation to themselves usually in reporting an event, even in the absence of criticism by others present at the event (cf. Ho et al. 2004: 70).

The results of broader infractions are assessed with idiomatic expressions like *δεν έχω μούτρα/πρόσωπο να τον δω/να του μιλήσω* roughly meaning 'I don't have face to see/speak to him'[5] or *δεν έχω μούτρα/πρόσωπο να βγω στην κοινωνία* 'I don't have face to appear in society'. These are also evaluative judgements made by individuals in relation to themselves. However, they refer to more serious offences possibly involving additional qualities of face and perhaps with long-lasting effects. Producers of such utterances express their embarrassment and/or shame for not having behaved according to expected norms in the past so that contact or interaction is currently difficult. These clearly illustrate Goffman's (1972: 320) claim that in order for someone to maintain face in the current situation s/he must have abstained from certain acts in the past that would be difficult to face up to later. They also illustrate my claim that one is normally understood to enter an interaction already possessing some kind of face.

Interestingly, the majority of collocations of the face lexeme involve the verb 'to have', a fact which indicates that face is conceptualised as a possession that everybody should have. Lack of expressions rendering 'I have face' may indicate that having face is taken for granted[6] and related comments involve mostly its absence through negative or interrogative constructions. For instance, both the negative *δεν έχω μούτρα να τον δω* 'I don't have face to see him' and the interrogative *έχει μούτρα και μιλάει ακόμα;* 'Has s/he still got face to talk?' indicate absence of face, the former being a negative evaluation of self and the latter a similar implied evaluation of the other. In other words, the latter questions the possession of face and implies that the addressees' previous conduct does not entitle them to face. Further evidence that face is conceptualised as an individual's possession is provided by expressions like *πήρε τα μούτρα του και έφυγε* 'He took his face and left', which means that one leaves an interaction or a place feeling embarrassed or shamefaced. It could be suggested that even the expressions discussed earlier involve possessions which are either dropped or fall down. Thus, face seems to be understood primarily as a possession that can be handled by individuals but not as something that can be given to others directly. Unlike East-Asian languages, but similar to French and English (Ervin-Tripp et al. 1995: 52), in Greek the idea of giving someone face is not verbalised. One's verbal involvement with somebody else's face can only be negative. Distantly related expressions include *του 'σπασα/'λειωσα τα μούτρα* 'I broke/crushed his face' which, in addition to their literal meaning, may also mean causing loss of face for somebody else. Interesting in this respect is the expression *του 'κανα τα μούτρα κρέας* 'I made his face meat', which implies that I deprived somebody of all the qualities of face. Similarly, *του πέταξε λάσπη στα μούτρα* 'He threw mud in his face' can have both a literal and a figurative meaning (cf. Haugh 2007a: 662 for the same expression in Japanese).[7]

As mentioned earlier, in Greek, most 'face' expressions refer to the absence of face, much like Chinese, Japanese and Korean (but unlike English where the concept of face-saving is more frequent; Ervin-Tripp et al. 1995: 53) since every human being, irrespective of status, has face or honour. By adhering to societal norms and behaving according to one's social standing, face is maintained (rather than enhanced) and may fall down if norms are disregarded. This situation may lead to feelings of embarrassment, shame or guilt, which are both private and public emotions. The presence of an audience and the possibility of negative comments may exacerbate these emotions.

Interestingly, even though rare, there are a couple of examples in my data where the speaker claims that his/her 'face fell' in private. For instance, in one case the speaker describes how at a christening ceremony she had met a little girl she thought was very unattractive and despite her attempts to identify just a single nice feature in her she could not. When she heard the mother summon her child with 'Where are you my beauty?' she felt extremely embarrassed ('My face fell from the nastiness of my thought'). Such examples are discordant with Lim's (1994: 210) contention that face is conceptualised as a distinctly and uniquely interactional phenomenon. This appears to be a rather restricted understanding of the notion of face, as examples like the above illustrate. Generally speaking, it is true that "one cannot gain face from a great feat that is not witnessed by others, and cannot lose face from blunders made in private" (Lim 1994: 210), but if significant, such events will be incorporated into one's projected image.

It is my contention here that even though face is relational, it is not constructed anew at every interaction but emerges over time as a cumulative effect of several interactions with the same individuals. The effects of just one positive or negative act may not influence face or they may do so but only temporarily. In fact, just one adverse act may cause empathy. To attribute qualities such as 'honesty' or 'integrity' to somebody, it normally takes more than single events. Similarly, more than single events are required for the withdrawal of face, unless the specific infraction has been assessed as very serious. If somebody's face 'falls', this may be relevant only for the current situation or may have repercussions for forthcoming ones. Face is relational but interlocutors start each interaction taking for granted the kind of face that has been constructed in previous encounters and which they bring to the interaction. This is the unmarked case where face may not be salient. A new version of face may surface when a mismatch between speaker's self-presentation and addressee's evaluation emerges. In other words, face is a significant though vulnerable socio-historical construct whose maintenance in interaction is important. As the popular Greek saying goes, 'It's better to lose your eye than your good name.'

4. Face and politeness

The above discussion reinforces the suggestion that facework is broader than politeness (see, for example, Watts 2003: 130; O'Driscoll, this volume). Not all contexts which involve impoliteness or rudeness entail loss of face and not all loss of face entails impoliteness. For instance, the former Greek prime minister described in the article mentioned earlier as dropping his face and asking Brussels for financial aid was clearly neither interpreted as being rude or impolite to Brussels' officials nor could he feel that way about himself. Similarly, the blogger who complained about the problems with his telephone service provider, as a result of which his landline was disconnected for 26 days, and wrote "I want to see if they [the providers] have the face to bill me" for this month, would not have evaluated the providers' behaviour as rude or impolite but rather as incompetent. In recounting an embarrassing experience, a hostess said to a friend 'My face fell because of the untidiness of my place.' However, she neither felt impolite to her unexpected visitors nor did they make any related comment. Moreover, dropping one's face may even serve politeness concerns, as in the case of a blogger who wrote that he had dropped his face and apologised to some friends in order to avoid the escalation of a conflict.

If one were to draw a link between face and politeness, face would appear more closely related to positive politeness. As O'Driscoll (1996: 6) suggests, it is positive face that "seems to accord very closely with the concern for honour and good reputation inherent in folk notions of face itself". It might be the breadth of positive politeness mentioned earlier (Section 2.3) that can better accommodate the concepts of honour and integrity. Moreover, these concepts, much like positive face, are perennial needs (Brown and Levinson 1987: 73). It is true, as Brown and Levinson (1987: 130) claim, that in western cultures it is negative politeness that is conjured up when we think of, or talk, about politeness. However, this may largely reflect a stereotypical understanding of politeness which equates it with formality. When Greeks (Sifianou 1992: 87–92) were asked to define politeness and provide relevant examples, interesting results emerged. A number of Greek informants included in their definitions attributes that might be better described in English in terms of altruism, generosity, morality and self-abnegation rather than formality.[8] This broad understanding of politeness is closely related to the broader and uniquely Greek concept of *φιλότιμο* (*filótimo*) 'love of honour' (see, for example, Triandis and Vassiliou 1972: 308–309; Sifianou 1992: 89–90; Koutsantoni 2007), which "is revealed, above all, in socially appropriate behaviour" (Herzfeld 1980: 343). The overlap between the two concepts is nicely illustrated in Herzfeld's (1980: 343) example in which it is *φιλότιμο* 'love of honour', rather than politeness, which is seen as demonstrated by the foreign visitor who later sends a postcard to thank a villager for their hospitality.

5. Conclusion

In this chapter I have attempted to explore the concept of face as conceptualised and used by lay Greek people. To this end, I considered dictionary definitions and related metaphorical expressions used in daily and web interactions. Even though the data is limited, it points to a conceptualisation of face as a taken-for-granted personal property one should maintain in interaction. Thus maintaining or saving face is not verbalised. What is verbalised is withdrawal or loss of face. The latter is verbalised as one's face falling down or one's negating their possession of face while the former is verbalised through questioning somebody else's possession of face. Interestingly, there are also cases where one may choose to drop their own face if other concerns are judged as more significant than maintaining face. These may even relate to politeness concerns.

Most collocations involve the verbs 'have', 'drop' and 'fall', a fact that indicates that face is conceptualised as an individual's possession. This does not mean that face is independent of others since it is interactionally constructed through verbal and non-verbal behaviour. It is, however, constructed over time in ongoing relationships through self- and other-evaluation and is present in any interaction but may or may not become salient. Thus, individuals enter interactions already possessing some kind of face, modification of which may or may not become relevant or salient in the specific encounter. It becomes relevant when speakers' and addressees' evaluations indicate a mismatch which may trigger change. However, any change may be either temporary or may have long-term repercussions reflecting poorly on the individual and/ or the group s/he belongs to.

If my interpretation is correct, namely that lay people conceptualise face as a kind of possession, then a related theory should be able to incorporate this conceptualisation at least as an option (cf. Haugh 2007b: 302). In other words, a theory cannot ignore lay people's notions of lay terms in use, unless it aims at formulating an abstract, higher level, universal theoretical construct (see, for example, Watts 2003: 9; O'Driscoll 1996, 2007; Terkourafi 2009).

Notes

This chapter is based on a larger project funded by the University of Athens (Special Research Account 70/4/5535). I would like to thank Eleni Antonopoulou and Villy Tsakona for our lengthy discussions and their constructive comments. Thanks are also due to the reviewers of the chapter and especially to the editors of this volume, who gave me the opportunity to explore an issue on which I have been pondering for some time.

1. Moreover, 'claiming' cannot involve a single speaker.
2. In fact, according to Brown and Levinson, most, if not all, of our acts are face-threatening.
3. See Triandafyllidis (2003: www.komvos.edu.gr/dictonlineplsql/simple_search.display_full_lemma?the_lemma_id=36032&target_dict=1).
4. I owe this comment to Villy Tsakona. An interesting example of this comes from a popular song: 'With what face does she ask to look me in the face? With what face will she apologise?' These are the betrayed lover's repeated questions to the late-night visitor who has supposedly come to seek reconciliation on her behalf.
5. Similar is the Turkish expression *onunla konuşacak/ona bakacak yüzüm yok* (A. Bayraktaroğlu p.c.) and the Chinese *meiyou lian jian ren* (Ho et al. 2004: 67). See Ervin-Tripp et al. (1995) for related expressions in Japanese, Chinese and Korean. See also Haugh (2007a) for Japanese and Ruhi and Işık-Güler (2007) for Turkish.
6. The only related expression is *θέλω/έχω το πρόσωπό/κούτελό μου καθαρό* 'I want/have my face/forehead clean' which expresses desire for or possession of integrity and honour (see also Koutsantoni 2007: 103).
7. In relation to self one can even say *έφαγα τα μούτρα μου* 'I ate my face' to mean that I risked but did not achieve my goal.

8. In fact, some respondents saw overt markers of politeness as habitual distancing devices which conceal 'real' 'innate' politeness (whatever that may mean).

References

Arundale, R. (1999) 'An Alternative Model and Ideology of Communication for an Alternative to Politeness Theory', *Pragmatics*, 9/1, pp. 119–153.

Arundale, R. (2005) 'Pragmatics, Conversational Implicature, and Conversation', in K.L. Fitch and R.E. Sanders (eds), *Handbook of Language and Social Interaction*, Mahwah, Lawrence Erlbaum Associates, pp. 41–63.

Arundale, R. (2006) 'Face as Relational and Interactional: A Communication Framework for Research on Face, Facework and Politeness', *Journal of Politeness Research*, 2/2, pp. 193–216.

Arundale, R. (2009) 'Face as Emergent in Interpersonal Communication: An Alternative to Goffman', in F. Bargiela-Chiappini and M. Haugh (eds), *Face, Communication and Social Interaction*, London, Equinox, pp. 33–54.

Babiniotis, G. (1998) *Λεξικό της Νέας Ελληνικής Γλώσσας* [*Dictionary of Modern Greek Language*], Athens, Lexicology Centre.

Bargiela-Chiappini, F. (2003) 'Face and Politeness: New (Insights) for Old (Concepts)', *Journal of Pragmatics*, 35/10–11, pp. 1453–1469.

Bargiela-Chiappini, F. (2009) 'Facing the Future: Some Reflections', in F. Bargiela-Chiappini and M. Haugh (eds), *Face, Communication and Social Interaction*, London, Equinox, pp. 307–327.

Bayraktaroğlu, A. (2000) 'A Repair Mechanism in Turkish Conversation: The Case of *Estagfurullah*', *Multilingua*, 19/3, pp. 281–310.

Bravo, D. (2008) '(Im)politeness in Spanish-Speaking Socio-Cultural Contexts: Introduction', *Pragmatics*, 18/4, pp. 563–576.

Brown, P., and Levinson, S.C. (1978) 'Universals in Language Usage: Politeness Phenomena', in E. Goody (ed.), *Questions and Politeness: Strategies in Social Interaction*, Cambridge, Cambridge University Press, pp. 56–289.

Brown, P., and Levinson, S.C. (1987) *Politeness: Some Universals in Language Usage*, Cambridge, Cambridge University Press.

de Kadt, E. (1998) 'The Concept of Face and Its Applicability to the Zulu Language', *Journal of Pragmatics*, 29/2, pp. 173–191.

Eelen, G. (2001) *A Critique of Politeness Theories*, Manchester, St. Jerome.

Ervin-Tripp, S., Nakamura, K., and Guo, J. (1995) 'Shifting Face from Asia to Europe', in M. Shibatani and S. Thompson (eds), *Essays in Semantics and Pragmatics: In Honor of Charles J. Fillmore*, Amsterdam and Philadelphia, John Benjamins, pp. 43–71.

Goffman, E. (1972 [1955]) 'On Face-Work: An Analysis of Ritual Elements in Social Interaction', in J. Laver and S. Hutcheson (eds), *Communication in Face-to-Face Interaction*, Harmondsworth, Penguin, pp. 319–346.

Gu, Y. (1990) 'Politeness Phenomena in Modern Chinese', *Journal of Pragmatics*, 14/2, pp. 237–257.

Haugh, M. (2007a) 'Emic Conceptualisations of (Im)politeness and Face in Japanese: Implications for the Discursive Negotiation of Second Language Learner Identities', *Journal of Pragmatics*, 39/4, pp. 657–680.

Haugh, M. (2007b) 'The Discursive Challenge to Politeness Research: An Interactional Alternative', *Journal of Politeness Research*, 3/2, pp. 295–317.
Haugh, M., and Hinze, C. (2003) 'A Metalinguistic Approach to Deconstructing the Concepts of "Face" and "Politeness" in Chinese, English and Japanese', *Journal of Pragmatics*, 35/10–11, pp. 1581–1611.
Herzfeld, M. (1980) 'Honour and Shame: Problems in the Comparative Analysis of Moral Systems', *Man* (n.s.), 15, pp. 339–351.
Hirschon, R. (2001) 'Freedom, Solidarity and Obligation: The Socio-Cultural Context of Greek Politeness', in A. Bayraktaroğlu and M. Sifianou (eds), *Linguistic Politeness across Boundaries: The Case of Greek and Turkish*, Amsterdam and Philadelphia, John Benjamins, pp. 17–42.
Ho, Y.-F.D. (1994) 'Face Dynamics: From Conceptualization to Measurement', in S. Ting-Toomey (ed.), *The Challenge of Facework*, Albany, State University of New York Press, pp. 269–305.
Ho, Y.-F.D., Fu, W., and Ng, S.M. (2004) 'Guilt, Shame and Embarrassment: Revelations of Face and Self', *Culture & Psychology*, 10/1, pp. 64–84.
Ide, S. (1989) 'Formal Forms and Discernment: Neglected Aspects of Linguistic Politeness', *Multilingua*, 8/2, pp. 223–248.
Koutlaki, S.A. (2002) 'Offers and Expressions of Thanks as Face Enhancing Acts: Tæ'arof in Persian', *Journal of Pragmatics*, 34/12, pp. 1733–1756.
Koutlaki, S.A. (2009) 'Two Sides of the Same Coin: How the Notion of "Face" Is Encoded in Persian Communication', in F. Bargiela-Chiappini and M. Haugh (eds), *Face, Communication and Social Interaction*, London, Equinox, pp. 115–133.
Koutsantoni, D. (2007) '"I Can Now Apologize to You Twice from the Bottom of My Heart": Apologies in Greek Reality TV', *Journal of Politeness Research*, 3/1, pp. 93–123.
Kriaras, E. (1995) *Νέο Ελληνικό Λεξικό* [*Modern Greek Dictionary*], Athens, Ekdotiki Athinon.
Lim, T.-S. (1994) 'Facework and Interpersonal Relationships', in S. Ting-Toomey (ed.), *The Challenge of Facework: Cross-cultural and Interpersonal Issues*, Albany, State University of New York Press, pp. 209–229.
Lim, T.-S., and Bowers, J.W. (1991) 'Facework: Solidarity, Approbation, and Tact', *Human Communication Research*, 17/3, pp. 415–450.
Locher, M.A. (2006) 'Polite Behaviour within Relational Work: The Discursive Approach to Politeness', *Multilingua*, 25/3, pp. 249–267.
Locher, M.A., and Watts, R.J. (2005) 'Politeness Theory and Relational Work', *Journal of Politeness Research*, 1/1, pp. 9–33.
Mao, L.M.R. (1994) 'Beyond Politeness Theory: "Face" Revisited and Renewed', *Journal of Pragmatics*, 21/5, pp. 451–486.
Matsumoto, Y. (1988) 'Reexamination of the Universality of Face: Politeness Phenomena in Japanese', *Journal of Pragmatics*, 12/4, pp. 403–426.
Nwoye, O.G. (1992) 'Linguistic Politeness and Socio-Cultural Variations of the Notion of Face', *Journal of Pragmatics*, 18/4, pp. 309–328.
O'Driscoll, J. (1996) 'About Face: A Defence and Elaboration of Universal Dualism', *Journal of Pragmatics*, 25/1, pp. 1–32.
O'Driscoll, J. (2007) 'Brown and Levinson's Face: How It Can – and Can't – Help Us to Understand Interaction across Cultures', *Intercultural Pragmatics*, 4/4, pp. 463–492.

Ruhi, Ş., and Işık-Güler, H. (2007) 'Conceptualizing Face and Relational Work in (Im)politeness: Revelations from Politeness Lexemes and Idioms in Turkish', *Journal of Pragmatics*, 39/4, pp. 681–711.

Scollon, R., and Scollon, S.W. (1995) *Intercultural Communication*, Oxford and Cambridge, MA, Blackwell.

Sifianou, M. (1992) *Politeness Phenomena in England and Greece: A Cross-Cultural Perspective*, Oxford, Clarendon Press.

Spencer-Oatey, H. (2000) 'Rapport Management: A Framework for Analysis', in H. Spencer-Oatey (ed.), *Culturally Speaking: Managing Rapport through Talk across Cultures*, London and New York, Continuum, pp. 11–46.

Spencer-Oatey, H. (2005) '(Im)politeness, Face and Perceptions of Rapport: Unpackaging Their Bases and Interrelationships', *Journal of Politeness Research*, 1/1, pp. 95–119.

Spencer-Oatey, H. (2007) 'Theories of Identity and the Analysis of Face', *Journal of Pragmatics*, 39/4, pp. 639–656.

Terkourafi, M. (2008) 'Toward a Universal Notion of Face for a Universal Notion of Cooperation', in I. Kecskes and L.R. Horn (eds), *Explorations in Pragmatics*, Berlin and New York, Mouton de Gruyter, pp. 313–344.

Terkourafi, M. (2009) 'Finding Face between *Gemeinschaft* and *Gesellschaft*: Greek Perceptions of the In-Group', in F. Bargiela-Chiappini and M. Haugh (eds), *Face, Communication and Social Interaction*, London, Equinox pp. 269–288.

Ting-Toomey, S. (2005) 'The Matrix of Face: An Updated Face-Negotiation Theory', in W.B. Gudykunst (ed.), *Theorizing about Intercultural Communication*, Thousand Oaks, Sage, pp. 71–91.

Ting-Toomey, S., and Kurogi, A. (1998) 'Facework Competenece in Intercultural Conflict: An Updated Face-Negotiation Theory', *International Journal of Intercultural Relations*, 22/2, pp. 187–225.

Triandafyllidis, M. (2003) *Λεξικό της Κοινής Νεοελληνικής* [*Modern Greek Dictionary*], accessed on 30 January 2010 from: http://www.komvos.edu.gr/dictionaries/dictonline/DictOnLineTri.htm.

Triandis, H.C., and Vassiliou, V. (1972) 'A Comparative Analysis of Subjective Culture', in H. Triandis (ed.), *The Analysis of Subjective Culture*, New York, Wiley, pp. 299–335.

Ukosakul, M. (2005) 'The Significance of "Face" and Politeness in Social Interaction as Revealed through Thai "Face" Idioms', in R. Lakoff and S. Ide (eds), *Broadening the Horizon of Linguistic Politeness*, Amsterdam and Philadelphia, John Benjamins, pp. 117–125.

Watts, R.J. (2003) *Politeness*, Cambridge, Cambridge University Press.

Watts, R.J. (2005) 'Linguistic Politeness Research. *Quo Vadis?*', in R.J. Watts, S. Ide and K. Ehlich (eds), *Politeness in Language: Studies in Its History, Theory and Practice*, 2nd edition, Berlin and New York, Mouton de Gruyter, pp. xi–xlvii.

Watts, R.J., Ide, S., and Ehlich, K. (1992) 'Introduction', in R.J. Watts, S. Ide and K. Ehlich (eds), *Politeness in Language: Studies in Its History, Theory and Practice*, 2nd edition, Berlin and New York, Mouton de Gruyter, pp. 1–17.

Werkhofer, K.D. (1992) 'Traditional and Modern Views: The Social Constitution and the Power of Politeness', in R.J. Watts, S. Ide and K. Ehlich (eds), *Politeness in Language: Studies in Its History, Theory and Practice*, 2nd edition, Berlin and New York, Mouton de Gruyter, pp. 155–199.

Part II: Im/politeness in Intracultural Interaction

4

Im/politeness, Rapport Management and Workplace Culture: Truckers Performing Masculinities on Canadian Ice-Roads

Louise Mullany

1. Introduction

This chapter analyses the interplay between linguistic im/politeness, gender and workplace culture in a series of interactions between groups of men working on Canadian ice-roads as seasonal truck drivers. The data are taken from the documentary series *Ice Road Truckers*, which has been broadcast on a number of commercial television networks in a range of locations including the USA, the UK, Australia, New Zealand and the Netherlands.[1]

The language of the workplace is becoming a burgeoning field of sociolinguistic enquiry and the approach of linguistic im/politeness has recently established itself as a productive framework through which workplace communication can be investigated. Studies have been published on linguistic im/politeness which cover a range of sociolinguistic issues (see Holmes and Stubbe 2003a), as well as research focusing upon the relationship between im/politeness, gender and language (Holmes and Schnurr 2005; Mullany 2006, 2007, 2008; Schnurr et al. 2008; Schnurr 2009).

However, the majority of previous research has tended to examine linguistic im/politeness and gender in interactions between 'white-collar' professionals, often in business meetings. There are a handful of exceptions, including 'blue-collar' factory research carried out in New Zealand (Holmes and Stubbe 2003b; Schnurr et al. 2008).[2] Baxter and Wallace (2009) have also recently examined the interactions of working-class builders in the UK, though their work does not examine im/politeness. Nonetheless, there is a lack of empirical evidence on the interactional im/politeness strategies of manual 'blue-collar' workers, especially with a combined focus on im/politeness, gender and culture.[3]

This chapter's focus on Canadian English will expand upon the language varieties that have been examined thus far in im/politeness and workplace research, most notably British and New Zealand English. In a similar vein to Baxter and Wallace's (2009) builders, the profession of ice-road trucking is an overwhelmingly male occupation. It thus provides a good opportunity to add to the developing focus on masculinities in language and gender studies (e.g. Coates 2003), specifically from a linguistic im/politeness perspective.

This study thus aims to fill a gap in the research field by producing a culturally-situated examination of the performance of im/politeness, masculinities and workplace culture in a group of all-male blue-collar workers in an intracultural Canadian setting. There will be a focus, in particular, upon analysing the linguistic im/politeness strategies of a group of truckers who form a specific community of practice (Eckert and McConnell-Ginet 1992). The chapter will demonstrate how the interplay between im/politeness, gender and workplace culture can be observed through a communities of practice approach.

2. Data

Ice Road Truckers is part of a recent development in western media culture to produce 'fly-on-the wall' documentary series focusing on 'real' men in manual blue-collar professions who place themselves in dangerous, potentially life-threatening situations, often as a direct consequence of the extremes of the weather in their workplace environments.[4] This focus can be viewed as part of the dominant discourse of 'hegemonic masculinity' (Connell 1995; see Section 4), whereby those who are held in the highest esteem are hard working, physically tough, resourceful male breadwinners who succeed in the face of adversity (cf. Baker 2008). Since the 1990s there has been much talk within the media and popular culture of masculinity being 'in crisis' in western culture (Cameron 2009). Part of this 'crisis' has been attributed to a major decline in traditional blue-collar industries and with it, prototypical male occupations, with the rise of a service-sector economy and more 'feminised' job roles (Cameron 2006). These gender-based documentary series are arguably part of a broader discourse within the media to reaffirm traditional values of masculinity and demonstrate that there are still some all-male groups working in traditional blue-collar occupations which require hard manual labour in harsh physical conditions.

In terms of the nature of the data source, workplace media documentaries focusing on particular professions have already been utilised in previous linguistic im/politeness research. Studies have focused upon the military (Bousfield 2007a, 2007b), traffic wardens (Culpeper et al. 2003; Bousfield 2007b), police officers (Bousfield 2007a, 2007b; Limberg 2008) and kitchen staff (Bousfield 2007a). The current study thus builds upon this trend. Such sources have the advantage of providing analysts with access to often inaccessible and/or physically dangerous workplace environments such as ice-roads where truckers need to drive over temporarily frozen lakes, rivers or stretches of ocean.

When analysing documentary media data, it is important to acknowledge that the first priority of programme makers is to entertain and gain as wide an audience as possible. Not all of the data collected will be shown and the editing process will be orientated towards this overarching desire to entertain and appeal to a broad audience (Limberg 2008). The process of having a camera crew following the truckers through their daily routines will inevitably affect the data, though this is the case with any data-collection context where participants are aware of being observed. The observer's paradox is always an issue for linguistic workplace research where, for ethical reasons alone, participants will be aware that the recording of interactions is taking place, though participants do have an additional awareness of recording for an unspecified overhearing public audience with media broadcast data.

The interactions can be described as authentic as they are unscripted stretches of discourse that take place spontaneously as the truckers engage in talk when fulfilling their everyday workplace roles. Another advantage of using documentary media sources is that the videoed nature of the recordings enables nonverbal as well as verbal features to be examined, enabling an additional layer to be added to the analysis.

In addition to interprofessional interactions, truckers also talk directly to the camera, providing another valuable data source to aid the analyst's interpretations, as well as producing fascinating linguistic texts to analyse in their own right. Other studies have also used these additional sources for analysis (see Bousfield 2007a).

When talking directly to the camera/to a member of the crew, the truckers frequently evaluate and reflect upon their own and others' behaviour, including linguistic behaviour. They engage in the process of constructing their own identities as well as the identities of fellow members of their workplace. Such data can arguably be loosely accorded with interviews conducted by linguistic analysts with speakers who have participated in a study to try to gain insight into their intentions and judgements in previous interactions. Such on-camera reflections in *Ice Road Truckers* provide valuable data on truckers' evaluations and judgements of one another, giving access to reflections on the identity construction of self and other.

The truckers are aware from the outset that there is the potential for their comments to be viewed by any of their workplace colleagues as well as by a broad public audience. Arguably then, there is a perpetual awareness of the overhearing audience, including individuals who are being talked about (but not necessarily present) at the time of recording.

3. Theorising politeness and impoliteness

In order to advance current thinking on im/politeness, this chapter draws on recent developments in im/politeness theory, often referred to collectively as socially constructed or postmodern approaches, where im/politeness is seen as discursively constructed within interaction (Mills 2003; Culpeper 2005; Haugh 2007). It is now established that in order to examine im/politeness from a discursive perspective it is important to analyse stretches of discourse and not just focus upon single utterances; a move away from the traditional analytical approach associated with Brown and Levinson (1987).

Another interrelated part of this approach is to examine the discourse of the speaker(s) *and* hearer(s) to ensure that both roles are seen as equally important in the process of discourse production. Again, early research based upon Brown and Levinson tended to prioritise speaker intention and, therefore, important clues as to how utterances were interpreted and judged were missing. Also, as signalled in this chapter by use of the term 'im/politeness', it is becoming more commonplace to examine data for strategies of impoliteness as well as politeness, as impoliteness establishes itself as a legitimate area of politeness research. Culpeper's (2005) definition of impoliteness is useful as it stresses the role of the hearer as well as the speaker, and should be employed as part of a discursive approach:

> Impoliteness comes about when: (1) the speaker communicates face-attack intentionally, or (2) the hearer perceives and/or constructs behaviour as intentionally face-attacking, or a combination of (1) and (2). (Culpeper 2005: 38)

The approach taken here blends Mills' (2003) advancements in gender and linguistic politeness theory with elements of Spencer-Oatey's

(2002, 2008) rapport management framework. Spencer-Oatey's framework has proven to be an effective approach to assess the intricacies of politeness and culture in inter and crosscultural workplace settings and this chapter illustrates its analytical value in an intracultural workplace context. Culpeper's impoliteness definition is also integrated within this approach to enable instances of impoliteness to be clearly identified (cf. Mullany 2008).

I adopt Mills' (2003) view that, instead of a 'universals' approach to politeness where a definition of politeness is put forward that should be analytically applicable across cultures (cf. Brown and Levinson 1987), im/politeness should instead be conceptualised from a communities of practice perspective (CofP). Following Eckert and McConnell-Ginet (1992), a CofP is defined as follows:

> An aggregate of people who come together around mutual engagement in an endeavor. Ways of doing things, ways of talking, beliefs, values, power relations – in short – practices – emerge in the course of this mutual endeavor. (Eckert and McConnell-Ginet 1992: 464)

The CofP approach originally developed as a theory of learning to investigate how apprentices learn established practices of workplaces over time. It characterises 'core', 'peripheral' and 'outsider' membership roles (Wenger 1998) which can be applied to distinguish workplace participants' relationships and to track how these change over time. From a CofP perspective, im/politeness is conceptualised as follows:

> A set of practices or strategies which communities of practice develop, affirm, and contest, and which individuals within these communities engage with in order to come to an assessment of their own and others' behaviour and position within the group. (Mills 2003: 9)

This approach therefore places the emphasis on the members of the CofP themselves to make their own assessments of im/politeness. These assessments made by workplace colleagues "reflect and reinforce the norms developed by a particular CofP" (Schnurr et al. 2007: 715).

It is useful at this stage to define 'workplace culture' and clarify how this relates to CofPs. Schnurr (2009: 80) defines workplace culture as "a system of shared meanings and values as reflected in the discursive and behavioural norms typically displayed by members, that distinguishes their workplace or organisation from others". CofPs exist within workplace cultures, and the culture of a workplace will be incorporated into the various practices of its CofPs.

Mills' CofP approach to im/politeness can be enhanced by Spencer-Oatey's (2002, 2008) rapport management framework, as the latter offers a nuanced perspective to analysing 'face' as well as adding an additional layer to the analysis with the introduction of the concept of 'sociality rights'. It enables the intricacies of im/politeness, gender identities and culture within particular CofPs to be emphasised. I apply the different components of face which Spencer-Oatey characterises in order to enhance the linguistic analysis along with her additional notion of 'sociality rights'.[5]

Spencer-Oatey (2002: 540–541) follows Goffman's (1967: 5) perception of face as "positive social value" and then splits this into 'quality' face, the desire for positive evaluation in our personal qualities including competence and abilities, and 'social identity' face, the desire for people to acknowledge and uphold our social identities and roles.[6] In addition to face, speakers also have 'sociality rights': personal and social *entitlements* in interaction. Spencer-Oatey splits sociality rights into two components: 'equity rights' and 'association rights'. Equity rights refer to interlocutors' entitlement to personal consideration and fair treatment from others by not being unfairly imposed upon, taken advantage of or exploited. They are dependent on a 'cost–benefit' continuum which must be kept balanced and on an 'autonomy–imposition' scale which gauges the extent to which others control or impose on us. 'Association rights' refer to interlocutors' entitlement to association with others, as is appropriate within our relationships. This includes 'affective association/disassociation': the extent to which our concerns, interests and feelings are shared, along with 'interactional association/disassociation', such as the amount of talk deemed relevant in particular contexts.

Unlike Spencer-Oatey I am not replacing im/politeness with the term 'rapport management' – the above elements of the rapport management framework are integrated into the CofP approach, alongside Culpeper's definition, to maintain an overall focus on im/politeness within CofPs and how this interrelates with masculinities and workplace culture. As such, this constitutes a new form of discursive politeness analysis, enabling the CofP approach to be expanded upon by including a more nuanced view of face, alongside sociality rights, which add valuable analytical layers to the CofP framework.

4. Theorising masculinities

In addition to the theoretical position taken in relation to im/politeness, gender identities in this chapter are also conceptualised as socially-constructed notions performed within interaction (Butler 1990, 2004). Butler's definition of gender performativity is of gender as a "doing, an incessant activity performed" and where "one is always 'doing' with or for another" (Butler 2004: 1). This draws attention to the importance of taking a discursive approach to analysing im/politeness and gender in interaction. Gender identities emerge across stretches of discourse and are co-constructed by ourselves and our fellow interlocutors.

Butler (1990: 33) emphasises that a "rigid regulatory frame" operates to regulate our behaviour and that, if we step outside of the normative boundaries of acceptable interactional patterns within a given society, we may be subject to negative evaluations or consequences. She characterises that such regulation "operates as a condition of cultural intelligibility for any person" (Butler 2004: 52). From the perspective of masculinities, this leads neatly on to Connell's aforementioned notion of hegemonic masculinity, which can be conceptualised as a core part of the 'rigid regulatory frame', encoding and regulating gendered behaviour.

Connell's (1995) definition draws on Gramsci's (1971) notion of hegemony, broadly defined as individuals' compliance in the societal exercise of power. Power is maintained through ideology and as a consequence there is consent in its enactment, as opposed to power being enacted by means of coercion. The foundation of hegemonic masculinity is held in place by ideologies which are embedded within broader social institutions.

Hegemonic masculinity needs to be constantly performed and negotiated and women and gay men are frequently placed in opposition to those who perform the most 'valued' characteristics of hegemonic masculinity (Coates 2003), with 'effeminate' or homosexual behaviour placed in direct opposition with hegemonic masculinity. Indeed, there are a range of masculinities backgrounded by hegemonic masculinity, including the "subordinate" categories of "wimp", "geek" or "nerd" (Baker 2008: 125). Fitzsimons (2002: 103) pinpoints that the hegemonic discourse of masculinity in the workplace is characterised by "competitiveness, power, rationality, emotional control and independence". Baker (2008: 124) summarises that the most dominant way to be a 'real man' is to be associated with heterosexuality, to be tough and competitive and to enact power and authority.

In this chapter, the analysis of masculinities and im/politeness will include a specific focus upon expletives and humour. Both are multifunctional devices which can be used to view hegemonic masculinity in action. Coates (2003: 46) comments that swearing "performs hegemonic masculinity" and that it has a long history of being uttered globally "by men in the company of other men as a sign of their toughness and of their manhood". Coates draws attention to the historical association of swearing with physicality and hard labour. She documents expletives as a way of maintaining solidarity within all-male subcultures.

The analysis will examine the multifunctionality of expletives and, as well as examining their role as solidarity-building politeness devices which build camaraderie and enhance rapport, there will also be a focus on how they can be used as impoliteness strategies to challenge and attack, damaging face and sociality rights. The linguistic function of expletives can be difficult to pinpoint. The same forms can be used by the same speakers on different occasions to convey very different linguistic functions, depending on context. The analysis will combine a focus on expletives with a detailed pragmatic analysis of the illocutionary and perlocutionary force of particular speech acts where expletives occur, combined with a focus on discoursal features including interruptions, adjacency pair sequences and discourse markers, which operate as further contextualisation cues to judge the force of interlocutors' linguistic strategies.

Investigating humour through a linguistic im/politeness lens has proved to be an effective means to analyse gender and im/politeness in workplaces. Humour is defined as follows:

> Instances where participant(s) attempt to signal amusement to one another, based on the analyst's assessment of interlocutors' paralinguistic, prosodic and discoursal clues. Humour can be a result of either intentional or unintentional humorous action, and can be classified as either successful or unsuccessful. (Mullany 2007: 88)

In addition to being used as a strategy to maintain solidarity/collegiality, it can also be used to contest/challenge power relationships, hide power relationships or express rivalry between equals (Mullany 2004). It is a powerful discourse device due to its ambiguous nature. Analysing humour also makes the "distinct characteristics and values of the culture of a workplace visible" (Schnurr 2009: 85).

5. Analysis

The ice-road truckers come together for a short but concentrated period of employment: trucking takes place for just two months every year when the ice becomes thick enough for a road to be formed. Up to 800 truckers transport goods from Yellowknife to the various bases of a diamond mine company. Documentary makers follow six drivers throughout the duration of the ice-road season.

The analytical focus of this chapter is on three drivers, Hugh, Rick and Drew, who form a distinct CofP. Hugh is the leader of this CofP – he owns a fleet of trucks and employs Rick and Drew to work for him. All three drivers live in Kelowna, British Columbia (893 miles from the ice-road) and have travelled together for the start of the season. While all of the truckers make individual wages, if Rick and Drew are successful this will also enhance Hugh's income. Hugh has worked on this ice-road for over 20 years. Rick has worked one previous season and Drew, although a professional truck driver, has never driven on ice-roads before.

Hugh also employs Rick for the rest of the year and they both describe themselves as 'best friends'. Hugh is the most central core CofP member, followed by Rick, with Drew as a peripheral member. Drawing on social network terminology, Hugh and Rick have 'multiplex' social ties (Milroy 1987), which arguably sets up an expectation of greater rapport management between them than between Hugh and Drew.

Example 1 is from the first episode. All truckers have to undergo a compulsory urine test before they are allowed onto the ice-road (transcription conventions are given at the end of the chapter):

Example 1

Rick has completed his drug test

1.	Rick:	go on in I'm good I've passed
2.	Drew:	he studied hard ((laughter))
3.	Rick:	yeah ((laughs))
4.		((camera turns to Hugh))
5.	Hugh:	if it comes out coloured we're good and if it comes out pink
6.		we're pregnant
7.		((laughter from many))

Drew and Hugh invoke humour to enhance solidarity and collegiality here in the form of 'one-liners'. The resultant laughter functions as a contextualisation cue signalling that both attempts are successful, thus enhancing their quality and social identity face. Humour also functions here as a tension releaser between these CofP members – this is a potentially embarrassing and challenging situation, especially with the presence of a camera outside of the bathroom where they give their samples. Hugh's turn derives its humour from the biological impossibility that any of the male truckers being tested could be pregnant. It can be classified as a humorous 'fantasy sequence' (cf. Holmes and Stubbe 2003a).

Hugh's status is further enhanced when he does his sample. He deliberately does not close the door and shows his bare backside to the other truckers and the camera. His performance is met with a great deal of laughter from the surrounding group of truckers, including Rick and Drew. Hugh thus constructs a 'joker' identity which can be seen as part of a performance encoded with hegemonic masculinity – he is bold, daring and funny. These examples provide illustrations of harmonious rapport management through humour within this CofP.

Competitive hegemonic discourses of masculinity are also observable from the start of the first episode. The profession is described by one of the other veteran drivers, Alex: 'It's called the dash for the cash.' This clip is replayed at the start of every episode. Alex also reports the following:

Example 2

Alex: ((to camera)) It's sort of like a he-man thing (.) you know who's got the biggest pecker you know ((laughing)) who gets the most loads ((smiles))

Alex directly aligns the nature of the competition with competitiveness between men regarding the size of their penises, referred to by the slang term 'pecker'. In specific relation to the CofP under study, the competitiveness to secure the most loads is frequently articulated by Rick, who expresses a strong desire to beat Hugh:

Example 3

Rick: ((to camera)) I have one thing that pushes me and one thing only and that's Hugh Rowland cos if (-) if I could beat him that's all I want to beat him (.) the competition with everybody that's up here is probably to beat him

Rick's comments set up Hugh as the "hero leader" (Holmes 2009: 189) – Hugh is the one person everyone wants to beat as he is the most successful. Rick's comments enhance Hugh's face while simultaneously setting up a direct competition between them; a typical example of the performance of hegemonic masculinity and of how masculinity is constantly being enacted and negotiated.

Despite this competitive, supposedly autonomous culture, the truckers do need to work together. They most often run in convoys and if anything goes wrong they are expected to help each other in potentially life-threatening situations, communicating via their truck intercom, known as very high frequency (VHF) radios, which work within a 10–15 mile radius. However, the vast majority of their exceptionally long working days are spent physically alone and their only option for interaction is via the VHF radio or mobile phone. A good deal of communication in this workplace therefore takes place remotely, without paralinguistic features and other contextualisation cues present in face-to-face interaction. They are thus solely reliant on verbal cues to assess their interactions when conversing remotely. While driving, the truckers regularly engage in both transactional and affective talk via radio or mobile phone.

In Example 4, Rick and Hugh are communicating via their VHF radios. They are running in separate convoys in opposite directions but they have just entered the 10–15 mile zone where they will be able to communicate with each other as they are about to pass on the ice:

Example 4

Rick: Where abouts are you at?

Hugh: It was a good trip til I got down to Charlie's Hill last night anyway (.) two or three guys spun out on Charlie's Hill and then one on thirty-two and err security just said 'if you're goin- if you're going any further you're putting chains on' (xxx) I just pulled her over and said 'I'm going to bed then fuck you' I've never put chains on yet and I don't intend to do it now for (.) somebody else's stupid fucking (-) idea

Rick: Yeah there's a whole lot of stupid rolling on the roads this year eh

Hugh: Yeah a whole lot of stupid is right fucking Christ err it's all all these new g- new guys I've seen more new guys this year than any other year

Rick: So what load you pulling now? Two? Three?

Hugh: You've only got fucking six or seven loads in (-) you've been running for two weeks shoulda had fucking ten in (-)

Rick: ((smiling to the camera)) Hu- Hugh won't fucking tell us he'll lie to us that's fucking Hughie he'll tell us he's got five loads

20.		for the rest of the year ((laughs))
21.	Rick:	What you pulling now? Two? Three?
22.	Hugh:	I think this one's five
23.	Rick:	((to camera smiling)) last one he said was five too
24.	Hugh:	Give me another week I'll be caught up to ya ((smiles))

Following Rick's opening question Hugh enters into a narrative report (lines 2–9), functioning to re-establish contact with Rick. Hugh tells him of the expletives and insults he used to security staff, using direct speech (line 7). Hugh can be assessed as performing a hegemonic masculinist 'hero' identity through his narrative (Coates 2003). He identifies himself as a competent, experienced driver who does not need chains to drive. In principle, stopping to fit chains onto a truck's tyres makes driving safer as it helps prevent slipping on the ice, but from Hugh's perspective, fitting chains would damage his self-reliance and 'toughness' and he therefore refuses.

Hugh's narrative performance enhances his own quality and social identity face, especially his professional trucker identity. Rick affirms this by agreeing, further enhancing Hugh's status, and then blaming the problems on what he calls 'a whole lot of stupid' (line 10). Rick uses the Canadian pragmatic particle, 'eh' at the end of this utterance as a tag to signal informality, rapport and camaraderie (line 11, see Holmes 2009 for discussion of 'eh' as a marker of masculinity and informality in New Zealand workplaces).

Hugh signals supportive agreement, directly echoing Rick's phrase, intensified by an expletive premodifying 'Christ' (line 12). He goes on to give the 'whole lot of stupid' a more specific identity through the additional noun phrase 'these new guys' (line 13). Rick and Hugh work together here in the joint production of discourse to enhance in-group solidarity and collegiality between themselves in opposition to the out-group, the 'new guys', including Drew (see Example 5), who are causing delays and blockages because they are 'stupid'. Hugh and Rick strengthen their CofP membership here, positively enhancing their relationship as good friends and colleagues by engaging in harmonious rapport management.

They then change topic and engage in competitive banter about who has pulled the most loads (lines 15–24). This competitiveness is a good example of hegemonic masculinity in action. Hugh refuses to answer Rick's question, instead criticising the number of loads Rick has pulled (lines 16–17). Rick's reaction demonstrates that he has not taken the illocutionary force of his boss's criticism seriously; instead it can be identified as part of banter between them – an avoidance strategy on Hugh's part not to let Rick know how many loads he has pulled. He completes the adjacency pair sequence at line 22 following Rick's repetition of his question, but Rick is convinced Hugh is lying (line 23). Hugh continues the banter by issuing a warning that in a week he will have caught up (line 24). It is clear from their contextualisation cues across this stretch of discourse that the banter between them is part of their dash for the cash 'competition' and ultimately functions to maintain rapport.

The next example is a radio interaction between Rick and Drew on their first convoy run:

Example 5

Rick's cab

1.	Drew:	Just remember I'm being nice to you Rick
2.	Rick:	yeah I might pull you out a ditch ((smiles))
3.	Drew:	I have no intention of GOING in a ditch bro
4.		and I haven't seen a ditch yet
5.	Narrator:	Soon after Drew had found his ditch
6.		((cut to a shot of Drew's truck in the ditch)

Drew and Rick engage in humorous banter (lines 1–4) while driving along. Moments afterwards Drew drives his truck into a ditch. Therefore, his combative response (lines 3–4) results in his quality face and social identity face, especially his professional trucker identity, being further damaged. All CofP members evaluate this event separately to the camera when back at base:

Example 6

Rick:	((to the camera)) he's now realized it isn't just a cake walk to bring the freight to the diamond mines it's a hard deal
Hugh:	((to the camera)) he just wouldn't listen…just big boy's pride was hurt (-) but he's lucky that his chin don't hurt ((makes a fist and a punching motion))
Drew:	((to the camera)) today a trailer came and bit me in the ass…Rick had said you know be prepared it's a little rough but Jesus I've had four-by-four roads better than this thing

Rick and Hugh's on-camera comments damage Drew's face further. Although Drew did not overhear these comments at the time, both

Hugh and Rick will be aware that he may well see them when the episode is broadcast. The implicature of Rick's evaluative utterance implies that Drew was overconfident on his first run. Hugh damages Drew's quality face by using 'big boy' sarcastically as a pejorative referring expression. He then explicitly states that Drew's 'pride', (his face, in politeness terms), has been 'hurt'. His paralinguistic action of making a fist, combined with the declarative in the final part of his utterance, functions as an indirect threat. Hugh performs his desire to punch Drew, constructing him as a bad employee deserving of physical violence due to his inability to listen, simultaneously constructing himself as physically strong and tough through his punching motion. Drew tries to save part of his social identity face by blaming the road quality, but the fact that the other truckers were fine draws attention to his inexperience.

Over time, CofP peripheral members may successfully integrate into the workplace culture and its CofPs, but in Drew's case this does not happen. He continues to have multiple problems, as in Example 7:

Example 7

Drew's truck has broken down for the fourth time. Mechanic Lee is in Drew's cab. Drew is standing by his open cab door.

1.	Drew:	((to the camera)) I'm leaving it up to the experts they've
2.		had it in the shop I went and picked it up and taken it down
3.		the road (-) got less than half a mile and she died (-) what do
4.		you know
5.	Lee:	I know you're just about close to getting your teeth punched
6.		down your throat I know that
7.	Drew:	Mine?
8.	Lee:	Yours
9.	Drew:	Why?
10.		((Lee walks away. Drew follows))
11.	Drew:	Why would I get MY teeth punched Lee?
12.	Lee:	You say it's in the shop you go half a mile and then the
13.	Lee:	fucking truck [dies
14.	Drew:	[I don't know [what the problem]
15.	Lee:	[You ran it out of fucking fuel]
16.		you stunned ass every problem you've had this winter has been
17.		because of your own stupidity

It is clear that Lee has interpreted Drew's comments (lines 1–4) as an accusation, albeit indirect, implying that he is responsible for the breakdown of Drew's truck. This is evidenced by Lee's aggressive face attack in response, including the threat of physical violence. In his impoliteness work, Bousfield (2007a: 2192) incorporates Jay's (1992) notion of an "offending event", which includes instances where offence stems from "slander, libel, verbal abuse, and 'fighting words'". Lee's response shows that the perlocutionary effect of Drew's utterance has been as an accusation of mechanical incompetence and thus the basis of slander/potential libel. Drew's comments can be perceived as attacking Lee's quality and social identity face, especially his professional identity. In his face attack act (FAA) (lines 5–6), Lee echoes the rhetorical part of Drew's previous utterance 'what do you know' to take the floor in direct response starting with 'I know' and terminating with 'I know that'. This linguistic framing of the FAA through partial repetition works to intensify Lee's threat to punch Drew. Lee's actions arguably perform hegemonic masculinity by issuing a physical threat to assert power.

A single-word adjacency pair exchange then takes place, with Lee breaking the Gricean quantity maxim (line 8). Drew then twice utters a wh- question (lines 9, 11), demanding more information, claiming not to understand. Lee repeats what Drew has said using the framing of direct speech with the insertion of an intensifying expletive by Lee (line 13). Drew attempts to offer an explanation but Lee successfully interrupts with two FAAs which damage Drew's quality and social identity face. Lee insults him with the derogatory term 'you stunned ass', and then refers directly to Drew's 'own stupidity', intensified by expletives, with 'fucking' as another premodifier (line 15) to emphasise Drew's trucking incompetence. Lee reports what has happened on the truck radio to Hugh:

Example 8

1.	Hugh's cab. Lee comes in on the radio	
2.	Narrator:	Lee the mechanic calls and fills him in on Drew's situation
3.	Hugh:	((to the camera)) Like if Drew don't fucking smarten up I'm
4.		gonna have to fire his ass (-) yapping all over {company name}
5.		and everything oh 'the fucking truck' well it's his own
6.		fault ... and he just looks like a fucking idiot now

Hugh draws attention to his power over Drew as his superior, emphasising his authority 'to fire his ass'. According to Hugh's evaluation and short vignette, Drew has been threatening Hugh's quality and social identity face by 'yapping all over' the company that the problem is with the truck Hugh has provided. As Lee has now told Drew that he is to blame on camera, this reaffirms Hugh's social identity face as Lee is a highly-valued professional in this workplace culture.

Drew decides to leave the ice-road shortly afterwards. He has frequently suffered damage to his quality and social identity face, but to justify his position he has blamed his equipment and Hugh in particular. In rapport management terms, from Drew's perspective, his equity and association rights have been infringed – Hugh has not given him fair treatment and has imposed faulty machinery on him. In terms of the 'cost–benefit continuum' the costs have now outweighed the benefits for Drew. Hugh willingly lets Drew leave as from his perspective there are benefits to this as Drew's incompetence has cost him money.

Toward the end of the season the relationship between Hugh and Rick also starts to break down:

Example 9

Rick's cab. He is talking to Hugh on his mobile phone

1. Hugh: what's wrong with truck now Rick every time I phone
2. you you've got a complaint
3. Rick: Well because I'm fucking tired of freezing in this
4. fucking thing (-) it's fucking cold in here
5. Hugh: If it's freezing I told you to get the fucking thing fixed take it
6. to the mechanic (-) you got a mechanic
7. Rick: So you get me running so I'm running with no heat
8. Hugh: Nobody's fault but your own go take it get it fixed
9. Hugh: [you've got a mechanic]
10. Rick: [No I'm fucking freezing] all of the time man fucking getting
11. pretty pretty tough to fucking want to go for a load when you're
12. freezing all other time (-) I'm kind of abandoned
13. he[re]
14. Hugh: [Aband]oned? What are you talking ab[out?]
15. Rick: [I'm just] left fucking
16. hanging here like is costing me a fortune just to feed myself
17. Hugh: What have you gotta eat I mean you went through like two
18. grand in a fucking week (-) so what are you what are y- what
19. are you spending it on going to the bar every night?
20. Rick: s- see that's what I mean Hugh you got a totally different
21. fucking attitude when you're up here you come up here and

22. just don't give a fuck as long as you're hauling loads and I
23. don't think that's fucking right
24. Hugh: You've got a mechanic Rick take it over there quit your
25. fucking whining about it

This stretch of discourse contains a series of FAAs and expletives by both speakers which function to intensify the conflict. 'Fucking' occurs as a premodifying intensifier on 12 occasions within speech acts where face attack is taking place as part of competitive and challenging discourse strategies.

Following Hugh's wh- question and an FAA that Rick complains every time Hugh telephones (lines 1–2), Rick "counters" with a "defensive" response (Culpeper et al. 2003: 1563), including a succession of expletives attacking Hugh's face, indirectly criticising his role as boss. Hugh counters using metalanguage 'I told you' and issues Rick with a direct, on-record aggravated directive including an intensifying expletive: 'get the fucking thing fixed'.

Rick counters again by expressing dissatisfaction with his working conditions (line 7), with pronoun usage '*you* get *me* running', signalling that Rick holds Hugh responsible. Hugh repeats that it is not his responsibility and that Rick is at fault as he has not followed Hugh's orders. Hugh repeats himself by uttering another two direct unmitigated directives (line 8). Rick then interrupts, complaining about how cold he is and utters an indirect accusation that Hugh has 'abandoned' him (lines 12–13). Hugh questions this, directly repeating 'abandoned', turning it into a question, immediately followed by another metalinguistic question challenging Rick to explain himself (line 14).

Rick switches topic to complain about food costs, leading Hugh to attack his face and accuse him of spending all his money in the bar. Rick counters by attacking Hugh's social identity face and his professional status, accusing him of having the wrong attitude towards his employees. He attacks on-record, and launches this with the aggressive discourse marker 'see' (line 20). He then issues the on-record accusatory declarative, including 'fuck' as a noun, 'you just don't give a fuck', followed by his own evaluation of Hugh's behaviour, functioning as an indirect accusation including 'fucking' as an aggressive intensifier (line 23).

To counter, Hugh issues two aggravated unmitigated directives, the first again for Rick to take his truck to the mechanic and the second, a direct threat to Rick's quality face, to stop 'fucking whining' (lines 24–25). The exchange goes on for some time until Rick terminates the interaction:

Example 10

1. Hugh: ((mocking laughter)) ahhhhhha
2. Rick: like
3. Hugh: you're so full of [(it xxxx]
4. Rick: [(ARRRRGH] ((Rick hangs up
5. and throws his mobile phone across the cab))

As Rick disruptively interrupts, shouts down the phone and then hangs up, it appears that he has interpreted Hugh's mocking laughter as contestive and challenging, signalling that he is not taking him seriously. Rick attacks Hugh's face by hanging up without warning, preventing Hugh from further counter-attack. Hanging up clearly marks out Rick's evaluation of Hugh's behaviour as impolite and beyond the boundaries of acceptable behaviour in this CofP. His evaluative comments to the camera following this interaction confirm this (see Example 11).

In terms of sociality rights, the linguistic evidence in this interaction demonstrates that Rick has different expectations of Hugh. From Rick's perspective, his equity rights have been infringed – he is being treated unfairly and is not getting personal consideration. His socio-cultural expectations of a decent working environment are not being met and he accuses Hugh of prioritising money over his well-being. He has been unfairly imposed upon and exploited as Hugh has not offered to come and sort his truck out for him; instead Hugh adopts the defensive counter-strategy of 'dismissing' that there is any problem, and then "makes light of face damage" (Bousfield 2007a: 2200) by joking at Rick's expense:

Example 11

Rick is in the bar drinking a beer

Rick: ((to a member of the documentary crew)) this is not how y- y- you treat your right-hand man (.) AND your best friend that's this is just unacceptable I'm freezing up there I tell him that and he laughs at me like it's a joke...I ain't gonna work for Hughie again (.) especially up here

Rick evaluates the mocking humour that he has received from Hugh as unacceptable and inappropriate. From Rick's perspective, Hugh has used humour to frame what Rick deems to be a genuine threat to his health as a joke. In Culpeper's terms, hearer Rick has perceived Hugh's comments as intentionally face-attacking, resulting in him eventually hanging up. Rick leaves the ice-road shortly after this comment is recorded without communicating again with Hugh.

Mills (2005: 268) observes that impoliteness can result from "a mismatch in the judgement of status, role or familiarity" and an often corresponding mismatch in assessments of members' positions in a CofP. This is the case here as Rick articulates a mismatch in his expectations of Hugh, who has failed in his roles as both boss and friend. This is unacceptable to Rick given the levels of familiarity between them and because of his self-perception as Hugh's 'right-hand man'.

Through Hugh's linguistic strategies there is evidence of affective disassociation. He does not expect Rick to impose on him by needing him to come and fix his truck. Hugh's expectation is that Rick should be autonomous and sort this out himself. Examples 12 and 13 give Hugh's evaluations of Rick following this conflict:

Example 12

Hugh: ((to a member of the documentary crew)) he hung up on me that's how mad he is ((laughs)) he's like a little fucking girl eh ((laughs))

Example 13

Hugh has got back to base and found out Rick has left

Hugh: Rick's the type of guy who always wants a pat on the back... and I told him yesterday (.) I said 'I haven't got time for your fucking needing a hug bull shit right now' that's my and exact words and he just fucking freaked... he was a carpet cleaner before I come and I got a hold of him and made a man out of him

In both examples Hugh damages Rick's face by constructing him as emotional, needy, vulnerable, not independent or tough enough, including the directly indexicalised gendered insult that he is 'like a little fucking girl'. His use of 'eh' as a tag here can be seen as an appeal to the camera operator and the wider audience to agree with his evaluation. Hugh has aligned Rick with the dominant discourse of femininity, placing him in direct opposition with the dominant discourse of hegemonic masculinity and thus in direct opposition with Hugh. This strategy is also an attempt at saving face for Hugh – Rick's departure has resulted in him losing his last crew member. He blames this on Rick's weakness and behaving like a 'girl'. He then claims that he was the one who made Rick a 'man' with the implicature that before he met Hugh, Rick lacked in masculinity, having no 'manly' status due to his role as a carpet cleaner.

6. Conclusion

This chapter has illustrated how documentaries such as *Ice Road Truckers* are rich data sources for the analysis of im/politeness, gender and culture. The analysis has shown a full range of politeness and impoliteness instances between colleagues in this CofP and how the im/politeness norms and conventions of the ice-road workplace culture change and develop over time. This type of workplace, which exists for only two months every year, arguably acts as a microcosm of workplace culture (from its annual inception to its termination), providing a rather unique opportunity to observe changes in CofP relationships and socio-cultural norms of im/politeness and rapport management at strategic points in the workplace cycle.

The data analysis highlights the multifunctional power and importance of expletives and humour within this workplace culture. Swearing is commonplace and can perform hegemonic masculinity, functioning as a device to establish and maintain solidarity/collegiality, often in conjunction with banter, as well as functioning as a face-attacking impoliteness device used to contest, challenge and threaten. The truckers use humour as a strategic politeness and impoliteness device through which their gender and professional identities are enacted. Humour is used as an in-group solidarity marker to establish, maintain and strengthen solidarity/collegiality, as well as to express rivalry and to contest and challenge one another.

At the end of the series Hugh 'wins' the 'dash for the cash' as he has pulled the most loads in his CofP. His triumph adds to his 'hero' identity status, being brave, hard working, physically tough and independent, succeeding against the odds, proving himself to be a 'real' man, which directly aligns him with hegemonic masculinity. However, his 'hero' status does not stretch to being an effective, successful 'hero leader' in this workplace (Holmes 2009). He has suffered relationship breakdowns with two subordinates who left his employment and damaged his profit margins, including one with whom he had long-term multiplex social ties. The findings could be used in future work as the basis to examine how conflict and the breakdown of workplace relationships could be avoided through a focalisation on the analytical tools offered by the im/politeness and rapport management framework in particular workplace cultures.

In overall conclusion, additional analytical layers have been added to the CofP approach to theorising and examining im/politeness in empirical linguistic analysis by combining the perspectives of Mills with techniques from Spencer-Oatey's rapport management framework. The focus on im/politeness and workplace culture through analyses of the linguistic practices in this ice-road CofP has provided a fruitful framework through which performances of gender and dominant hegemonic masculinity can be viewed in an under-researched Canadian workplace setting.

Transcription conventions

(.)	a pause of two seconds or less
(-)	a pause of over two seconds
(xxx)	material was impossible to make out
{xxxx}	material changed for purposes of confidentiality
[ ]	simultaneous speech
[ ]	
RIDICULOUS	Capital letters indicate material was uttered loudly
((laughs))	Material in double brackets indicates additional information

Notes

I am very grateful to Ron Carter and Sara Mills for their perceptive comments on an earlier draft of this chapter. I also wish to express many thanks to Francesca Bargiela-Chiappini and Daniel Kádár for their unfettering enthusiasm, support and patience. This chapter is dedicated to my father-in-law Bob Green, who has spent many a cold winter working on ice-roads as a mechanic in the Canadian Arctic.

1. *Ice Road Truckers* is produced by *The History Channel*, now known as *History*. All of the data in this chapter have been transcribed from Series 1, recorded in Yellowknife and surrounding areas of the Northwest Territories, Canada. It was first broadcast on 17 June 2007 in the USA and then on 6 February 2008 in the UK.
2. The terms 'white collar' and 'blue collar' derive from a historical tradition of different colours of workplace clothing depending upon occupation. The term 'blue collar' refers to blue shirts/overalls worn by those engaged in manual labour whereas 'white collar' refers to white shirts worn by those in offices, engaged in non-manual work. The *Oxford English Dictionary* (1989) cites the terms as originating in the USA from 1919 onward. They are still frequently used to signify a contrast between manual and non-manual labour in locations including North America and Europe.

3. While 'working class' could arguably be an appropriate classification to assign to groups of manual workers working in countries including the UK, as Canada has a 'weak discourse' of social class (Kerswill 2007: 53), I have avoided using any socio-economic class distinction to refer to the truckers (see Chambers 2003 for further details on Canadian government systems for occupational rankings).
4. Other examples include the UK-based *Trawlermen* and the US-based *Ax Men*.
5. Another recent framework for analysing politeness beyond 'face' which also takes a discursive approach is Locher and Watts' (2005) 'relational work'. They place impoliteness and politeness on a continuum, including a crucial distinction between 'politic' behaviour and 'politeness'. In certain contexts this can attempt to clarify the distinction between socio-culturally determined behaviour ('politic') and behaviour which aims to make someone feel better about themselves ('polite'). However, this distinction can often be 'counter-intuitive' as 'politic' behaviour is taken to stand for politeness, particularly if interactants' perceptions of politeness are assessed (Mills 2003: 68). Additionally, the distinction often creates more problems than it aims to solve as it is frequently difficult to see when one definition starts and the other ends (Harris 2005).
6. Spencer-Oatey (2005: 102) includes an additional category termed 'respectability face' to account for different concepts of face in Eastern cultures and Chinese in particular. This chapter focuses on the concepts of quality face and social identity face defined in her 2002 work, as these best correlate with the intracultural setting and the interactionally based analysis focused on in this chapter.

References

Baker, P. (2008) *Sexed Texts*, London, Continuum.

Baxter, J., and Wallace, K. (2009) 'Outside In-Group and Out-Group Identities? Constructing Male Solidarity and Female Exclusion in UK Builders' Talk', *Discourse & Society*, 20, pp. 411–429.

Bousfield, D. (2007a) 'Beginnings, Middles and Ends: A Biopsy of the Dynamics of Impolite Exchanges', *Journal of Pragmatics*, 39, pp. 2185–2216.

Bousfield, D. (2007b) *Impoliteness in Interaction*, Amsterdam, Benjamins.

Brown, P., and Levinson, S. (1987) *Politeness: Some Universals in Language Usage*, Cambridge, Cambridge University Press.

Butler, J. (1990) *Gender Trouble*, New York, Routledge.

Butler, J. (2004) *Undoing Gender*, New York, Routledge.

Cameron, D. (2006) *On Language and Sexual Politics*, London, Routledge.

Cameron, D. (2009) 'Theoretical Issues for the Study of Gender in Spoken Interaction', in P. Pichler and E. Eppler (eds), *Gender and Spoken Interaction*, Basingstoke, Palgrave, pp. 1–17.

Chambers, J. (2003) *Sociolinguistic Theory*, 2nd edition, Oxford, Blackwell.

Coates, J. (2003) *Men Talk*, Oxford, Blackwell.

Connell, R. (1995) *Masculinities*, Cambridge, Polity Press.

Culpeper, J. (2005) 'Impoliteness and Entertainment in the Television Quiz Show: The Weakest Link', *Journal of Politeness Research*, 1/1, pp. 35–72.

Culpeper, J., Bousfield, D., and Wichmann, A. (2003) 'Impoliteness Revisited: With Special Reference to Dynamic and Prosodic Aspects', *Journal of Pragmatics*, 35, pp. 1545–1579.

Eckert, P., and McConnell-Ginet, S. (1992) 'Think Practically and Look Locally: Language and Gender as Community-Based Practice', *Annual Review of Anthropology*, 21, pp. 461–490.

Fitzsimons, A. (2002) *Gender as a Verb: Gender Segregation at Work*, Aldershot, Ashgate.

Goffman, E. (1967) *Interaction Ritual*, New York, Anchor Books.

Gramsci, A. (1971) *Selections from the Prison Notebooks* (trans. Q. Hoare and G. Nowell-Smith), New York, Lawrence and Wishart.

Harris, S. (2005) 'Review of Power and Politeness in Action: Disagreements in Oral Communication', *Journal of Politeness Research*, 1/1, pp. 165–169.

Haugh, M. (2007) 'The Discursive Challenge to Politeness Research: An Interactional Alternative', *Journal of Politeness Research*, 3/2, pp. 295–317.

Holmes, J. (2009) 'Men, Masculinities and Leadership: Different Discourse Styles at Work', in P. Pichler and E. Eppler (eds), *Gender and Spoken Interaction*, Basingstoke, Palgrave, pp. 186–210.

Holmes, J., and Schnurr, S. (2005) 'Politeness, Humour and Gender in the Workplace: Negotiating Norms and Identifying Contestation', *Journal of Politeness Research*, 1/1, pp. 121–149.

Holmes, J., and Stubbe, M. (2003a) *Power and Politeness in the Workplace*, Harlow, Pearson.

Holmes, J., and Stubbe, M. (2003b) '"Feminine" Workplaces: Stereotype and Reality', in J. Holmes and M. Meyerhoff (eds), *The Handbook of Language and Gender*, Oxford, Blackwell, pp. 573–599.

Jay, T. (1992) *Cursing in America*, Philadelphia, Benjamins.

Kerswill, P. (2007) 'Social Class', in C. Llamas, L. Mullany and P. Stockwell (eds), *The Routledge Companion to Sociolinguistics*, London, Routledge, pp. 51–61.

Limberg, H. (2008) 'Threats in Conflict Talk: Impoliteness and Manipulation', in D. Bousfield and M. Locher (eds), *Impoliteness in Language*, Berlin, Mouton, pp. 155–179.

Locher, M., and Watts, R. (2005) 'Politeness Theory and Relational Work', *Journal of Politeness Research*, 9/1, pp. 9–33.

Mills, S. (2003) *Gender and Politeness*, Cambridge, Cambridge University Press.

Mills, S. (2005) 'Gender and Impoliteness', *Journal of Politeness Research*, 5/1, pp. 263–280.

Milroy, L. (1987) *Language and Social Networks*, 2nd edition, Oxford, Blackwell.

Mullany, L. (2004) 'Gender, Politeness and Institutional Power Roles: Humour as a Tactic to Gain Compliance in Workplace Business Meetings', *Multilingua*, 23/1–2, pp. 13–37.

Mullany, L. (2006) '"Girls on Tour": Politeness, Small Talk and Gender Identity in Managerial Business Meetings', *Journal of Politeness Research*, 2/1, pp. 55–77.

Mullany, L. (2007) *Gendered Discourse in the Professional Workplace*, Basingstoke, Palgrave.

Mullany, L. (2008) '"Stop Hassling Me!" Impoliteness in the Workplace', in D. Bousfield and M. Locher (eds), *Impoliteness in Language*, Berlin, Mouton, pp. 231–255.

Oxford English Dictionary (1989) online edition, available at: http://dictionary.oed.com.

Schnurr, S. (2009) *Leadership Discourse at Work: Interactions of Humour, Gender and Workplace Culture*, Basingstoke, Palgrave.

Schnurr, S., Marra, M., and Holmes J. (2007) 'Being (Im)polite in New Zealand Workplaces', *Journal of Pragmatics*, 39, pp. 712–729.

Schnurr, S., Marra, M., and Holmes, J. (2008) 'Impoliteness as a Means of Contesting Power Relationships in the Workplace', in D. Bousfield and M. Locher (eds), *Impoliteness in Language*, Berlin, Mouton, pp. 211–229.

Spencer-Oatey, H. (2002) 'Managing Rapport in Talk', *Journal of Pragmatics*, 34, pp. 529–545.

Spencer-Oatey, H. (2005) '(Im)politeness, Face and Perceptions of Rapport', *Journal of Politeness Research*, 1/1, pp. 95–119.

Spencer-Oatey, H. (2008) *Culturally Speaking: Managing Rapport across Cultures*, 2nd edition, London, Continuum.

Wenger, E. (1998) *Communities of Practice*, Cambridge, Cambridge University Press.

5
Why Are Israeli Children Better at Settling Disputes Than Israeli Politicians?

Zohar Kampf and Shoshana Blum-Kulka

1. Introduction

One of the most popular metaphors in political communication research is the 'game' metaphor (Patterson 1993), whereby similarities are drawn between political practices and practices connected to sports. A related metaphor, probably unique to Israeli political culture,[1] and used especially for news coverage of parliamentary debates, is politics as a 'kindergarten'.[2] For Israelis, this metaphor suggests a basic similarity in the behaviour in conflictual situations in the two communities, evoking a derogatory view of the interactions between children. In this chapter we examine conflict-resolution mechanisms in two Israeli Communities of Practice – that of politicians and that of children – against the backdrop of the metaphors of 'game' and 'kindergarten'. We follow Miller (1979) in arguing that such metaphors are essential for making manifest the 'intelligible structure' of a political reality. According to Miller, metaphors cannot be verified by direct comparison to reality. However, using 'metaphorical thinking' can shed new light on the reality examined. Accordingly, we examine the nature of conflict resolution within two very different Israeli communities and their characteristic activities.

Our broad aim is to explore the mechanisms of conflict resolution in both communities and to examine if and to what extent cultural ways of speaking are echoed in the relational facework of Israeli children and politicians. We use materials and data collected in two different research projects (Blum-Kulka 2005; Hamo and Blum-Kulka 2007; Kampf 2008, 2009). Without drawing direct comparisons between them, we argue that by analysing interactions within the two communities under the umbrella of politeness, we gain a new focus and fresh insights regarding both these communities and Israeli culture in general.

This chapter presents two main arguments. On the one hand, the kindergarten metaphor does not hold: there is no basis for the assumption of similarity between politicians and children which lies at the core of the metaphor – not because politicians do not behave in what is generally considered a 'childish' manner but because children themselves refute the stereotype. As we shall demonstrate, children use highly sophisticated strategies to pre-empt, mitigate and resolve conflictual situations. On the other hand, the game metaphor is an adequate one for capturing the nature of political discourse, particularly Simmel's notion of the 'antagonistic game' (1955 [1908]).

In politeness terms we examine the construction of self and other 'face' during negotiations over conflicts and their resolutions within the two Israeli Communities of Practice. We take a dynamic view of 'face' as both a given and a sequentially negotiated driving force of human interaction. This linkage between what is intuitively perceived as opposite fields of human interaction will allow us to explore two notions basic to all discussions of im/politeness – sociality and relational facework.

2. Theoretical background

The focus of this study is an analysis of discursive struggles which include 'corrective actions' (Goffman 1971) – such as accounts, apologies and reconciliatory gestures – implemented by Israeli politicians and children in order to settle disputes with their rivals/peers. In line with current trends in linguistic politeness research, we adopt a participants' perspective in order to understand how im/politeness is perceived and achieved in interactions between members of both communities (Eelen 2001; Mills 2003; Watts 2003).

Our exploration of dispute resolution in two such different communities as children and politicians rests on two further major considerations.

Firstly, both groups are treated in the literature as distinctive communities, characterised by a specific language use and operating in specific fields of human interaction. Children's peer talk has recently emerged as a major area for understanding how a range of discourse skills is developed during peer interactions and how childhood culture, including modes of appeasement (Kampf and Blum-Kulka 2007), is created by children's distinctive practices (Blum-Kulka and Snow 2004). As for politicians, sociologists as well as discourse scholars have demonstrated the unique distinctive logic of the political world (Thompson 2000), which influences both the way in which members of the political community perceive face and the way that they use language (Bull et al. 1996; Lakoff 2000; Kampf 2008, 2009). In what follows, we demonstrate that, although interactional patterns displayed by both groups with their peers are characterised by cooperation and power struggles (Sheldon and Johnson 1994; Chilton 2003), the range and nature of discourse practices used differ from group to group. Hence, it is of theoretical interest to unveil the dynamics of dispute-resolution discourse unique to each.

Secondly, and specific to this study, we assume that both groups are exposed to and manifest cultural ways of speaking related to their being 'Israelis'. Earlier studies, conducted during the 80s and the 90s within the purview of linguistic politeness research, underline the culturally unique perceptions of politeness in Israeli society (Blum-Kulka 1992). The collective values dominating Israeli culture during the first decades of its existence were manifested in the *dugri* speaking style, characterised as assertive, direct and sincere 'straight talk' (Katriel 1986). In the political arena, the highly confrontational style of Israeli politicians was shown to have roots in traditional Jewish modes of argumentation (Blum-Kulka et al. 2002). Accordingly, 'face' considerations in Israeli speech favoured values such as clarity and authenticity over elaborate relational facework. These values were shown to be upheld especially in close relationships, with styles of politeness still varying greatly according to social situation within Israeli society (Blum-Kulka et al. 1985). Later studies drew attention to the process of erosion of this distinctive Israeli style of speech, paralleling the decline in collective values in Israeli society. This process brought about both mitigated and elaborated scripted types of speech, and, on the other hand, the emergence of an offensive and hostile style of talk, termed *kasah* (Katriel 1999). Tracing the role of Israeli cultural values in the discourse of the two communities allows for a better understanding of the current Israeli system(s) of politeness.

3. Data and method

The data for this study was collected during two different research projects, one concentrating on the apologetic behaviour of children and the other on that of politicians.

The first project focused on pragmatic development and was based on ethnographic observations of peer interactions of Israeli preschool children. The study followed two cohorts – young preschoolers and fourth graders of 20 children each –for three years (2001–2003); the children were observed and taped during natural peer interactions (Blum-Kulka et al. 2004). Among the studies derived from this data were two dealing with mechanisms for settling disputes: Kampf and Blum-Kulka (2007) on children's apologies and Zadunaisky-Ehrlich and Blum-Kulka (2010) conflict resolution. The second project analysed the role of apologies in conflict resolution in the Israeli political arena (Kampf 2008, 2009). The data consists of events reported in the printed press between 1997 and 2004 of struggles between political figures that included apologies as a means of appeasement. Additional occurrences of disputes and their aftermaths were collected from the Israeli media and analysed for this chapter.

The materials for these studies are very different, some would say even incomparable. We use our knowledge of these two communities and their discursive modes to crystallise our conclusions regarding conflict resolution in both. In our study, we use illustrative examples from both data sets to demonstrate (1) ways of *settling* conflicts among Israeli children and (2) ways of *magnifying* conflicts among Israeli politicians. We end each section with a discussion of the role of culture on conflict-resolution mechanisms. Lastly, we conclude by suggesting that what underlies the differences observed between the two communities is a difference in face concepts – collective as opposed to individual.

4. The negotiation of conflict in childhood: indicators of sociality in disputes

Our linguistic-ethnographic studies of young children rest on the view of children's peer talk as a double opportunity space – as a space that allows for children's active co-construction of their social worlds in the present of their childhood and concurrently as the space that provides a wide gamut of occasions for children's overall development in chronological time. This view considers recent constructivist approaches to the study of childhood, which call for a new appreciation of children's self-constructed social and moral worlds to be a vital and necessary complementary addition to the more traditional developmental psychological approaches (Corsaro 1985; Blum-Kulka 2005; Hamo and Blum-Kulka 2007; Cromdal 2009). Hence, in looking at children's management of disputes we shall focus particularly on the goals such events serve in children's co-construction of their local social world. We argue that one of the major goals motivating and explaining much of children's conduct on such occasions is their deep commitment to 'sociality': in other words, children direct their efforts to managing disputes in ways that will not threaten the basic ties of friendship – ties which serve as the precondition for peer communication and play (Kampf and Blum-Kulka 2007).

Theoretically we embrace the claim that human culture and cognition are rooted in the character of human interaction, which is unique in the animal kingdom. In this view, children are born into the world with an innate drive for sociality. It is this 'interaction engine', in Levinson's terms, which enables and explains their linguistic, social and cognitive development through meaningful interaction with others (Levinson 2006). The management of disputes by preschool-age children is no exception: it is an occasion for enlisting a wide range of strategies, some unique to children and some appropriated from the adult world, to negotiate social relations while being engaged in argumentative discourse (Zadunaisky-Ehrlich and Blum-Kulka, 2010). In what follows we examine such occasions at four stages of conflict management: pre-empting a conflict, managing sociality as the conflict unfolds, finding creative solutions to conflicts and finally, when/if needed, engaging in remedial action.

4.1. Pre-empting conflictual situations: drawing on the world of fantasy

Sensitivity to face concerns may lead children to adopt pre-emptive strategies which work to nullify the possibility of direct conflict. In our first example, two boys are standing next to the 'book corner' in the preschool, leafing through a picture book with animal pictures and pointing out and naming the animals in the book. At one point one of the boys introduces a pretend play framing, inviting his friend to join in a game of fantasy:

Excerpt 1. The Squirrels[3]

1. Raphael: Le::t's say that **we** turned **it** into a pet. (3.7) let's say **I** took let's say [**we** took- ((took out))
2. Rami: **let's say we put a spell on it that it will be two, that it would become two.**

(Raphael, m, 6;3; Rami, m, 5;11. Date: 5 May 2000, 'Galit' Kindergarten, Jerusalem.)

The two children collaborate in perfect synchrony in the magical transformation of the squirrel in the picture to a virtual pet. As they are talking, each 'lifts' his squirrel from the book and walks away holding it in the palm of his hand. Collaboration is enabled through two pre-emptive strategies. First, by the insistence on 'inclusive joint action': Raphael begins his suggestion by naming both himself and his friend as the 'doers' in the suggested plot, then slips into 'I' but immediately self-repairs back to 'we'. In this way he makes sure that both children are granted equal rights in the realisation of the pretend play to emerge. In the next turn Rami goes a step further: exploiting the unlimited possibilities of the fantasy frame, in which anything can happen, he suggests using magic to double the symbolic object of the play. This move reflects children's occupation with issues of ownership (Cobb-Moore et al. 2009), whether real (over toys) or symbolic, as in the case of the virtual squirrels. The magic transformation of doubling the squirrel acts as a 'pre-emptive move': once there are two virtual squirrels no conflict can arise over ownership of the symbolic object(s) of the play. Thus the play can continue in perfect synchrony: the children move around putting their respective squirrels in imaginary cages, singing them lullabies and planning ahead for the return of the pets to the book ('When they'll get up let's say they want to go back to the book').

4.2. Managing disputes while maintaining sociability: verbal strategies for mitigation

The high value placed by young children on maintaining friendship even under conditions of conflict gives rise to several sophisticated mitigating verbal strategies used. One such strategy is the maintenance of 'high textual density' between oppositional turns, keeping up an appearance of sociality (Zadunaisky-Ehrlich and Blum-Kulka, 2010). On one occasion five boys argue over who has won a computer game. When one of the children declares himself the winner, he is immediately contradicted by another boy.

Excerpt 2: Arguing in harmony

42. Yoav: ((0) I won::.- (clapping his hands)
43. Rami: <you lost>.-
44. Guy: you lost, good for you (.......).-(clapping his hands)
45. Yoav: °no no°, I didn't lose-
46. Rami: yes, it's a loss because the sun disappeared – (0).(sounds of the computer).

((continued))

(Rami (5;8), Rafael (6), Guy (6), Danny (5;9) and Yoav (4;4) are sitting around the computer playing a game.)

The oppositional moves in this extract are performed very directly, bold on record, with no apparent concern for face-saving. However, the interchange displays close ties between turns and speakers. The children rely on the immediately prior discourse in formulating their next utterances, using the technique of repeating parts or structures from a previous move called 'format tying' (Goodwin 1990). Thus turn 43 counters turn 42 with the same form (inflected verb), substituting the verb previously used with an antonym from the same semantic field.

Additional ties between turns are achieved by the repetition of words based on different forms of the same stem ('lost/lost/lose/loss'). These strategies help to maintain topical continuity and build cross-turn cohesion in a way that lends the discourse high textual density. This density, in turn, indicates a high level of conversational cooperation, which is at odds with the clearly oppositional nature of the exchange.

Another way to maintain conversational cooperation in argumentative events is face-saving through adult-like modes of mitigation (Caffi 2007). In the following case, this is done by the avoidance of direct refusals. Given the highly direct argumentative style associated with Israeli discourse (Blum-Kulka et al. 2002), such avoidance of direct refusals in the children's discourse came as a surprise to us. In the following example of children's negotiation over a highly valued possession (here, a particular Pokemon sticker), the negotiation unfolds in a complex manner, displaying a gamut of persuasive strategies countered by indirect, sophisticated – and polite – modes of refusal. The children are sitting around the drawing table, drawing Pokemons, looking at a booklet of Pokemon stickers and talking. Amir has finished drawing a maze to reach the Pokemons. We shall concentrate only on the design of the refusals.

Excerpt 3. The Pokeball sticker: how to avoid saying 'no'

1. Amir: Gadi, Gadi, are you will – (2.5) Gadi,
2. Gadi: °what°
3. Amir: (1.9) Gadi, <could you give me a Po:ke:ball sticker?> PLEASE ONLY one
4. Gadi: **BUT I [HAVE] ONLY SIX↑**
   ((turns 5 to 15 omitted – Amir explains to Gadi why he needs the Pokeball sticker so badly))
16. Gadi: ((turning the pages of the stickers' booklet, pointing to a sticker and directing his body and gaze to Dani.)) He WANTS me to give him <u>such</u> a Pokeball sti<u>cker</u>. (1.3) ONLY FOR HIS MAZE (2.5) AND THEN I'LL HAVE ONLY <u>FIVE</u>↑

17. Amir: Five is also a lot.
((turns 18–25 omitted – the children continue arguing the value of 'five'))
26. Amir: (1.3) [then_]
27. Gadi: [NU] RIGHT, AND IF I GIVE YOU ONE (0.9) THEN I'LL HAVE (0.6) I'LL HAVE FIVE AND THEN (0.7) AND THEN MY SISTER WILL SCREAM AT ME (0.9) THAT I GAVE ONE FOR FREE↑. ((continued))

(Amir (m) (6;5); Gadi (m) (6;5). 'Pokeball' is the name of the ball where Pokemons 'live'; Gadi's older sister is 7 years 9 months.)

The argumentative event between the two children starts with a polite request (almost a plea) for a particular sticker (turn 3). Instead of overtly refusing, Gadi counters by using the strategy of justifying his refusal. As the bargaining continues, Gadi continues to avoid overt and direct refusals, opting for various indirect strategies. Thus in turn 16 he tries to enlist the aid of his audience, and speaks of his opponent in the 3rd person, changing him from an addressee into an 'overhearer' (Goffman 1981). In his next refusal (turn 27) Gadi combines several strategies. First, he makes a concession that helps retain the illusion of conversational cooperation (Antaki and Wetherell 1999); second, he uses a conditional statement that constrains the concession; and, finally, he evokes the voice of his older sister, an authoritative third party, to completely annul the possibility of compliance with his opponent's request.

The above example shows that as the children negotiate over the sticker they concurrently negotiate social relations. Due to their deep commitment to sociality, they express clearly oppositional acts by face-saving indirect moves. In this case they are drawing on adult practices: as in business negotiations, the participants avoid direct moves of correction or disagreement and try to manage disagreement by not displaying it too overtly (Stalpers 1995).

4.3. Conflict resolutions: the 'both of us' compromise

One recurring source of conflict in children's play is the assignment of roles at the planning stage of pretend play. Some roles (like the mother or father, or the lion) are more coveted, carrying more prestige and symbolic power than others (like the baby or some small animal). The simple and elegant solution to such conflicts is the 'both of us' strategy: many short exchanges in the form 'I'm the X', 'No, I'm the X' end when one of the children announces 'both of us' (in Hebrew *shnenu,* literally 'the two of us'). This solution works for a wide range of play characters (like animals or siblings in the family frame) but not for all. In some cases, more creative solutions are called for. Mor's (forthcoming) study of pretend play in the preschool reveals several creative modes for conflict resolution. For instance, in one case two girls are playing family: one of them is the 'mother', and the other her 'daughter', sister to a 'baby' (doll). At some point in the game the mother leaves, asking her 'daughter' to take care of the 'baby'. When she returns, negotiations over the roles in the play reopen: the girl playing the sister complains fiercely 'I don't want to (be the sister), no, no, no, no, no, you are always the mother, you are always the mother, it's cheeky' (in Hebrew *chutzpa*, literally 'impertinence'). The other girl protests ('I'm not cheeky'), her friend counters and the argument continues in highly emotional tones for several turns, with the girl unhappy with her role threatening to turn to the teacher to complain and also to stop the play. Finally, her friend offers a solution: 'So let's be both the same age, okay?' At this point the two smile at each other, move closer together, whisper and walk away. Apparently, the fierce dispute over roles in the play did not threaten the children's friendship outside of play.

4.4. Remedial action: apologising

In our earlier study on children's apologies we demonstrated how apology events among peers index the centrality of friendship in the social world of young children (Kampf and Blum-Kulka 2007). The next episode demonstrates how reconciliation is sophisticatedly co-constructed by peer rivals. The confrontational event stems from a fight over a stick, during which Yoav receives a blow from Ariel.

When Ariel realises the seriousness of the blow he repeats 'sorry' (*slixa, slixa*) no fewer than 14 times, but to no avail. An adult's intervention also fails to appease Yoav, and the boys part, avoiding each other for a few minutes, until Ariel approaches Yoav with a new proposition.

Excerpt 4. Let's make a party picnic

78. Ariel: ((walks up to Yoav)) Let's have a picnic Yoav.
79. Yoav: em, let's have a parTY↑!
80. Ariel: Come↑! take it Amichay. [Amichay!]
81. Yoav: [>It's a birth↑day that] we are preparing.<
82. Ariel: Yoav **I didn't mean to do it to °you°. ((gives him the stick.))***
83. Yoav: Tha↑nks.
84. Ariel: (3.3) **I didn't mean at all↑** to do it to you- >Come here.< (to do it to YOU:) lets make A PI↑CNI::#::C,#= ((sings))
85. Yoav: =With par#TY::# ((also sings in same intonation.))

86. Ariel: Let's make a party picnic. yala?
87. Yoav: YES! [(I only need to take)-]
88. Ariel: PARTY PI↑CNIC! =

(*Our emphasis. Yoav, m, (4;8); Ariel, m, (4;11).)

As Ariel approaches Yoav with a new idea for play and Yoav concedes (Ariel: 'Let's have a picnic'; Yoav: 'Let's have a party' 78–79), the previous incident seems at first to have been completely forgotten. But Ariel's reference to the unpleasant incident in turns 81 and 83 – 'I didn't mean to do it to you' and 'I didn't mean at all to do it to you' (meaning, to hurt you) – sheds a new light on the whole exchange, turning it into a carefully planned remedial action performed in stages. In fact, Ariel's moves seem to resemble the 'confidence-building measures' diplomats talk about in the context of international conflict resolution. The first stage consists of an attempt to re-establish mutual trust as friends by proposing a joint play using solidarity politeness markers ('let's') that suggest common ground. It is only after the offer is fully embraced by the other child, and a shared commitment to renewed friendship is firmly established, that reference is made to the previous incident. The renewal of friendship – which is expressed verbally through each child echoing the other's 'let's' utterance – works here to build the trust needed for allowing a reconciliation. In this mutually supportive context Ariel's repeated denial of intent (see turns 81, 83) is accepted, and we can indeed witness its success through the two children's full collaboration in the new play frame.

5. The uniqueness of children's modes of conflict resolution

From a cultural perspective, two constructs of 'culture' can be evoked to explain the children's modes of conflict resolution: that of the adult world and that of the world co-constructed by the children themselves. Our analysis shows that while the children employ a wide range of strategies, some adult-like and some child-unique, the underlying social motivations and the goals achieved in such events are motivated by local concerns. Not all children's disputes manifest the strategies of pre-empting, mitigation and remedial action that we have demonstrated, but, on the whole, the children seem more oriented to cooperation and face concerns than could be expected from the direct *dugri* norms of Israeli culture (Katriel 1986). This disposition is even more surprising given that Israeli norms of solidarity (historically, the underlying justification for the *dugri* style) are in a constant process of erosion. Thus in our view it is 'culture' in the second sense – the social world co-constructed in the present of childhood – which is most responsible for young children's modes of conflict resolution.

6. The negotiation of conflict in politics: mechanisms for magnifying disputes

Our definition of politicians as members of a Community of Practice is based on what Thompson (2000) entitles the 'double logic' of politics. In contemporary mediated political arenas, politicians are compelled to manage their personas vis-à-vis the general public in the broader political field, as well as with respect to their peers/rivals within the political sub-field. Within the broader political field, politicians are involved in various types of interactions that are oriented mainly toward the general public such as speeches, political interviews and more recently, infotainment genres; in these types of interactions, politicians manage their public face in order to gain the electorate's support. Within the political community, politicians are involved in various types of interactions, some hidden from the camera's eye (such as private letters, telephone calls and face-to-face personal conversations), others monitored as part of everyday political activity (such as committee meetings, parliament speeches etc.); in these types of interactions, politicians are oriented mainly toward peer politicians, manoeuvring themselves according to the community's demands: obeying their parties' decrees, constructing and deconstructing coalitions etc.

In order to achieve political goals, politicians, as public representatives, are compelled to manage their faces in multi-recipient arenas with conflicting interests. Moreover, most of their engagement with other members of the community is constantly scrutinised by journalists and surveillance technologies. These characteristics of contemporary politics contribute to the polemic confrontational discourse typical of political arenas in western representative democracies (Tannen 1998).

The implications of these structural features are apparent in patterns of facework typical of members of the political community. Sociologists as well as discourse scholars have argued that the 'face' of professional politicians (sometimes replaced by the concepts of 'image' and 'prestige') is perceived as a resource which one must continually nurture and maintain in order to keep her/his official position (Bull et al. 1996; Thompson 2000; Kampf 2008, 2009). It is a crucial component in a politician's symbolic power and failing to maintain one's political face may result in harsh consequences. In the broader political field the meaning of 'damaged face' is a lower chance of being re-elected; within the political Community of Practice, the meaning of 'losing face' is a weakened capacity "to persuade others ... to secure bonds of trust and to turn words ... into deeds" (Thompson 2000: 102).

The close connection between image considerations and political power may explain why face maintenance in political contexts is 'an end in its own right' (Bull et al. 1996: 271). During their various types of interactions, politicians are constantly occupied with the mission of enhancing their own face and that of their allies on the one hand, and threatening their rivals' face on the other hand (Bull et al. 1996: 271). Observing these practices in everyday politics may leave one with the impression that politics is nothing but "an esoteric world of internal squabbles, of Byzantine power struggle" (Thompson 2000: 99). However, for the politicians themselves, "these subtle distinctions are part of the very essence of politics, for political conduct within the sub-field is inseparable from the activity of distinguishing one's own positions from those of one's opponents and of criticising and denouncing the latter" (Thompson 2000: 99).

Hence, in looking at the ways in which politicians manage disputes we shall focus on the goals such events serve in their continuous efforts to gain and maximise symbolic power at the expense of other members within the political fields. In the following sections we examine such occasions at two stages of conflict management: promoting conflicts and keeping conflicts alive on the public agenda. Since political interests of different members in the community sometimes coincide, we will mention conflict-resolution mechanisms that allow individuals and parties to bridge gaps in order to achieve mutual goals.

6.1. Promoting conflictual situations: doing 'being insulted'

Our first example demonstrates how insisting on a particular interpretation of a rival's words leads to a dispute in which the interpreter performs the role of the insulted in order to initiate the public denunciation of the allegedly insulting politician. The following dispute erupted during a meeting of the Education Committee of the Israeli Knesset in 2008. During a speech by the chairman of the Israeli Teachers' Union, the Minister of Education, Yuli Tamir, whispered a comment concerning the former director of the Ministry, Ronit Tirosh, who happened to be sitting next to her. Tamir complained that she was working to clean up the 'garbage and shit' that Tirosh had left behind in the Ministry. In response to this impolite and unprofessional form of criticism, Tirosh made a 'scene' (Goffman 1956) and treated Tamir's words as a personal insult.

Excerpt 5. 'She is calling me a piece of shit'

1. Tirosh: [your honoured chairman, the minister] of education has just called me- >called me< a piece of shit.
2. Tamir: [no, that is not what I said]
3. Tirosh: [I wasn't speaking to her]
4. Tamir: [I said that the garbage and shit you] left-
5. Tirosh: [it is precisely, it is recorded]
6. Tamir: [I said that the ga::rbage,]
7. Tirosh: [I can't believe it] I am sitting here and listening (.) and she is calling me a piece of shit↑

   4 turns of duelling omitted

12. Tirosh: [your honored chairman, I pro::test. She will not call me shit. I am asking that in the education committee, a university professor, I am [sitting and listening
13. Tamir: [sorry]
14. Tirosh: [to the chairman of the teachers union]
15. Tamir: [according to the]
16. Tirosh: and she is calling me a piece of shit
17. Tamir: your personal bitterness cannot be a work plan, there is nothing you can do

   The committee chairman hushes them up and encourages the Teachers' Union chairman to finish his address.

(Yuli Tamir, the Minister of Education and a professor of education; Ronit Tirosh, the former Minister of Education and a Likud MK; 8 July 2008, the Education Committee of the Israeli Knesset.)

Following her dramatic announcement of the Minister of Education's insult (turn 1), Tirosh rejects Tamir's explanation that she has been misinterpreted. In fact, during the entire interaction she refuses to negotiate regarding the apparent misunderstanding (Weizman and Blum-Kulka 1992) and chooses to simply ignore Tamir's words, treating her (in Goffman's 1981 terms) as a non-ratified participant and directing her protest to the committee chairman and other participants. This strategy can be understood in Garfinkel's (1956) terms as an effort to degrade the Minister of Education: in denouncing Tamir and ignoring her at the same time, Tirosh tries to build up a coalition of denunciation against Tamir which could result in a loss of status not only here, but – with the help of the media – in the general public.[4] It is interesting to note that Tirosh ignores the potential threat to her own political face in being called 'a piece of shit' (she mentions these words no less than four times) or in taking part in such a quarrel (headlined by Y-net on 8 July 2008 as 'The Preschool of the Education Committee'). The utilitarian logic of doing 'being insulted' in this case is that damaging the face of the rival may benefit the insulted, despite the potential damage to her own face as part of an embarrassing situation.

6.2. Keeping conflicts alive on the public agenda

The second example focuses on the ways in which the offended party invests efforts to keep his insult on the public agenda in order to gain greater public exposure in the competitive mediated political arena. Involving two allied politicians,[5] this incident at the 2002 Labour Party convention began with an insult directed by Minister Benjamin Ben-Eliezer, the Labour Party Chairman, at Dalia Itzik, the Minister of Industry and Trade. Itzik had spoken against the unity government of Labour with the right-wing Likud Party, and Ben-Eliezer, a supporter of the unity government, went to the podium and called her critical remarks 'a big bluff' (*Yediot Aharonot,* 4 October 2002); in response, Itzik demanded an apology. Ben-Eliezer, who needed Itzik's support in order to stabilise his position as party chairman, subsequently made two separate apologies, both rejected by the offended party. After Itzik refused to accept his telephone apology, Ben-Eliezer made a second attempt to placate her: in front of the entire assembly of Labour Party government ministers, Ben-Eliezer turned to Itzik and said

> I love you Dalia. You are an excellent minister. I apologise for the thing I said that hurt you at the party convention. (*Haaretz,* 4 October 2002)

Alongside a realisation of an IFID ('apologise') and acknowledgment of responsibility for the misdeed ('for the thing I said that hurt you'), Ben-Eliezer also supported Itzik's political positive 'face'. He expressed his affection ('I love you') and called her by her first name.[6] After attempting to secure solidarity with the offended, he continued to reinforce her political face by complimenting her professional virtues. However, despite Ben-Eliezer's efforts, Itzik rejected this apology too, and made her forgiveness conditional on one more statement, to be performed publicly before a large audience. Itzik's refusals and insistence on a spectacle of public apology can be understood as a means for keeping the chairman's debt to her on the public agenda, as evidenced in her comment to Ben-Eliezer after he had fulfilled her demand: 'Your offense was very helpful. I should have sent you a huge bouquet of flowers' (*Haaretz,* 4 October 2002).

Itzik's reference to the advantages that issue from serving as the voice of dissent may indicate that her taking offense was not authentic, but rather a calculated attempt to gain political points and at the same time detract from the political face of Ben-Eliezer. As we have argued elsewhere (Kampf 2008), in politics, the sincerity condition is frequently replaced by the 'embarrassment condition', that is, the extent to which the gesture is perceived by the forgiver as threatening the apologiser's political face. Like Tirosh in the previous example, Itzik violated the sincerity condition by 'doing "being insulted"', and she justified her recurring refusals and her demands for reparation for the transgression in terms of giving equal publicity to the apology statement. Her self-positioning as a victim within the political community of practice 'awarded' her a higher position in the political hierarchy as a person central enough to be the recipient of an apology and to award absolution. Within the broader political field, keeping the insult on the public agenda granted her greater public exposure in the mediated political arena.

6.3. Paving the way out of conflicts: the role of mediators in the political arena

The examples above demonstrate how political face considerations motivate politicians to prolong their disputes. However, even in an arena with an overt conflict of interests among its members there is, from time to time, a need for cooperation in order to achieve mutual goals. When opponents are unable to settle a conflict on their own, there is a need for the intervention of some public figure functioning as an arbitrator to help rivals constrain their confrontations. The basic condition for such political bridging is the existence of a mediator – either a person or an institution accepted by all parties – the Attorney General, the Knesset Ethics Committee or the Chairman of the Knesset, for example (Kampf 2008), or some other public actor.

Our last example demonstrates how a journalist can serve as a mediator, facilitating rapprochement between rivals. The case was initiated and brought to closure by Sima Kadmon in the course of several interviews in the weekend political section of *Yediot Aharonot* in 2001–2002.

The incident began several weeks before the 2001 primary elections in the Labour Party with a transgression on the part of Labour MK Avraham Burg's 'best political friend' (*Haaretz,* 4 October 2002), Labour MK Haim Ramon. Ramon refused to support Burg's candidacy for party chairmanship against MK Binyamin Ben-Eliezer, who won the election, and the result was a rift between the two political colleagues. A year later Ramon declared his intention to replace Ben-Eliezer as party chairman. Needing support, he wanted Burg's forgiveness and Kadmon came to his aid. Reflecting on her conversation with Ramon, Kadmon wrote in *Yediot Aharonot*:

> Ramon has excellent communication skills and good interpersonal skills. Nevertheless, he is much more complicated than he looks. Something is sitting on the tip of his tongue and he has difficulty saying it ... 'I think I made a mistake'. He finally says it, as if someone is extracting it from his mouth with pliers. (5 July 2002)

The next step in Kadmon's mediation was to deliver Ramon's acknowledgment to his rival Burg.

> I told Burg what Ramon said and he laughed. It was a laugh of relief ... He commented fondly on Ramon's expression of regret: One should frame these words. I think it is the only time that Ramon has ever admitted he made a mistake. I know it's hard to apologise in the world of politics and I appreciate Haim's act. (*Yediot Aharonot,* 5 July 2002)

The active mediation by Kadmon bore fruit: Burg forgave Ramon and later even declared his support for Ramon's candidacy (*Haaretz,* 4 October 2002). This outcome demonstrates that in some cases the need for mediation in order to resolve conflicts between peer politicians is crucial.

From a crosscultural point of view, Israeli ways of speaking in the political arena are highly confrontational and direct. If in the British Parliament, for example, threats to the rival's face are mitigated by forms of deferential address ('institutional hypocrisy' in Perez de Ayala's terms [2000]), insults in the Israeli Parliament are often unmitigated. Every year more cases of insults are referred to the Knesset Ethical Committee, increasingly raising its status (Kampf 2008). In a society characterised over the past three decades by processes of fragmentation (Kimmerling 2001), not attending to the face of the other may be interpreted by political representatives as a useful strategy for appealing to one specific sector at the expense of another. From a historical perspective we are witnessing a hardening of the Israeli *dugri* speaking style but apparently without the underlying values of solidarity traditionally associated with this style. In its current version, 'straight talk' (*dugri*) has been transformed into 'smash talk' (*kasha*) (Katriel 1999).

7. Politics as kindergarten?

We began this chapter by pointing out a metaphor popular among journalists which compares the emotional confrontations between politicians to disputes between preschool children. The authentic examples of children's modes of conflict management in natural peer talk suggest that the metaphor is unjust to the children. In actual fact, children manifest a gamut of sophisticated strategies for conflict management and resolution which are geared towards maintaining cooperation despite disagreements. In contrast, the game metaphor aptly characterises the internal logic of the political world. Politicians employ sophisticated strategies for magnifying conflicts while maintaining cooperation according to the norms of the political Community of Practice. Political dispute may be considered what Simmel (1955 [1908]) calls an 'antagonistic game'. In 'antagonistic games' such as sport or play, which are carried out "under the mutually recognized control of norms and rules ... the fascination of fight and victory itself is the exclusive motivation" (Simmel 1955: 34).

Admittedly, in both communities conflicts may end in the opposite direction, with escalation and separation in children's conflicts and cooperation and resolution in politician's conflicts. However, we argue that different face-concerns motivate the conduct of the members in the respective communities: collective-face concerns in the children's Community of Practice, and ego-centred (or party-centred) face concerns in the political world.

There are two ways to explain how collective-face concerns arise in the world of children; both of them associated with the centrality of friendship. Corsaro (1985) argues that children's play constitutes a 'fragile interactive space' shared by a group of playmates. In this view the concept of friendship in the preschool years is mainly built on the need for collaboration in play – your friends are the children you play with; and since peer interactive spaces are difficult to enter yet easily disrupted, "children develop relations with several playmates as a way to maximize the probability of successful entry" (Corsaro 1985: 186). Our observations shed a different light on the concept of friendship in the preschool years. Friendship in itself seems to be conceived of as the major *precondition* for gaining access to play: once the interactive space of play is created by friends, the children share a collective goal to maintain the space (Hamo and Blum-Kulka 2007). Thus the children's norms for face threat and remedial action are driven by local child-world-specific concerns: friendship is *the* central motivating force for interpersonal relations and there are (mostly) unspoken norms governing appropriate behaviour between friends. Disputes may be taken as face threatening not only to the offended party but also to the collective shared face of the children as friends. Since it is friendship that is jeopardised, children make efforts to minimise the threat.

In the political arena, collective face (for example, that of the party) seems secondary to the ego-centred face of the individual politician. Nurturing and enhancing one's own face may determine the politician's success in being elected to public positions and in influencing processes within the political arena (Thompson 2000). As for all public figures, the construction of a unique impressive *persona* is essential and part of this construction consists of face management during particular interactions, leading to particular modes of image stylisation (Corner and Pels 2003). In an era of political personalisation, with a growing need for media attention, politicians have to adopt a wide range of strategies to achieve/attain visibility. Threatening the face of your opponent becomes one of the ways of enhancing your own face and magnifying conflicts a useful strategy to enhance the image of the politician.

Transcription conventions

word	emphasis
Wo::rd	stretch
WORD	loud volume
°word°	low volume
↑↓	pitch changes
<words>	slow rhythm
>words<	fast rhythm
#words#	unique tone
-	pause
[words]	overlap
word=	overlatch
wor-	cut-off
(word)	transcription doubt
((comment))	comments
(... .)	unclear talk

Turn numbers reflect the original numbering in the full recorded session the excerpt is taken from.

Notes

1. We would like to thank an anonymous reader for pointing out that this metaphor is not universal and our political science colleagues Tamir Sheafer, Sahul Shenhav and Gadi Wolfsfeld for confirming this observation, and Paul Frosh for his useful suggestions on the subject of 'metaphorical thinking'.
2. For example, from *Y-net*, the most popular Israeli news website: "Kindergarten in the Knesset in the discussion on the 'nurse law'" (headline, 13 July 2009); and "The preschool of the education committee" (*Y-net*, 8 July 2008). Politicians also use the kindergarten metaphor for describing problematic interpersonal relationships. Members of the Labor Party said about an argument between party chairman Ehud Barak and party secretary-general Raanan Cohen: "It's a kindergarten" (*Haaretz*, 16 April 2000).
3. For fuller transcripts and analyses of the children's peer-talk excerpts see Blum-Kulka (2005) (excerpt 1), Zadunaisky-Ehrlich and Blum-Kulka (2010) (excerpts 2 and 3) and Kampf and Blum-Kulka (2007) (excerpt 4). See below for transcription conventions. Contextual information for each excerpt consists of name, gender, age (years; month), date, and place.
4. See Garfinkel's definition of degradation ceremonies: "Any communicative work between persons, whereby the public identity of an actor is transformed into something looked on as lower in a local scheme of social types" (1956: 420).
5. See Kampf (2008) for an elaborated analysis of the event.
6. Although Ben-Eliezer's use of first name and declaration of love may sound patronising and chauvinistic, this use of *dugri* direct colloquial style is not unfamiliar in Israeli political discourse.

References

Antaki, C., and Wetherell, M. (1999) 'Show Concessions', *Discourse Studies*, 1/1, pp. 7–27.

Blum-Kulka, S. (1992) 'The Metapragmatics of Politeness in Israeli Society', in R.J. Watts, S. Ide and K. Ehlich (eds), *Politeness in Society*, Berlin, Mouton de Gruyter, pp. 255–280.

Blum-Kulka, S. (2005) 'Modes of Meaning-Making in Children's Conversational Storytelling', in J. Thornborrow and J. Coates (eds), *The Sociolinguistics of Narrative*, Amsterdam and Philadelphia, John Benjamins, 149–170.

Blum-Kulka, S., and Snow, C.E. (2004) 'Introduction: The Potential of Peer Talk', *Discourse Studies*, 6/3, pp. 291–306.

Blum-Kulka, S., Danet, B., and Gerson, R. (1985) 'The Language of Requesting in Israeli Society', in S. Forgas (ed.), *Language and Social Situations*, New York, Springer, pp. 113–136.

Blum-Kulka, S., Blondheim, M., and Hacohen, G. (2002) 'Traditions of Dispute: From Negotiations of Talmudic Texts to the Arena of Political Discourse in the Media', *Journal of Pragmatics*, 34/10–11, pp. 1569–1594.

Blum-Kulka, S., Avni, H., and Huck-Taglicht D. (2004) 'The Social and Discursive Spectrum of Peer Talk', *Discourse Studies*, 6/3, pp. 307–329.

Bull, P., Elliott, J., Palmer, D., and Walker, L. (1996) 'Why Politicians Are Three-Faced: The Face Model of Political Interviews', *British Journal of Social Psychology*, 35/2, pp. 267–284.

Caffi, C. (2007) *Mitigation*, Amsterdam and Philadelphia, John Benjamins.

Chilton, P. (2003) *Analyzing Political Discourse: Theory and Practice*, London and New York, Routledge.

Cobb-Moore, C., Danby, S., and Farrel, A. (2009) 'Young Children as Rule Makers', *Journal of Pragmatics*, 41/8, pp. 1477–1493.

Corner, J., and Pels, D. (2003) *Media and the Restyling of Politics: Consumerism, Celebrity and Cynicism*, London, Sage.

Corsaro, W.A. (1985) *Friendship and Peer Culture in the Early Years*, Norwood, Ablex.

Cromdal, J. (2009) 'Childhood and Social Interaction in Everyday Life: Introduction to the Special Issues', *Journal of Pragmatics*, 41/8, pp. 1473–1476.

Eelen, G. (2001) *A Critique of Politeness Theories*, Manchester, St. Jerome.

Garfinkel, H. (1956) 'Conditions for Successful Degradation Ceremonies', *American Journal of Sociology*, 61/5, pp. 420–424.

Goffman, E. (1956) *The Presentation of Self in Everyday Life*, Edinburgh, University of Edinburgh Press.

Goffman, E. (1971) *Relations in Public*, New York, Basic Books.

Goffman, E. (1981) *Forms of Talk*, Philadelphia, University of Pennsylvania Press.

Goodwin, M.H. (1990) *He-Said-She-Said: Talk as Social Organization among Black Children*, Bloomington and Indianapolis, Indiana University Press.

Hamo, M., and Blum-Kulka, S. (2007) 'Apprenticeship in Conversation and Culture: Emerging Sociability in Preschool Peer Talk', in J. Valsiner and A. Rosa (eds), *The Cambridge Handbook of Social-Cultural Psychology*, Cambridge, Cambridge University Press, pp. 423–444.

Kampf, Z. (2008) 'The Pragmatics of Forgiveness: Judgments of Apologies in the Israeli Political Arena', *Discourse & Society*, 19/5, pp. 577–598.

Kampf, Z. (2009) 'Public (Non-)apologies: The Discourse of Minimizing Responsibility', *Journal of Pragmatics*, 41/11, pp. 2257–2270.

Kampf, Z., and Blum-Kulka, S. (2007) 'Do Children Apologize to Each Other? Apology Events in Young Israeli Peer Discourse', *Journal of Politeness Research*, 3/1, pp. 11–27.

Katriel, T. (1986) *Talking Straight: Dugri Speech in Israeli Sabra Culture*, Cambridge, Cambridge University Press.

Katriel, T. (1999) *Milot Mafte'ah: Dfusei Tarbut Vetikshoret Beisrael* [*Keywords: Patterns of Culture and Communication in Israel*], Haifa, University of Haifa Press and Zmora-Bitan.

Kimmerling, B. (2001) *The Invention and Decline of Israeliness: State, Society and the Military*, Berkeley, University of California Press.

Lakoff, R.B. (2000) *The Language War*, Berkeley, University of California Press.

Levinson, S. (2006) 'On the Human "Interaction Engine"', in N.J. Enfield and S.C. Levinson (eds), *The Roots of Human Sociality*, Oxford and New York, Berg, pp. 39–69.

Miller, E.F. (1979) 'Metaphor and Political Knowledge', *American Political Science Review*, 73/1, pp. 155–170.

Mills, S. (2003) *Gender and Politeness*, Cambridge, Cambridge University Press.

Mor, E. (forthcoming) '"I Was the Firstborn Because I'm Really Older Than You": Between Reality and Fiction in Children's Pretend Play', in M. Hamo and S. Blum-Kulka (eds), *Child Talk*, Tel Aviv, The Center for Educational Technology (in Hebrew).
Patterson, T.E. (1993) *Out of Order*, New York, Knopf.
Perez de Ayala, S. (2001) 'FTAs and Erskine May: Conflicting Needs? Politeness in Question Time', *Journal of Pragmatics*, 33/2, pp. 143–169.
Sheldon, A., and Johnson, D. (1994) 'Preschool Negotiators: Gender Differences in Double-Voice Discourse as a Conflict Talk Style in Early Childhood', in B. Sheppard, R. Lewicki and R. Bies (eds), *Research on Negotiation in Organizations*, 4, Greenwich, JAI Press, pp. 25–57.
Simmel, G. (1955 [1908]) 'Conflict', in K. Wolff (ed.), *Conflict and the Web of Group Affiliation*, New York, Free Press, pp. 11–123.
Stalpers, J. (1995) 'The Expression of Disagreement', in K. Ehlich and J. Wagner (eds), *Discourse of Business Negotiation*, Berlin and New York, Mouton de Gruyter, pp. 275–299.
Tannen, D. (1998) *The Argument Culture: Moving from Debate to Dialogue*, New York, Random House.
Thompson, B.J. (2000) *Political Scandal*, Cambridge, Polity Press.
Watts, R.J. (2003) *Politeness*, Cambridge, Cambridge University Press.
Weizman, E., and Blum-Kulka, S. (1992) 'Ordinary Misunderstanding', in M. Stamenoff (ed.), *Current Advances in Semantic Theory*, Amsterdam and Philadelphia, John Benjamins, pp. 419–434.
Zadunaisky-Ehrlich, S., and Blum-Kulka, S. (2010) 'Peer Talk as a "Double Opportunity Space": The Case of Argumentative Discourse', *Discourse & Society*, 21/5, pp. 211–233.

6

Korean Honorifics and 'Revealed', 'Ignored' and 'Suppressed' Aspects of Korean Culture and Politeness

Lucien Brown

1. Introduction

Korean is well known for possessing one of the most elaborate honorifics systems observed in the world's languages. Through the addition of verb endings and vocabulary substitutions the speaker is able to express subtle degrees of deference towards the hearer or sentence referents. At times, this results in sentences of identical referential meaning being rendered in altogether different ways depending on whether the speaker is addressing (or referring to) a status superior (as in 1a) or status equal/subordinate (1b):[1]

(1) a.	진지를	잡수셨습니까?	b.	밥을	먹었어?
	cinci-lul	capswusi-ess-supnikka?		pap-ul	mek-ess-e?
	meal:HON-ACC	eat:HON-PAST-SUPNITA		meal-ACC	eat-PAST-E?
	'Have you eaten your meal?'				

Although the two sentences above are identical in meaning, whereas (1a) contains the honorific lexical items for 'meal' and 'eat', (1b) contains the plain counterparts. In addition, whereas (1a) is rounded-off with the 'completely raised' *–(su)pnita* speech style ('hearer honorific') ending, (1b) is rendered in the 'generally lowered' *–e*.[2]

With languages that possess special categories of honorific forms being relatively few and with honorifics appearing to directly encode language-specific politeness phenomena in the very fabric of the language, their study should be crucial to discussions of politeness and culture. However, previous studies within politeness research have tended to focus on the Japanese rather than the Korean system. And even when the Korean system has been considered, research has too frequently adopted essentialised positions regarding the function of honorifics, not to mention their cultural meanings and relationship to 'politeness'. It has been too readily assumed that honorifics constitute neat 'closed sets' of linguistic forms that are applied 'obligatorily' according to social convention (Sohn 1986). In addition, it has been taken for granted that the social function of honorifics is to communicate 'respect' or 'deference' (Hwang 1990) and that their existence in the Korean language is connected to Confucian values (Yoon 2004). Finally, at least within accounts of honorifics within politeness research, descriptions have focused almost entirely on the idealised Seoul standard at the expense of dialectal variations, not to mention the use of honorifics in North Korea.[3]

The current chapter sets out to disentangle the ideologies that surround honorifics from their actual patterns of usage and to reconsider the place of honorifics within notions of Korean culture and politeness. In order to paint a more complete picture of the cultural-specific meanings of honorific forms I adopt a tripartite model of culture from Walker (2000: 232): 'revealed culture', 'suppressed culture' and 'ignored culture'. Under the first of these monikers I discuss visible, ideologically loaded norm-abiding usages of honorifics. Rather than accepting these social norms as being stable and uncontested I look critically at how the media, popular press and traditional academic texts work to create and perpetuate the ideology of 'correct' and 'obligatory' honorifics use, not just in South Korea but also in the communist North. Then, under the headings of 'suppressed culture' and 'ignored culture' I examine alternative usages of Korean honorifics that are only recently coming into relief thanks to new lines of academic research and emerging social discourses. Before engaging these three modes of honorific use in Sections 4 and 5, I sketch a model of culture and politeness in Section 2 and provide background information regarding Korean culture and politeness in Section 3.

2. Towards a working model of culture and politeness

The exploration of culture-specific modes of politeness requires the adoption of a culture-specific so-called politeness1 or emic perspective. Such a perspective should take as its focus culture-specific values and meaning systems that influence the ultimately subjective social judgments of what constitutes politeness. In this section, I argue that the adoption of such a perspective requires careful consideration of the different facets of politeness1 and also of the ideological aspects of politeness. After considering these problems, I outline the approach to 'culture' adopted in this chapter and explain how this approach helps to bring the different levels of politeness1 into focus.

Originally defined as "the various ways in which polite behavior is talked about by members of sociocultural groups" (Watts et al. 1992: 2), politeness1 actually possesses at least three facets (Eelen 2001: 35), all of which are important for an emic perspective. In addition to the way that politeness is conceptualised in layman discourse – what Eelen (2001: 35) dubs 'metapragmatic politeness1' – politeness1 may also refer to 'expressive' (politeness as encoded in speech) and 'classificatory' (politeness as spontaneous hearer judgments during interaction) aspects. These distinctions, however, are not always made explicit within politeness research, where metapragmatic layman politeness concepts are at times unquestionably correlated with expressive and classificatory aspects of politeness1. One obvious example of such problems concerns the use of the term *wakimae* (Ide 1989). Although rightfully recognised as a metapragmatic layman term associated with politeness in Japanese, this emic concept is too unproblematically conflated with actual linguistic structures (notably honorifics) and it is too readily assumed that it can explain their distribution in (idealised forms of) Japanese. To make matters worse, *wakimae* is also discussed as a relatively stable and uncontested value that all members of the given culture are assumed unquestionably to aspire to. As a final confusion, culture-specific *wakimae* then gets translated as 'discernment' and is offered up as a cross-linguistic theoretical politeness2 term.

I am not claiming here that metapragmatic layman terms such as *wakimae* are unhelpful to the study of politeness. To the contrary, they can be illuminating, provided that the cultural ideologies behind them are properly deconstructed and the relationships between them and expressive and classificatory politeness are problematised rather than just assumed. In order to do this, the approach to politeness adopted in this chapter plugs into research on language ideologies (Silverstein 1979) and, in particular, work on politeness ideologies (Kienpointner 1999) and honorific ideologies (Irvine 1998; Koyama 2004). From this approach, rather than being taken to correspond directly to the way that politeness is actually negotiated in authentic communication, metapragmatic conceptualisations of politeness are seen as rationalisations that attempt to assign order to language and its association with culture. Such rationalisations are seen as being power-laden and tied up with "viewpoints that serve the interests of specific groups and help to implement social value structures" (Held 1999: 21).

In order to examine the ideologies surrounding Korean honorifics and their place within Korean politeness and at the same time provide a more complete picture of the culture-specific usages of these forms, the current chapter adopts a three-pronged model of culture. The model follows the observation of Walker (2000) that culture has three facets: 'revealed culture', 'ignored culture' and 'suppressed culture'. Discussed in the context of Japanese language learning, Walker (2000: 232) defines 'revealed culture' as "cultural knowledge that a native [i.e. native speaker or person who is 'native' to the culture] is generally eager to communicate to a non-native [i.e. a non-native speaker or someone who is not 'native' to the culture]". More broadly, 'revealed culture' corresponds to 'normative' aspects of culture about which 'natives' have a high conscious awareness of and that are reified through power-laden channels.

Relating the model to notions of politeness, 'revealed culture' encapsulates highly visible metapragmatic beliefs pertaining to what it means to 'be polite' according to assumed culture-specific patterns. 'Ignored culture' is to do with knowledge or behaviour that 'a native is generally unaware of'. Such modes of behaviour may be specific to a particular community, but their importance is not recognised and they are not imbued with the same powerful cultural ideologies as 'revealed' aspects. These modes of behaviour encapsulate culture-specific politeness phenomena at the expressive or classificatory level which, however, are rarely acknowledged at the layman metapragmatic level. Finally, 'suppressed culture' is concerned with cultural knowledge or behaviour that 'natives' are aware of, but 'that a native is generally unwilling to communicate to a non-native'. Put simply, these are aspects of culture that exist outside of or even contradict ideologically invested social norms and are considered as 'substandard' or 'inferior' by those in positions of power. Such cultural modes may include patterns of behaviour that are involved in the negotiation of politeness in real-world interaction but these patterns are considered 'incorrect' by established societal norms. This model connects to the observation of Silverstein (1979) that native perceptions of language are neither the same as how interactions are actually negotiated in context nor to how they may be observed by an outsider. Furthermore, the model allows for the consideration of non-mainstream, alternative and suppressed cultural meanings and perceptions of Korean honorifics.

3. 'Korean' culture and 'Korean' politeness

Before analysing 'revealed', 'ignored' and 'suppressed' cultural meanings of Korean honorifics, I pause briefly to problematise 'Korean' as a target for culture-specific analysis of politeness. I also provide a brief critique of previous definitions of what politeness means in the 'Korean' context.

Accepting 'Korean' as representing a unified language, culture and set of politeness norms requires considerable caution, particularly given the high congruity that is assumed between ideas of Korean race, nation, culture and language. Until the partition of the Korean peninsula in 1948, Korea did indeed hold a remarkably close 'fit' between these aspects (King 2007: 200). Moreover, even after the partition, governments in both Koreas have promoted mutually exclusive ideals of Korea as a 'unitary nation' that is ethnically and culturally unique and homogenous.[4] In addition to equating nation with race and culture, Korea maintains a high congruity between speech community and nation: "whoever speaks Korean, is a Korean" (Coulmas 1999: 48). Both Koreas display a high degree of language patriotism, with Korean being equated on certain levels with the unique national and ethnic characters of the Korean people (King 2007: 219).

Korean honorifics, frequently quoted as the most complex and advanced in any of the world's languages[5] are a focus for some of this patriotism, with their complexity being equated with traditional modes of Confucian etiquette and also, in the North, with communist morals. To quote the North Korean leader Kim Jong-il, "because our language can express etiquette and politeness exactly, it is also extremely useful for educating communist morality" (from King 2007: 223). However, it should be noted that Korean language patriotism, rather than focusing predominantly on honorifics (as is the case for Japanese, see Koyama 2004; Wetzel 2004), has more commonly targeted the Hangul script (King 2007: 219) and sound-symbolism (King, personal communication). With language seen as important to ethnic and cultural identity both Koreas have promoted active policies to encourage unified standard versions of the language, including linguistic etiquette (see below).

However, the idea of 'Korean' as representing a unified language and culture comes with obvious contradictions. Firstly, a degree of linguistic divergence has been noted between the languages spoken in the North and South, extending to the use of honorifics (Cho et al. 2002; Yeon 2006). This divergence, as well as resulting from a simple lack of contact, has been accentuated by opposing political systems, ideologies and language policies. Secondly, in addition to being spoken on the Korean peninsula, Korean is spoken by large populations of ethnic Koreans settled overseas. This includes populations such as the *Zainichi* Koreans in Japan, the *Koryŏ-saram* in post-Soviet states and the *Chosŏnjok* in

China, who predate Korean partition and who hold Korean identities and use forms of the language distinct from either Seoul or Pyongyang standards. Thirdly and most fundamentally, although both the North and the South promote ideals of homogenous populations aspiring to speak standardised languages, this does not correlate with linguistic reality. Of particular significance to the current study, regional dialects of Korean have been shown to differ markedly in terms of honorifics.[6] Although discussions in the current chapter focus on Seoul Korean with some reference to the Pyongyang standard, I am keen to stress the need for further research into honorifics and the social meanings attached to them in different 'Korean' populations.

With this powerful ideology of ethnic and cultural homogeneity, previous research attempting to define politeness in the Korean context has tended towards adopting relatively stable and non-contested definitions of linguistic etiquette. The closest equivalent to the English word 'politeness' is taken to be *kongson*. This Sino-Korean word combines the Chinese characters 'respect' and 'humility' and these two concepts are seen as being important properties of Korean politeness (Yu 2003: 146). Also viewed with importance is *chondae* 'respect, deference', which is commonly taken to encapsulate the use of honorific forms – *chondaenmal* 'respect-speech'. *Chondae* is understood by some theorists to represent a different dimension of behaviour to *kongson* in that it is obligatory and does not rely on individual speaker strategy (Sohn 1986; Hwang 1990). However, it appears doubtful that separating *chondae* from *kongson* corresponds with lay conceptualisations of Korean politeness. As shall become obvious in Section 4, the 'correct' use of honorifics is central to popular discourse on linguistic etiquette.

The concept of 'face', or *cheymyŏn*, resonates strongly with researchers looking at the normative meaning of 'Korean' politeness. S. Kim (2001: 123) notes that "to Koreans, *cheymyŏn* is much more precious than fortune and more precious than life". Central to this concern for face is the importance of adhering to form and meeting societal expectations which are identified as being key Confucian values (T. Lim 1995). This need to conform to social norms is motivated by a high concern for how others perceive one's behaviour; "the eyes and ears of others", as S. Kim (2001: 123) describes it. Considering the specific content of Korean face, Lim (1995) suggests five components: *chŏshin* 'proper conduct', *inp'um* 'ethos', *p'umŭi* 'refinement', *yŏngnyang* 'ability' and *sŏngsuk* 'maturity'. Put simply, normative 'Korean' face is established through recognition as a person of ability, refinement, good character and adequate maturity who follows the paths of proper conduct. The use of 'polite' language, particularly respectful language and honorifics, has been identified as important to the establishment of face. Cho (1988: 131) notes that inappropriate use of honorifics results in the face of both the addressee and the speaker being threatened; the former feels that his social status is being neglected and the latter runs the risk of being branded rude and ill-bred.

With adhering to form constituting a powerful Korean social ideology, it perhaps follows that both Koreas rigorously pursue attempts to promote and to standardise politeness norms. These attempts include government-sponsored publications of language-courtesy handbooks – *Chosŏnmal ryeyjŏlbop* (*Rules of Courtesy in the Korean Language*) (Kim 1983) in North Korea and *Uri mal-ŭi yeyjŏl* (*The Etiquette of Our Language*) (Kungnipkukŏwon 1992) in the South. In South Korea, as noted previously in Lee and Ramsey (2000: 238) and Yoon (2004), the use of 'correct' honorifics is also widely promoted through the media and popular press.

4. 'Revealed' aspects of Korean honorifics

Traditional academic and popular accounts of the use and social meanings of Korean honorifics typically assume that these forms constitute 'closed' sets that express the fixed social meaning of 'deference', that are markers of Confucian cultural values and that must be applied obligatorily according to stable social conventions. In this section, I argue that such descriptions represent the 'revealed' aspect of Korean honorifics rather than the linguistic reality of how these forms are actually applied at the 'expressive' level.

Honorifics systems in languages such as Korean are highly iconic and appear to be composed of regular vocabulary sets and segmentable morphemes seemingly reserved for encoding aspects of politeness. Highly developed as these honorifics systems may be, Koyama (2004; for Japanese) and Irvine (1998; for Javanese, Wolof, Zulu and ChiBemba) argue that their assumed regularity in actual fact represents an ideal standardisation that corresponds only partially to actual language use. Analysis of the way that Korean honorifics (particularly speech styles or 'hearer honorifics') are organised in traditional descriptions supports this point of view. According to the Seoul standard, six speech styles are arranged in the order of deference displayed below.[7] In this model, forms described as 'raised' are honorific forms that are assumed to 'raise' (and therefore show respect, deference to etc.) the hearer of the utterance. Conversely, forms described as 'lowered' are non-honorific forms that 'lower' the hearer.

STYLE	DECLARATIVE	INTERROGATIVE	IMPERATIVE
'completely raised'	*–(su)pnita*	*–(su)pnikka*	*–(u)psio*
'generally raised'	*–a/eyo*	*–a/eyo*	*–a/eyo*
'conventionally raised'	*–(s)o*	*–(s)o*	*–o*
'conventionally lowered'	*–ney*	*–na/–nunka*	*–key*
'generally lowered'	*–e*	*–e*	*–e*
'completely lowered'	*–ta*	*–ni/–(nu)nya*	*–ca*

The neat six-way divide and the normative labels are problematic on a number of levels. The model assumes that declarative, interrogative and imperative forms grouped as the same 'style' express the same normative degrees of deference, that these degrees of deference are stable semantic values and that the endings listed under each style differ only in terms of honorification and are otherwise parallel forms. These assumptions, however, do not stand up to scrutiny. Considering the 'completely raised' *–(su)pnita* style and 'generally raised' *–a/eyo* style, the model assumes that the former operates as an isolated style that is essentially higher than the latter. However, in honorific discourse, speakers frequently switch between these two styles. In such circumstances, rather than being associated with differing degrees of deference, each style takes on separate discourse–pragmatic functions (see Section 5). In addition, at times the *–a/eyo* style can be perceived as 'more respectful' than *–(su)pnita* due to the increased propensity for *–a/eyo* to combine with epistemic modal endings (K. Lee 2003: 206).

The fact that models attempting to organise honorific forms into neat categories are tied up with the promotion of normative patterns of politeness and 'revealed' cultural values becomes particularly clear when the South Korean model of speech-style organisation is compared with that of the North. Whereas Seoul recognises six separate styles, Pyongyang has simplified this to three (Nam and Chŏng 1990). The 'polite level' can be understood as encompassing honorific forms that may normatively index respect to the hearer, whereas the 'low' level represents non-honorific forms. The term 'equal' can be understood as correlating to language used between 'status equals', presumably when reduced intimacy or the formality of the situation does not allow for downgrading to the 'low' level.

STYLE	DECLARATIVE
'polite level'	*–(su)pnita* (some use of *–a/eyo* allowed)
'equal level'	*–a/eyo* *–(s)o* *–supte*
'low level'	*–ta*

As noted by H. Lee (1990: 79), it is the manner of classification rather than the content that differs from the Seoul system. The North Korean system conflates endings with different declarative forms under one category and includes the *–a/eyo* ending under two possible levels. These simplifications, and most notably the recognition of an 'equal level' represents attempts to correlate honorific forms with North Korea's special brand of communist ideology: "we have three levels ... suitable for the people engaged in the construction of a socialist country ... whereby we can respect seniors, express affection to juniors, and be friendly with colleagues and friends" (quoted in H. Lee 1990: 79). Here, the turn of phrase "express[ing] affection to juniors" is interesting for the way that it aligns the use of non-honorific forms with a positive social value (rather than, for example, exerting authority or power over juniors). In summary, the organisation of honorifics into neat categories and the labels attached to these represent rationalisations that attempt (whether consciously or not) to align the said forms with ideologically loaded social values.[8]

As can be seen in the way that speech styles are ascribed values of 'raising' and 'lowering', the cultural value most readily attached to honorific forms is the communication of respect towards status superiors. Indeed, as has been well documented in previous research (Sohn 1986; Hwang 1990; Koo 1995), the application of honorifics according to social hierarchy is markedly strict. When addressing notable superiors such as teachers, bosses and grandparents, it is difficult to imagine using anything except the highest honorific forms. Having said this, the value of 'respect' commonly associated with honorifics is not necessarily inherent to the semantics of these forms nor the only possible social 'meaning' that they can communicate. As pointed out by Irvine (1998: 52), the expression of deference associated with honorifics is conventionalised; in other words, it requires shared understanding of social knowledge rather than merely being communicated by compositional semantics. Put simply, rather than being automatic markers of respect, honorifics take on such meanings through application in specific contexts along recognised social norms and through knowledge of the cultural meanings that are associated with such usage. When applied in different contexts, interpretations of 'respect' may cease to become available. Thus, when used towards intimates of younger/equal age, honorifics are not taken as markers of social hierarchy but instead signal a lack of intimacy. Likewise, when applied towards intimates, honorifics can take on interpretations of humour, sarcasm or anger.

The importance of applying honorifics according to social hierarchy is typically explained through reference to the influence that

Confucianism exerts on Korean culture. The literature on honorifics frequently associates the use of these forms with highly visible neo-Confucian cultural slogans such as *changyuyusŏ* ("the old and the young know their place") (Lee and Ramsey 2000), *kyŏngnosasang* ("respecting the elderly") and *hyo* ('filial piety') (Yoon 2004). These metadiscourses emphasise that people are not of equal status and that it is desirable, proper and a sign of good breeding to index status differences in (linguistic) behaviour (Yoon 2004: 194–197).

Important as these values may be, it should be recognised that the association between them and honorific forms is a cultural construction at the 'revealed' level rather than something inherently embodied by honorific forms. As noted by Yoon (2004: 198), these Confucian metadiscourses and the use of honorifics associated with them are "promoted very actively and widely at the national level" through education and the popular press. In the South Korean publication *Uri mal-ŭi yeyjŏl*, for example, 'younger generations' are criticised for their 'incorrect' use of honorific forms and the lack of knowledge of Confucian social order that this betrays. Although the systematisation of honorifics probably has much to do with the promotion of neo-Confucian ideology, the actual existence of honorifics in the Korean language appears to predate the spread of Confucianism to Korea. According to Baek (1985), Korean honorifics were probably used in ancient times when referring to gods and kings and the use according to strict Confucian social hierarchy developed much later. Irvine (1998: 52), in her comparison of the honorfics systems of Javanese, Wolof, Zulu and ChiBemba, concluded that no correlations can be found between the existence of honorifics in a language and any particular form of social structure. Rather, these relationships only flourish at the ideological level – in "the complex systems of ideas and beliefs through which people interpret linguistic behaviors".

The final ideology regarding the 'revealed' culture of honorifics is that the use of these forms is obligatory. To be sure, the pressure in mainstream society to apply honorifics according to social expectations can be weighty and the social sanctions for non-use towards social superiors can be quite tangible. The example given by Koo (1995: 23) that a Korean student may be expelled from school for failing to use honorifics towards his/her teacher is no exaggeration. However, the 'obligation' that is perceived in the use of honorifics needs to be identified as an ideological construct at the metapragmatic level rather than something inherent to the forms themselves at the expressive level, as has sometimes been assumed in politeness literature. To take an example, Hwang

(1990: 42) claims that Korean honorifics represent "a matter of social code which is imposed upon the participants in communicative interactions". These comments echo the more well-known observations of Ide (1989: 227) regarding Japanese that honorifics are "socio-pragmatically and grammatically obligatory".

This ideology of obligation has been perpetuated in the Korean context by the grammatical tradition of analysing referent honorification as a form of agreement. Referent honorific forms, and the subject honorific morpheme *–si–* in particular, are frequently assumed within traditional grammatical descriptions to be 'triggered' by honorific properties of the noun phrase, typically the inclusion of the respectful suffix *–nim*.[9] From this traditional viewpoint, in examples such as the following, the addition of *–si–* (and, perhaps to a lesser extent the honorific nominative marker *–kkeyse*) is made 'obligatory' by the inclusion of the honorific subject sensayngnim 'teacher-HON':

(2)	선생님께서	오셨어요
	sensayng-**nim**-**kkeyse**	o-**si**-ess-eyo
	teacher-HON-NOM:HON	come-HON-PAST-EYO
	'teacher came'	

This theory of 'agreement' has been discredited by Kim and Sells (2007: 315) who argue that deletion of *–si–* (and *–kkeyse*) in sentences such as the above may typically result in awkwardness due to the deviation from 'understood social norms' but not in ungrammaticality. In fact, Kim and Sells (2007: 315) demonstrate several contexts in which *–si–* (and *–kkeyse*) may be quite naturally dropped. For example, if the teacher in question is actually a colleague of the same social level, the speaker may refer to him/her as *sensayngnim* to show respect for his professional position, but then omit *–si–* (and *–kkeyse*) due to the equal status. In another example, even if the speaker is the teacher's student, it may be acceptable (or even preferable) to omit *–si–* (and *–kkeyse*) if the addressee happens to be the teacher's father. In this situation, use of *sensayngnim* 'elevates' the teacher, but omission of *–si–* (and *–kkeyse*) avoids elevating the teacher higher than the hearer, who is, after all, the teacher's father. Kim and Sells (2007: 313) further point out that application of *–si–* cannot be viewed as agreement since it may quite naturally occur with noun phrases that have no inherent 'honorific feature', including the wh-phrase *nwukwu* 'who' and the negative polarity item *amwuto* 'nobody'.

Despite these obvious problems with the assumption of 'agreement', it appears that honorification is still frequently understood along these lines not just by grammarians but from a layman perspective. The assumption that *–si–* is 'triggered' by a noun with honorific properties underlies the way that honorification is taught in South Korean schools and also frequently in Korean classes for second-language learners. An example of the latter can be found in the textbook designed and published by South Korea's longest standing Korean language programme at Yonsei University – *Yonsei Korean* (book 1). When honorifics are first introduced (page 84), a table is presented showing honorific verb forms in one column and non-honorific forms in the other. The 'honorific' column is headed by a picture of an elderly woman labelled *halmŏni-kkesŏ* 'grandmother-NOM:HON', signalling that these forms have to be used when an elder is the subject of the sentence. The column of non-honorific forms, on the other hand, is headed by a picture of a small girl and the title *ydŏngsaeng–i* 'younger sister-NOM'.

The claim of 'obligation' can be better understood when the social ideologies that lie behind this ideal are deconstructed. As previously noted, the ideology of adhering to form holds high capital at the normative level of Korean culture, as indeed appears to be the case in other East Asian societies. At least according to normative description, East Asians are said to value obedience to elders, traditions and social norms and to experience satisfaction and to actively 'like' conforming to societal expectations (as stated in Kim and Markus 1999: 786). Conformity is associated with positive social values such as balance, harmony, maturity and inner-strength, whereas independence and individuality are branded unnatural, immature and disruptive (Kim and Markus 1999: 786). What such descriptions ignore, however, is that conformity constitutes a 'revealed' cultural discourse that does not necessarily extend to 'suppressed' and 'ignored' aspects of culture. For Koreans, I would argue, being *seen* to adhere to form is important. However, when away from the 'ears and eyes' of others – or in certain closed social groups – the cultural importance of conforming becomes more negligible. As shall be examined in Section 5, this may result in the 'hidden' application of patterns of honorifics use that actually contradict dominant cultural discourses.

Further light can be shone on the ideal of adhering to form when we consider the different patterns of prescribed honorifics in North and South Korea. In South Korea, the obligatory use of referent honorifics is most readily associated with expressing deference towards elders or *noin* (Yoon 2004) and notable superiors. In North Korea, these associations also hold true. However, in addition, prescriptive accounts of North Korean honorifics place stress on the forms that are obligatory when addressing the leader Kim Jong-il. Not only is a special ultra-high honorific form combining *–si–* and the morpheme *–op–* reserved for addressing Kim, but North Koreans are also instructed to use referent honorifics for the leader alone when talking in his presence and to suppress them in reference to other superiors (*Chosŏnmal ryeyjŏlbop*, Kim 1983, quoted in Cho et al. 2002: 238–239). This example shows that the 'rules' surrounding the obligatory nature of honorifics are not inherent to the forms themselves but are socially constructed.

5. 'Suppressed' and 'ignored' applications of honorifics

The 'revealed' patterns of honorifics usage discussed above provide an important sketch of the place that these forms occupy within Korean culture and politeness and the powerful social values that are normatively associated with them. However, as my critique has shown, the norms of honorifics use and the ideologies behind them are superficial and correspond only partially to the distribution of honorifics in real-world usage. To provide a more complete picture of the role of honorifics in Korean society, the current section discusses three alternative honorifics patterns identified in recent research: (1) egalitarian use within the nuclear family, (2) so-called over-honorification and (3) use to demarcate discourse types. In addition to illustrating the superficial nature of the ideologies surrounding 'revealed' applications of honorifics, these 'suppressed' or 'ignored' patterns reveal alternative explanations for the way that 'Korean' politeness is negotiated at the expressive and classificatory levels. Although these discussions cover three accounts of non-normative honorifics use, space restrictions do not allow for a wider discussion of shifting between different levels of honorification. Readers are referred to C. Lee (1996) or, in Korean, J. Lee (2001) and Yoo (1996).

Recent studies into the use of honorifics within the nuclear family reveal movements away from traditional hierarchical modes of interaction towards a new kind of 'polite' egalitarianism (Kim-Renaud 2001; Hi-Jean Kim 2003). Traditionally, families were expected to retain hierarchical patterns of honorifics use in line with the Confucian hierarchical family structure, with children addressing their parents in honorifics and wives applying honorifics towards their husbands. Despite this, the emerging dominant pattern within urban nuclear families is for universal reciprocation of non-honorific speech, or *panmal* (lit. 'half-speech') as it is commonly known. This change, however, is frequently blamed upon 'westernisation' in the popular press and is suppressed rather than being recognised as a fully fledged social norm.

This lack of recognition is evident first of all in its low level of representation in the media and press. Although a degree of shift has been observed in recent years, television dramas still only infrequently show wives and children using *panmal*. To illustrate this point from a television drama running at the time of press, the popular family drama *Sol yakkuk chip adŭl-dŭl* ('The Sons of Sol Pharmacy House', 2009/2010, KBS) depicts the wife of the family and the sons all faithfully using honorific *chondaenmal* but receiving *panmal*. Elsewhere, under some social pressure to show more gender equality (but also to respect traditional 'norms'), dramas are increasingly depicting couples (particularly younger couples) reciprocating honorific *chondaenmal*. This can be seen, for example, between the leading couple in the drama *Chŏnman pŏn saranghae* ('Loving You a Thousand Times', 2009/2010, SBS). By opting for universal *chondaenmal*, dramas manage to avoid questions of gender bias but at the same time circumvent overtly challenging the traditional social norm of wives showing respect to their husbands.

Continuing pressure to conform to social norms appears to frequently result in the creation of dual patterns of honorific use: a 'revealed' pattern applied in 'public' for forms' sake and a 'suppressed' pattern used behind closed doors. In a study of speech-style use by 'young' Korean couples, H.-J. Kim (2003: 204) found wives used *panmal* towards their husbands 91% of the time in recordings made in private. However, this decreased to 39% when in the presence of friends and to 1% when in the presence of their parents-in-law. Moreover, when wives were asked which speech style they believed they used to their husband in private interaction, only 69% reported that they used *panmal*. Similarly, Soh (1985: 32) notes that children generally use *panmal* to their parents, but upgrade to *chondaenmal* when in the presence of others, such as when visiting the house of family friends. This division between how you use honorifics at home and how you should use them in public is even recognised by the South Korean prescriptive politeness guide *Uri mal-ŭi yeyjŏl*. On page 23, the book is critical of the case of a 32-year-old teacher for using *panmal* and for addressing his mother as *ŏmma* 'mom' in front of his students. Although the writers seem to accept that this may be the way people talk at home, the teacher's speech is seen as unsuitable for the public sphere. Such observations confirm the at times superficial nature of ideologies of adhering to form in Korean culture.

Although popularly characterised as being indicative of westernisation and the breakdown of Korean social values, I follow Kim-Renaud (2001) in recognising the increased use of *panmal* as representing a new politeness 'strategy'. With the modernisation of South Korean society, Kim-Renaud (2001: 42) points out that being overtly power-conscious, subservient or self-effacing has simply fallen out of fashion, to be replaced by a 'friendlier' and 'nicer' mode of politeness. Thus, use of *panmal* by children and wives, rather than being interpreted as disrespectful or impolite, becomes associated with positive social values such as intimacy, closeness and being 'modern'.

Another application of honorifics that is 'suppressed' within Korean culture is the practice called 'over-honorification'. This refers to the inclusion of the 'honorific marker' *–si–* in sentences in which the intended target of deference does not appear as the sentence subject. This phenomenon is particularly common in service talk and is widely acknowledged in recent literature:

(3) a. 혹시 아르바이트 들어오시면 소개 좀 해; 주세요 (university junior to senior)
hoksi arupaithu tuleo-**si**-myen sokay com hay cwu-si-eyo
'if a part-time job becomes available, please let me know'
(J. Lee 1996: 288)

b. 가격이 얼마세요? (customer to cashier)
kakyek-i elma-**si**-eyo?
'how much is the price?'
(D. Lim 2000: 58)

c. 색상 교환 비용은 구매자 부담이십니다 (clerk to customer)
sayksang kyohwan piyong-un kwumayca pwutam-i-**si**-pnita
'the expense for exchange for a different colour will be charged to the buyer'
(Kim and Sells 2007: 319)

In the examples, the use of honorifics can be considered 'incorrect' from the normative viewpoint in that the subjects of the sentence are not the intended targets of deference but inanimate objects (part-time job, price, expense). Although linguists recognise the proliferation of such utterances, they are typically characterised as 'errors' or 'mistakes' resulting from 'misanalysis' as to the grammatical relationship between the target of honorification and the verb (Kim-Renaud 2001: 37–38). In layman discourse, such 'errors' are identified with the speech of 'younger generations' and blamed on the influence of Japanese beautification honorifics.

Rather than 'errors', I recognise such usage as an additional politeness strategy available at the expressive level for the use of *–si–*. Although such usage may be seen as clumsy by some (Kim-Renaud 2001: 37), I would argue that the inclusion of *–si–* nonetheless communicates the speaker's eager intention to pay deference towards the hearer when under situational pressure to speak with optimal attention to politeness. I would largely agree with Kim-Renaud (2001: 37) that such usage represents a shift in which *–si–* is now more discourse-bound rather than syntactically governed and that such usage represents a newly emerging politeness strategy.

The two examples considered so far in this section represent 'suppressed' cultures of honorifics use that are widely acknowledged but considered 'incorrect' or substandard. The third use I consider, however, represents a pattern of usage of which native speakers have low metapragmatic awareness and thus represents an 'ignored' culture of honorifics use: alternation between the 'completely raised' *–(su)pnita* style and 'generally raised' *–a/eyo*. Although it is traditionally assumed that *–(su)pnita* is more deferential and also more formal than *–a/eyo*, in natural conversation speakers frequently switch between the two. Analysis of public discourse has found that such switching is governed by shifts between new and shared information (Eun and Strauss 2004) and by the speaker moving between on-stage 'presenting' and off-stage 'commentating' (Brown 2007). Put simply, whereas *–(su)pnita* tends to occur with strong statements of factual new information presented in the speaker's on-stage persona, *–a/eyo* accompanies common knowledge, conjecture and personal comments.[10] Interestingly, the use of *–(su)pnita* to index a 'presentational' stance largely mirrors Cook's (2008: 45) analysis of the Japanese *masu* style.[11]

(4) Professor appearing on Muŏt-idŭn mulŏ poseyo (KBS 2006)

1 오히려 우리 나라의 경우 (.) 가끔 이: 보도 자료를 보면은: (0.1) 그마약성 진통제 같은 경우를; 너무 적게 쓰는 게 문제가 되기도 **합니다** 실제로.
ohilye uli nala-uy kyengwu (.) kakkum i: poto: calyo-lul po-myen-un: (0.1) ku mayakseng cinthongcey kath-un kyengu-lul: nemwu cekkey ssu-nun key mwuncey-ka toy-ki-to ha-**pnita**- silcey-lo.
'rather, in our country's case, if you look at the reported data using narcotic pain killers too sparingly can be a problem actually'

2 많이 안 쓰거든**요**.
manhi an ssu-ketun-**yo**.
'because we don't use a lot'

3 그래서 환자 삶의 질을 본다면; (.) 어: 마약성 진통제 같은 경우 필요할 때 꼭 써 주는 것이 좋을 것 같다는 생각이 들고**요**.
kulayse hwanca salm-uy cil-ul po-nta-myen (.) e: mayakseng cinthongcey kath-un kyengwu philyoha-l ttay kkok sse cwu-nun kes-i coh-ul kes kath-ta-nun sayngkak-i tul-ko-**yo**.
'so I think that if we consider patients' quality of life, uh, when really needed, definitely giving narcotic painkillers would seem to be a good thing'

4 자료에 의하면 오히려 우리 나라 같은 경우: (.) 세계 평균에 비해서 반도 안 되는 모르핀을 쓴다고 **합니다**.
calyo-ey uyha-myen ohilye wuli nala kath-un kyengu: (.) seykyey phyengkyun-ey pihayse pan-to an toy-nun moluphin-ul ssu-ntako ha-**pnita**.
'according to the data, actually, in our country's case, we don't even use half the global average for morphine'

In lines 1 and 4, use of *–(su)pnita* accompanies the presentation of factual objective information regarding the use of painkillers. Both utterances make reference to 'data' and employ statistical information. These utterances contrast with the more subjective presentation of information in lines 2 and 3, where the speaker aligns the quoted low use of painkillers with his own personal experience and gives his own opinion.

The fact that native speakers have low metapragmatic awareness of such shifting was evinced by C. Lee (1996: 151), whose interview data revealed a strong belief that only *–(su)pnita* is appropriate in public discourse. However, despite this lack of awareness on the metapragmatic level, switching between *–(su)pnita* and *–a/eyo* to index speaker stance and information status would appear to be relevant to the way that politeness is negotiated in Korean public discourse at the expressive and classificatory levels. By using the *–(su)pnita* style, the speaker converges to the social norm of applying the highest speech style in public discourse and makes the factual content of his presentation sound authoritative and believable. But then, by indexing more personal comments with the *–a/eyo* style, he/she appeals to the solidarity of the audience and avoids sounding too power-conscious. In addition, the switch to *–a/eyo* works as a politeness mechanism in the way that it acknowledges the ultimately subjective nature of the speaker's own comments and highlights that the speaker is not attempting to pass them off as objective facts.

The description of *–(su)pnita* in cases such as this differs notably from the traditional 'revealed' analysis and provides a final reminder of the nature of politeness as a subjective social judgement. Whereas traditional accounts of *–(su)pnita* posit that this form normatively signals the respect of a subordinate towards a superior, the usage described here shows *–(su)pnita* taking on quite different functions. In particular, the way that a speaker may use *–(su)pnita* in public discourse not only to mark 'new' or 'factual' information but also to index his/her own authority can be seen as almost contrary to the traditional view of honorific forms as markers of social status. Interestingly, in addition to indexing subservience when used by a status subordinate, the use of the highest forms of Korean honorifics in formal settings or by those in positions of power also becomes associated with authority and even masculinity (Okamoto 2004: 50). These connotations of *–(su)pnita* mark an interesting contrast with Japanese, where the use of honorifics is commonly associated with values such as beauty and femininity. As pointed out by Okamoto (2004: 50), this contrast "illustrates the subjective and arbitrary nature" of links between honorifics and social ideologies.

6. Conclusion

The current chapter has demonstrated that the 'revealed' picture of Korean honorifics at the metapragmatic level only partially explains the linguistic distribution of these forms. Through the deconstruction of the ideologies that surround 'correct' use of honorifics and through consideration of 'suppressed' and 'ignored' patterns, I have provided a more critical and detailed picture of the multiple cultural meanings that these forms possess. Rather than merely constituting 'closed' sets of linguistic forms that are applied obligatorily to index Confucian social hierarchies, honorifics are involved in the culture-specific negotiation of politeness on a number of levels.

The extension of 'culture' to 'suppressed' and 'ignored' meanings advocated in this chapter comes with obvious implications for politeness research. Firstly, the three-pronged model and my findings display the need for further consideration of what a politeness1 perspective may constitute. Until now, such perspectives have at times too readily accepted layman metapragmatic beliefs as direct representations of linguistic reality. Secondly, my discussions have demonstrated the need for politeness research to further investigate the role of ideologies in the construction of politeness. Metapragmatic beliefs regarding politeness, rather than being formed spontaneously, come into being against a backdrop of ideological discourse regarding 'correct' behaviour that is inevitably coloured by the interests of those in positions of power. Thirdly, the consideration of 'alternative' cultural meanings in the study of politeness emphasises the need for researchers to depart from stable national standard languages in their research into politeness phenomena. Rather than discussing 'Korean culture' and 'Korean language' as stable social realities, research needs to unpack the ideology behind such cultural identities and to include investigation of politeness in non-mainstream social groups. In the case of Korean honorifics, further research is required into the way that these forms are used amongst different social groups, speakers of dialects and Korean populations overseas to provide a more detailed picture of how their usage is involved in the struggle for politeness.

Notes

1. For Romanisation, the current chapter employs the Yale system for linguistic data and the McCune–Reischauer system elsewhere. Proper nouns are rendered according to given Romanisations when available.
2. Due to space restrictions, this chapter provides no lengthy description of the Korean honorifics system. Readers are referred to Lee and Ramsey (2000: 224–272).
3. There do, however, exist some noteworthy sociolinguistic or dialectology studies that consider the use of honorifics in South Korean regional dialects, including Wang (1994) and K. Lee (2003).
4. In recent years the South Korean government has started to change policy on this issue. Faced with a growing number of overseas residents and mixed-race marriages, in 2006 the South Korean government decreed that official documents and school textbooks should drop the 'unitary nation' slogan and replace it with the description of Korea as "a multiethnic and multicultural society" (Shin 2006).
5. See, for example, page 235 of the South Korean Politeness Manual *Uri mal-ŭi yeyjŏl* where it is stated, "In our language, honorifics are more complex than in any other language", or the North Korean didactic journal *Chosŏn ŏmun* (2003, Vol. 2: 213), where it is claimed that Korean is "the most superior language in speech levels" (quoted in King 2007: 223).
6. For complete discussion of honorifics in Korean dialects, see K. Lee (2003). Among the differences noted is that whereas the Seoul standard contains six speech styles, some dialects (including Gyeongsang and Jeju) feature only three.
7. It should be noted that this is only one of several models used to organise speech styles in South Korea (see Yeon 1996 for further discussion).
8. As insightfully pointed out by one anonymous reviewer, in addition to social ideologies, the systematisation of honorifics is also tied up with the ideologies of structural linguistics and the assumption that language can be organised into discrete rule-based categories which show one-to-one correspondence between form and meaning.
9. One notable study written in English that adopts the 'agreement' perspective is Yun (1993), who actually concludes that the noun 'triggering' honorification may belong to the more general category of 'topic' rather than 'subject'.

10. The propensity for *–a/eyo* to index a more interpersonal and subjective stance is increased by the fact that this speech style may freely co-occur with affect particles and other sentence endings, whereas such co-occurrence is restricted in the case of *–(su)pnita* (see Byon 2007).
11. Although the function of *–(su)pnita* appears to mirror that of *masu*, there is one important difference between Korean and Japanese regarding the shifting of styles to mark presentational/interpersonal stances. Namely, whereas the style that *masu* alternates with in Japanese is the non-honorific plain form, the style that *–(su)pnita* alternates with (*–eyo*) is also considered 'honorific'. Given this fact, it appears likely that this pattern of shifting in Korean is less marked than its Japanese equivalent.

References

Baek, E. (1985) 'Semantic Shifts in Korean Honorification', in J. Fisiak (ed.), *Historical Semantics: Historical Word Formation*, Berlin, Walter de Gruyter, pp. 23–32.

Brown, L. (2007) 'Alternation between "Polite" and "Deferential" Speech Styles in Korean Public Discourse', paper presented at the International Pragmatics Association Conference, Göteborg, Sweden, 12 July.

Byon, A. (2007) 'Teaching the Polite and the Deferential Speech Levels, Using Media Materials: Advanced KFL Classroom Settings', in D. Yoshimi and H. Wang (eds), *Selected Papers from Pragmatics in the CJK Classroom: The State of the Art*, available at: http://nflrc.hawaii.edu/CJKProceedings.

Cho, E. (1988) 'Some Interactions of Grammar and Pragmatics in Korean', PhD thesis, University of Illinois.

Cho, E., Kim, Y., and Park, T. (2002) *Nambukhan ŏnŏ-ŭi ihae* [*Understanding the Language of North and South Korea*], Seoul, Youkrack.

Cook, H. (2008) *Socializing Identities through Speech Styles: Learners of Japanese as a Foreign Language*, Bristol, Multilingual Matters.

Coulmas, F. (1999) 'The Far East', in J. Fisherman (ed.), *Handbook of Language and Ethnic Identity*, Oxford, Oxford University Press, pp. 399–413.

Eelen, G. (2001) *A Critique of Politeness Theories*, Manchester, St. Jerome.

Eun, J., and Strauss, S. (2004) 'The Primacy of Information Status in the Alternation between Deferential and Polite Forms in Korean Public Discourse', *Language Sciences*, 26, pp. 251–272.

Held, G. (1999) 'Submission Strategies as an Expression of the Ideology of Politeness', *Pragmatics*, 9/1, pp. 21–36.

Hwang, J. (1990), ' "Deference" versus "Politeness" in Korean Speech', *International Journal of the Sociology of Language*, 82, pp. 41–55.

Ide, S. (1989) 'Formal Forms and Discernment', *Multilingua*, 8/2, pp. 223–248.

Irvine, J. (1998) 'Ideologies of Honorific Language', in B. Schieffelin, K. Woolard and P. Kroskrity (eds), *Language Ideologies: Practice and Theory*, Oxford, Oxford University Press, pp. 51–67.

Kienpointner, M. (1999) 'Foreword', *Pragmatics*, 9/1, pp. 1–4.

Kim, D. (1983) *Chosŏnmal Ryeyjŏlbop* [*Rules of Courtesy in the Korean Language*], Pyongyang, Kwahak paekhwasajŏn chulp'ansa.

Kim, Hi-Jean (2003) 'Young Couples' Communication in Changing Korea', *Modern Studies in English Language and Literature*, 47/3, pp. 197–217.

Kim, Hee-jung and Markus, H.R. (1999) 'Deviance or Uniqueness, Harmony or Conformity? A Cultural Analysis', *Journal of Personality and Social Psychology*, 77/4, pp. 785–800.
Kim, J., and Sells, P. (2007) 'Korean Honorification: A Kind of Expressive Meaning', *Journal of East Asian Linguistics*, 16, pp. 303–336.
Kim, S. (2001) *Uri sahoe sok-ŭi urimal* [*Our Language in Our Society*], Seoul, Hankoookmunhwasa.
Kim-Renaud, Y. (2001), 'Change in Korean Honorifics Reflecting Social Change', in T. McAuley (ed.), *Language Change in East Asia*, London, Curzon, pp. 27–46.
King, R. (2007) 'North and South Korea', in A. Simpson (ed.), *Language and National Identity in Asia*, Oxford, Oxford University Press, pp. 200–234.
Koo, J. (1995) 'Politeness Theory: Universality and Specificity', PhD thesis, Harvard University.
Koyama, W. (2004) 'The Linguistic Ideologies of Modern Japanese Honorifics and the Historic Reality of Modernity', *Language and Communication*, 24/4, pp. 411–435.
Kungnipkukŏwon, C.I. (1992) *Uri mal-ŭi yeyjŏl* [*The Etiquette of Our Language*], Seoul: Kungnipkukŏwon, Choson Ilbo.
Lee, C. (1996) 'Variation in the Use of Korean Honorific Verbal Endings: An Interactional Sociolinguistic Study', PhD thesis, Boston University.
Lee, H. (1990) 'Differences in Language Use between North and South Korea', *International Journal of the Sociology of Language*, 82, pp. 71–86.
Lee, I., and Ramsey, S.R. (2000) *The Korean Language*, Albany, State University of New York Press.
Lee, J. (1996) 'Koryŏ kayo-e ssŭ-in hyŏngt'aeso '-si-' uy chaehaesŏk' [A Reanalysis of the Use of –si– in Koryŏ kayo], *Kwanak Emun Yenkwu* [*Kwanak Linguistics Research*], 21, pp. 267–296.
Lee, J. (2001), *Kugŏ kyŏngŏbŏp-ŭi chŏllyakchŏk* [*The Strategic Characteristics of Korean Honorifics Use*], Seoul, Thaehaksa.
Lee, K. (2003), *Kugŏ pangŏn munpŏp* [*Grammar in National Language Dialects*], Seoul, Thaehaksa.
Lim, D. (2000) *Hangukŏ ŏmi '–si–' ŭi munpŏp* [*Grammar of the Korean Ending –si–*], Seoul, Kukŏhakhoe.
Lim, T. (1995) *Chŏng, cheymyŏn, yŏnjul kŭrigo hanguk-in-ŭi ingan kwangyey* [*Affection, Face, Connections and Korean Human Relationships*], Seoul, Hannarae.
Nam, S., and Chŏng, C. (1990), *Pukhan ŭi ŏnŏ saenghwal* [*Linguistic Life in North Korea*], Seoul, Koryŏwŏn.
Okamoto, S. (2004) 'Ideology in Linguistic Practice and Analysis: Gender and Politeness in Japanese Revisited', in S. Okamoto and J. Shibamoto Smith (eds), *Japanese Language, Gender, and Ideology*, New York, Oxford University Press, pp. 38–56.
Shin, H. (2006), 'Korea Greets New Era of Multiculturalism', *The Korea Herald*, 3 August.
Silverstein, M. (1979) 'Language Structure and Linguistic Ideology', in P. Clyne, W. Hanks and C. Hofbauer (eds), *The Elements: A Parasession on Linguistic Units and Levels*, Chicago, Chicago Linguistic Society, pp. 193–247.
Soh, J. (1985) 'Social Changes and Their Impact on Speech Levels in Korean', in J.D. Woods (ed.), *Language Standards and Their Codification: Process and Application*, Exeter, University of Exeter, pp. 29–41.

Sohn, H. (1986) *Linguistic Expeditions*, Seoul, Hanshin.
Walker, G. (2000) 'Performed Culture: Learning to Participate in Another Culture', in R. Lambert and E. Shohamy (eds), *Language Policy and Pedagogy: Essays in Honor of Richard Lambert*, Amsterdam, John Benjamins, pp. 221–236.
Wang, H. (1994) 'Honorific Speech Behaviour in a Rural Korean Village', PhD thesis, University of California, Los Angeles.
Watts, R., Ide, S., and Ehlich, K. (1992) *Politeness in Language: Studies in Its History, Theory and Practice*, Berlin, Mouton de Gruyter.
Wetzel, P. (2004) *Keigo in Modern Japan*, Hawai'i, University of Hawai'i Press.
Yeon, J. (1996) 'Some Problems in Teaching Korean Speech Levels', *Hangungmal kyoyuk* [*Korean Language Education*], 7, pp. 281–294.
Yeon, J. (2006), '"Standard Language" and "Cultured Language"', in H. Sohn (ed.), *Korean Language in Culture and Society*, Hawai'i, University of Hawai'i Press, pp. 31–43.
Yoo, S. (1996) 'Kwuke chengca taywu emi-uy kyochey sayong(switching)-kwa chengca taywupep cheykyey – him(power)-kwa yutay(solidarity)-uy ceng-toseng-ey uyhan tamhwa pwunsekcek cepkun' [Korean Speech Style Shifting and Speech Style Organisation: A Discourse Analysis Approach Focusing on Power and Solidarity], PhD thesis, Korea University.
Yoon, K. (2004) 'Not Just Words: Korean Social Modes and the Use of Honorifics', *Intercultural Pragmatics*, 1/2, pp. 189–210.
Yu, K. (2003) 'Characteristics of Korean Politeness: Imposition Is Not Always a Face Threatening Act', *Tamhwa-was inji* [*Discourse and Cognition*], 10/3, pp. 137–163.
Yun, S. (1993) 'Honorific Agreement', PhD thesis, University of Hawai'i.

7
Modern Chinese Politeness Revisited

Yueguo Gu

1. Introduction

The literature on Chinese politeness, as for that on other languages, is very large, and one has to find a cut-off point to start with. Since the present volume is mainly concerned with linguistic politeness, Gu's paper (1990) provides an easy solution. Additionally, a good amount of research produced during the interim period is related to his research in one way or another. This chapter therefore first makes a round-up review of the existing literature. The major problem found in Gu (1990, 1992) is his view of the Chinese language, which is over-simplistic and monolithic. Consequently, his examination of Modern Chinese politeness is similarly simplistic and monolithic (see Section 3). This chapter attempts to overcome these weaknesses by examining Chinese politeness in four major modes of discourse which correspond with the view of the Chinese language as a four-dimensional city of historicity (Sections 3 and 4). Politeness will no longer be confined to linguistic politeness but also includes non-verbal politeness. Furthermore, it will be examined not in terms of verbal usage but as lived experience. Some theoretical implications are examined in the final section.

2. Chinese politeness studies: the state of the art

2.1. Historical backdrop

In China, the politeness phenomenon is arguably as old as Peking Man (*Homo erectus*, 400,000–200,000 BP; see Fairbank 1997: 31), who was excavated in a Beijing suburb in 1929. One has no way of knowing if Peking Man had formed, in oral-aural speech, any concepts of politeness, for example, address terms differentiating status and familial relations. However, one does have some definitive evidence for making such inferences – the evidence found, for example, in Hemudu, situated in the present-day Zhejiang Province.[1] The hard written-word evidence for concepts of politeness is found in oracle bone scripts, that is, a writing system quite extensively used in the Shang Dynasty (1765–1122 BC). As pointed out in Gu (1992), the modern concept of Chinese politeness, typically encapsulated in the lexical item *limao* is derived from the ancient concept of *li*. The foundational conceptualisations of *li* are attributed to Confucius and his disciples prior to and during the Han Dynasty (including the Former and Later Hans dating from 206 BC to AD 220). Although the first occurrence of *li* and *mao* used together is found in the literature as early as Mengzi,[2] conceptualisations of *limao* separate and independent of those of *li* date from the founding of New China in 1949. This is due to the fact that *li* during the successive feudal dynasties lasting 3,000 years or so was extremely broad and comprehensive. According to Gou (2002), *li* has evolved into five components: (1) *lizhi* (礼治), a political-ideological theory about how to use *li* to govern the country; (2) *lizhi* (礼制), a social-political infrastructure for implementing *li*; (3) *liy*i (礼仪), specific rules and rituals that materialise *li*; (4) *lijiao* (礼教), referring to the practice of indoctrinating *li* to such a degree that individual rights, particularly those regarding women, were savagely denied and (5) *lixue* (礼学), studies of *li* as an academic discipline.

Gu (1990), being the revised version of Gu (1985), is the first attempt at examining *limao* as a phenomenon of linguistic politeness analysable within pragmatics. Studies of *limao* were also conducted by other Chinese scholars, though within the perspective of Chinese *xiuci xue* (修辞学, i.e. stylistics) (see e.g. Wang 1983). Recently, China has witnessed an upsurge of *guoxue chao* (国学潮), that is, enthusiastic campaigns for the study of Chinese classics, including the restoration of some traditional values that had long been lost. For example, traditional fine manners, rituals such as weddings and funerals, formal ceremonial protocols etc. are being promoted (e.g. Jin 2007, 2008; Jiang 2008; see Section 2.6 below for further discussion) and practiced (cf. the SCCSD,[3] which contains quite a few videotaped samples of traditional wedding and funeral ceremonies). This classic upsurge obviously covers areas that go beyond *limao* in pragmatics or stylistics and has extended into the classic territory of *liyi* mentioned above.

So much for the historical backdrop. Let us turn to Chinese linguistic politeness proper.

2.2. Limao: linguistic politeness in pragmatics

The relevant literature can be divided into the following categories: (1) the Leech–Gu line, that is, studies carried out under the influence of Leech (1983) and/or Gu (1990, 1992); (2) the Brown–Levinson line, that is, studies that adopt Brown and Levinson's framework, and apply it to Chinese data analysis; (3) the blended line, that is, studies that incorporate selectively Brown–Levinson, Leech and Gu and (4) the indigenous line, that is, studies that attempt to use native home-grown concepts and frameworks.

Note that the four 'lines' are intended primarily to serve as threads in the tracking of patterns of research development and at the same time as an organisational structure for the review of the works below. Therefore they are not to be regarded as devices to rule out the original contributions the individual works make to the field.

2.3. The Leech–Gu line

Six studies are to be reviewed in this subsection, and are arranged according to the year in which they were first published. Shu and Wang Hong (1993/2001) adopt Leech's six maxims of politeness, the approbation maxim and modesty maxim in particular, as a reference framework against which they examine the speech acts of upgrading self/other and downgrading self/other in Chinese. Self-upgrading violates Leech's maxim of modesty, hence being impolite. Downgrading other violates Leech's maxim of approbation, hence being impolite too. Other-upgrading and self-downgrading, on the other hand, will be polite, since they abide by the approbation and modesty maxims, respectively. Since these studies seem to be unaware of Gu (1990, 1992), their treatment of upgrading self/other and downgrading self/other is not related to Gu's maxim of self-denigration and other-elevation. On the surface, both seem to cover more or less the same phenomenon. There is, however, a difference between them: Gu's maxim of self-denigration and other-elevation is derived from the ancient Chinese concept found in *li Ji* (礼记), thus it has indigenous origins, as it were. Shu and Wang's study, in contrast, takes Leech's maxims of politeness for granted, regarding them as being fully applicable to the Chinese context.

Rong Chen (1996) examines instances of food-plying events which he collected in Xi'an, North China. Food-plying, being a straight act of imposing in Brown and Levinson's theoretical framework, is regarded as showing warmth and care, which is one of the four fundamental values underpinning Chinese politeness (Gu 1990). Chen argues that Gu's concept of 'attitudinal warmth' cannot be reconciled with Brown and Levinson's 'imposition' – the avoidance of which is fundamental to their conceptualisation of negative politeness. Chen therefore takes issue with Brown and Levinson about their claim of universality.

Li and Li (1996) examine the concept of Chinese self associated with Gu's maxim of self-denigration and other-elevation. Li and Li share with anthropologists and sociologists the view that the family is "the primary and central social organisation in Chinese culture". "Remarkably, and this is where the Chinese concept of a family differs sharply from that in the Anglo-Saxon culture, the family includes not only everyone who is related by descent or marriage, but also those quasi-relations who are sufficiently close to be regarded as 'one of the family' " (Li and Li 1996: 132–133). The Chinese conception of 'self' thus "includes both the ego and his/her intimate relations whom he/she regards as 'the family' or 'us' " (Li and Li 1996: 133). Li and Li have shown that the frequent uses of self-denigration are a politeness strategy, including the use of pejorative references to one's spouse, children and other intimate relations.

Zhu (1998) put to test Gu's two maxims (the 'self-denigration maxim', and the 'address maxim') by examining 261 written letters, 86 of which are between family members, and the remaining between friends, students and teachers, colleagues and even between lovers. The parameters being analysed include addressing on the envelope, salutation, complimentary close and signature. It was found that in the family letters, self- and other-referring do not abide by the self-denigration and other-elevation maxim. Neutral and kinship terms are used instead. In the non-family letters the conformity with the two maxims is very high. It is interesting to note too that in the five letters between students and teachers there was no self-denigration but other-elevation only and that in the 31 letters between prospective lovers only neutral terms were found. Zhu's study clearly shows that the operation of the self-denigration maxim and address maxim is governed by the participants' care for deference, solidarity and interpersonal power hierarchy even in non-face-to-face situations.

Kádár (2007) is a monograph focusing on Chinese terms of address which draws data from traditional Chinese written texts. This work is reviewed in the Leech–Gu line because it is closely related to Gu's address maxim. Leech's theory of politeness does not contain the use of address terms as politeness usage. Gu (1990) argues that it is, however, an important part of the Chinese politeness system, and what makes it all the more so is the fact that it is crucially associated with the self-denigration maxim. As far as Chinese address terms are concerned, Kádár's contribution is twofold. First, he is the first to examine Chinese traditional address terms against the international context of politeness research. He has laid a framework in which one can look at the Chinese data from the inside as well as from the outside. Second, he has shown, quite convincingly to me, that "in the traditional setting, as opposed to the modern one, there is no 'neutrally' polite addressing". It is so because "*traditional Chinese polite terms of address compulsorily express denigrating/elevating meaning* or, vice versa, in polite register only elevating/denigrating address terms...are applied" (Kádár 2007: 23; italics original).

Gu (1990, 1992) maintains, at least conceptually, a sharp distinction between the act itself and the verbal means in which the performance of the act is materialised. The act of denigrating or elevating or addressing is thus conceptually distinct from the verbal means that are used to perform it. Research can focus on the act itself or on the verbal means or the interactive relation between the two. Therefore, the paradox that Kádár has found in Gu's study (see Kádár 2007: 23) is illusory and will dissolve when the switch from one focus to another is kept in mind.

2.4. The Brown–Levinson line

Li (1996/2005) is the only paper I managed to find that fits this category but I am sure there must be some more which I am unaware of. Li accepts Brown and Levinson's claim of universality. He holds, without offering his arguments for it, that their framework applies equally well to both spoken and written discourse. He attests this by examining the politeness strategies in book review articles found in English and Chinese academic journals. The analysis reads like a demonstrative exercise: Brown and Levinson's list of on-record and off-record politeness strategies is selectively matched with textual data.

2.5. The blended line

Liao (1994) is a monograph-length study of strategies, maxims and development of refusal in Mandarin Chinese. She draws her data from Mandarin Chinese used in Taiwan, which is extremely valuable in providing a complementary database for the field. "The theoretical framework of the study", she writes, "is Grice's cooperative principles (CP), Leech's six maxims of absolute interpersonal maxims (1983) and Brown and Levinson's (1978/1987) four super-strategies for doing FTAs, and Gu's (1990) seven maxims of Chinese politeness" (Liao 1994: 7).

The strength of Liao's study lies in her assembly of 22 strategies of refusal found in Taiwan Mandarin usage. It is also valuable that she looks at elementary school children's language development in the use of refusal strategies. Though the data of refusal are quite solid, the analytic framework is questionable. However, her observations on face are worth quoting: "We would like to emphasize that face is one's dignity in front of another person or another's opinion of us. This 'another person' includes one's husband or one's wife; for example, a Chinese husband may feel loss of face because his salary is lower than the wife's. He may also feel loss of face because his educational background is not so high as his wife's" (1994: 12).

I quite share Liao's intuition about the Chinese husband's fear of loss of face in front of his wife for earning less or receiving less education, but she has failed to show how this notion of face is to be reconciled with Brown and Levinson's face just discussed in the paragraph immediately above or with Goffman's notion of face summarised two paragraphs above.

Pan (2000) is also a monograph-length study, but on Chinese politeness in three social situations: business encounters, official meetings and family gatherings. What makes her study distinctive are the two thorny issues she attempts to tackle. The first issue concerns sweeping and impressionistic generalisations people in crosscultural encounters tend to make about how polite or how rude the Chinese can be. One person's evaluative remark can run in total contradiction to another's. The second issue, being closely related to the first, is more theoretical. It is a question about "what should be included in our study of politeness behavior" (Pan 2000: 4). Although the term 'Chinese politeness behaviour' occurs in 15 different places in Pan's work, none of them provides a working definition of it. However, she does explicitly address what politeness is: "Politeness is part of our world knowledge about how to behave appropriately in a given situation and how to maintain smooth interactions and good social relationships with other people." She observes further: "In face-to-face interaction, linguistic politeness, that is, the use of language to attend to each other's face needs, helps to mitigate utterances that may otherwise impose a threat to other people's face" (Pan 2000: 5). This is basically a restatement of Brown and Levinson's conception of linguistic politeness via face-threatening acts. It is worth pointing out that Brown and Levinson's notion of positive face is imported to Pan's study without revision.[4] As for their negative face, while reviewing the Chinese concept of self, Pan reaches a conclusion similar to Gu's (1990, 1992): "the desire to be independent and unimpeded in one's actions (negative face) is almost alien to Chinese" (Pan 2000: 102).

In a sense, Pan's approach to the study of politeness can be characterised as situation-based, which is undoubtedly a very viable alternative to Gu's framework as far as Chinese politeness is concerned. Gu's framework, under the influence of Grice and Leech, is primarily pragmatics-based; that is, its main concern is to look for general principles and maxims that underpin the usage of language. It can achieve a high-level generalisation at the expense of simplifying the complexity of real happenings in a situation or discourse. Pan's framework, in contrast, lays bare the complexity of real happenings in situation or discourse but loses the ability of reaching high-level generalisations so as to weave a coherent picture (although this may not necessarily be Pan's aim). This weakness becomes apparent when she deals with the concept of face and its connection with politeness. Gu (1990, 1992, 2008) insists that in Chinese culture face and politeness belong to different orders of conceptualisation. Similarly, in the realm of discourse practice, there can be intense face concerns without invoking politeness and there can be politeness concerns without involving face. Pan herself provides an instance of this. The encounter in the state-run store between a female customer and the sales assistant is regarded as an outsider interaction. "Thus no facework is called for" (Pan 2000: 13). Since there is no facework involved, there should be, by Pan's adopted view of politeness quoted above, no politeness required either. But this runs counter to the social practice in China. *Limao dai guke* (礼貌待顾客) is a public politeness norm pursued in all stores, state-run or private-run alike. In fact, many stores nail permanent posters on the entrance walls clearly publicising this politeness norm.

2.6. Indigenous line

The past decade or so in China has witnessed a boom of publications on Chinese *liyi* (礼仪, i.e. etiquette, rituals), for example, Wang et al. (1992), Huang (1995), Zhong (2001), Duan (2007), Jin (2007, 2008) and Jiang (2008).

Wang et al. (1992) and Zhong (2001) aim at providing a comprehensive coverage of *liyi* dating from the Pre-Qin times to the present-day New China. The former is written in a dictionary format. It is actually a mini-encyclopaedia of Chinese *liyi*, divided into over 80 categories with 4,000 or so entries. The latter, on the other hand, is not an academic monograph proper but a source book for information on all sorts of etiquette and rituals. The significance of these two works, apart from their comprehensiveness, lies in the fact they have made a great many classic ideas and practices easily accessible to the contemporary reader.

The remaining four references cited above all deal with *liyi* of Modern China. Huang (1995) is written as a textbook for business school programmes. The works by Duan, Jin and Jiang deal with *liyi* in banquets, offices and business transactions, respectively. A theoretical exploration of *liyi* is only briefly dealt with in the first part of Huang's work, while the rest of the book is practice-oriented.

Gou (2002) is a long monograph focusing on *li* from Pre-Qin times. It provides a scholarly treatment of the origins, practices, essential concepts and major conceptualisations of *li* found in Pre-Qin classics. It is monumental for its scope and in-depth analysis. Although it is a historical study, it is still highly relevant to contemporary studies of modern politeness as the foundations of Chinese *li* were laid during Pre-Qin times.

Looking from either the global or home context, the *liyi* studies reviewed above have made no fresh contributions to politeness theory-building. Having said this, they should not be undervalued. They are part of the *guoxue* campaigns mentioned in Section 2.1 above. The resurrection of some traditional values, customs and politeness practices in itself is significant in the Chinese context. As is commonly known, the so-called Great Cultural Revolution (1966–1976) virtually cut off contemporary China from its long-standing cultural heritage. With the post-Mao open-door policy and the influx of globalisation, China is getting increasingly anxious that it might become disconnected from its history and eventually lose its identity. The indigenous line of pursuit may act as a counterbalance to the forces of globalisation.

The review so far has been selective due to lack of space. The three research lines discussed in Section 2 (i.e. the Leech–Gu, Brown and Levinson and blended lines) all share the following three features:

(1) The Chinese language is treated as a self-contained abstract symbolic system;
(2) The Gricean theories of intentional communication, and of pragmatics in particular, are taken as the default theoretical framework;
(3) Linguistic politeness, by way of avowed research interest, is separated from non-verbal politeness and is examined in terms of language usage.

The first feature is derived from Saussurean linguistics, while the last inherits the legacy of Leech and of Brown and Levinson. The limitations of Saussurean linguistics have long been pointed out (see e.g. Stewart 1995, 1996). Watts (2003: 204) holds that the basic tenets of Gricean pragmatics, given the present state of our knowledge of the processes of social interaction and communication, become highly questionable. He calls for a 'postmodernist approach' to politeness studies (Watts 2005: xiii). As for the separation of linguistic politeness from non-linguistic politeness, it is obviously justifiable only on methodological grounds. In real-life, verbal and non-verbal politeness are intertwined and even mutually defining; that is, the non-verbal behaviour can override the polite import of verbal behaviour and vice versa. In what follows we explore a fresh way of looking at politeness, hoping to provide a more adequate account of Chinese politeness.

3. Politeness as lived experience

3.1. A 'postmodernist approach'

Watts' postmodernist approach mentioned above shares Scannell's critique of modern views of language. In this connection Scannell is worth quoting in full here.

> Modern views of language encourage a view of an external reality that is outside the subject and outside language, because language is thought in ways that remove it from the world. The effect is to establish language as an object of knowledge only by uncoupling it from praxis and being. (Scannell 1998: 262)

The 'uncoupling' is achieved through theoretical abstractions, such as the Saussurean *langue* abstracted from *parole*, language as an 'abstract symbolic system', 'signification' and so on. Scannell argues that:

> we must surely admit that we are closer to language than this. Human being is being-in-language, which is another way of saying that language *worlds*. The world in which we dwell includes language. Our world *languages*. It speaks us and we speak it. This is its nearness to us. It is what we live in. (Scannell 1998: 263; italics original)

The postmodernist approach, instead of looking at politeness as a 'static logical concept', that is, 'an object of knowledge', defines it as a 'dynamic, interpersonal activity', that is, sees it as rooted in praxis and being (Watts 2005: xviii).

The author of this chapter is quite sympathetic with Scannell's critique of the modern view of language, and his 'phenomenological' (Scannell 1998: 251) approach to language. Gu (2002, 2009a) has outlined an ecological approach to language, which happens[5] to share Scannell's view that language is what we live in. In the remaining part of this chapter I would like to sketch an outline for researching politeness in a post-Saussurean or post-Gricean way, playing perhaps a complementary role to Watts' postmodernist approach.

3.2. The language city: four-borne discourses

Gu (2009a: 99) argues for language to be understood as an experiential phenomenon coexistent with a society/culture. It is likened to a city, such as depicted by Wittgenstein (1958/1997: 8[e]):

> Our language can be seen as an ancient city: a maze of little streets and squares, of old and new houses, and of houses with additions from various periods; and this surrounded by a multitude of new boroughs with straight regular streets and uniform houses.

In regard to Chinese, the Chinese language city arguably started being built as early as Peking Man (see Section 2.1 above). From Peking Man to the Shang Dynasty there was only oral-aural discourse (i.e. 'land-borne situated discourse', LBSD) or what calls 'primary orality'. The use of Chinese characters gave birth to written-word-borne discourse (WWBD), an extra-dimension, as it were, on the language cityscape. The use of telecommunications technology first in telephony, then radio and TV broadcasting dispatch oral messages, thus creating what Ong calls 'secondary orality', or air-borne situated discourse (ABSD). The ABSD in China is less than a hundred years old and constitutes a third dimension on the Chinese language cityscape. Finally the web-borne situated discourse (WBSD) in China is only a very recent phenomenon, and becomes a fourth dimension of the existing language cityscape.

The LBSD involves what Goffman calls 'bodily activity' on the speaker/performer's side, and 'naked senses' on the addressee/receiver's side. "A frown, a spoken word, or a kick is a message that a sender conveys by means of his own *current* bodily activity, the transmission occurring only during the time that his body is present to sustain this activity" (Goffman 1963: 14; italics original). The speaker's 'current bodily activity' makes 'embodied messages' (Goffman's terminology):

> When one speaks of experiencing someone else with one's naked senses, one usually implies the reception of embodied messages. This linkage of naked senses on one side and embodied transmission on the other provides one of the crucial communication conditions of face-to-face interaction. (Goffman 1963: 15).

As emphasised by Goffman, ordinarily in using the naked senses to receive embodied messages from others, one also makes oneself available as a source of embodied messages for others. In other words, in face-to-face co-present interaction one is both a giver and receiver of embodied messages via natural multimodality. The term 'total saturated experience' (TSE) has been proposed to refer to Goffman's face-to-face interaction through naked senses and embodied messages. The term 'total saturated signification' (TSS) is used to talk about the total meanings constructed out of the total saturated experience by the acting co-present individuals (for detailed discussion of TSE and TSS, see Gu 2009b).

It is the natural multimodality and total saturated experience in the LBSD that are being mediated and transformed in the WWBD, ABSD and WBSD. This is one of the crucial aspects in which the present study differs from the existing literature on mediated discourse. The four-borne discourses vary in experiential qualities. Their differences can be illustrated through the consumption of a Peking roast duck. In the LBSD the Peking duck gets tasted by actually eating it – it is a 'taste-by-tongue experience'. In the WWBD, the Peking duck is reduced to a piece of orthographic text, which is 'tasted' by reading comprehension – it is a 'taste-by-comprehension experience'. In the ABSD and the WBSD, where still and moving images, photos, sounds and animations about the duck are made available, the Peking duck is 'tasted' by visual/aural processing – it is a 'taste-by-eye/ear experience' (see Section 3.3 below for further discussion).

The contribution of the four-borne discourse perspective to the study of the Chinese language is at least threefold:

(1) The discourses represent an enriched understanding of the modes of existence of the Chinese language;
(2) They reinforce one another by recycling some of the resources available within the system;
(3) The four-borne discourses can be transformed from LBSD to WWBD, and/or to ABSD and/or to WBSD, and vice versa. Broadcasting live LBSD is an instance of transforming LBSD into ABSD and WBSD. To turn a WWBD into a TV series is an instance of transforming the WWBD into ABSD.

It is essential to note that the distinction between the four-borne discourses is not, in essence, a distinction about discourse mediation or about the effects mass media exert on discourse. The notion of discourse mediation is only one parameter, a minor one among other more important ones, which are: (1) situatedness of discourse, (2) human spatial-temporal movement, (3) social space-time, (4) multimodality, (5) sedimentation of discourse processes and (6) accessibility and availability (for a detailed discussion of these parameters see Gu 2009a).

3.3. Politeness phenomenon in the four-borne discourse-constructed language city

We take politeness as being relational in essence; that is, it only makes sense in the self-versus-other context. The case of being polite or rude to oneself without an audience is a sheer play of polite or rude words, a form of self-amusement, as it were. The self being im/polite to other presupposes, between self and other, (1) spatial-temporal engagement and (2) personal involvement. In the four-borne discourse-constructed language city, politeness phenomena allow for four-dimensional modes of experiential existence and invoke four distinctive forms of spatial-temporal engagement and personal involvement.

In the LBSD the engagement is immediate, co-present and here-and-now. Politeness, if experienced, is a taste-by-tongue type: it is embodied (in the sense as discussed in Section 3.2 above), personalised and identified. The experience of politeness hence will be saturated and potentially intense, which can be borne out inversely by the negative experience of incoming impoliteness. That it is 'personalised' means that im/politeness in the LBSD is being experienced not as something impersonal or neutral or abstract, but as something from a particular person with a specific role identity.

The LBSD's immediate, co-present here-and-now engagement with embodiment, personalisation and specified identity serving as a reference dimension allows for the four-borne discourses to thus be contrasted as shown in Table 1.

Table 1 aims to evaluate politeness as it is experienced by the interactants. It is assumed that im/politeness in LBSD is a totally saturated experience; that is, a taste-by-tongue type. In the remaining modes the experience is assumed to be less saturated to variable degrees than in LBSD. In the net-conferencing of WBSD the experience of im/politeness is assumed to be less saturated than that in LBSD but more saturated than that in the remaining others; that is, it is a taste-by-eye type. The im/politeness in WWBD is being experienced by reading a text; that is, a taste-by-comprehension type experience.

The three types of politeness experience can be illustrated by the activity of entertaining guests with a banquet, which is one of the commonest

Table 1 Spatial-temporal engagement and personal involvement compared

Mode	sub-category	Spatial-temporal engagement			Personal involvement		
		immediacy	co-presence	here-and-now	embodied	personalized	identity specified
LBSD		yes	yes	yes	yes	yes	yes
ABSD	studio	yes	yes	yes	yes	yes	yes
	air-borne	false immediacy	no	no, except for live broadcast	one-way	one-way	one-way
WBSD	text-based	no	no	no	no	mainly anonymous	mainly generic
	voice chat	false immediacy	no	here= displaced, now=yes	voice modality only	yes	yes
	net-conferencing	false immediacy	no	here= displaced, now=yes	voice and visual modalities	yes	yes
	email/blog	no	no	no	no	yes	yes
WWBD	personal writing	no	no	no	no	yes	yes
	non-personal writing	no in general, false immediacy via literary creativity	no	no	no	no	mainly generic

and also most important ways of showing politeness in Chinese society. In the SCCSD there is an instance of a UK delegation attending a banquet held by a Chinese hostess. The restaurant is the Beijing Roast Duck Restaurant in Qianmen (Beijing). The choice of this restaurant, of the majestic-looking room (in fact it used to be the room reserved for the emperor's visit), the ways the guests are addressed, the seating arrangements (who sits where next to whom), the priority of who should be served first, and who next and the guests' table manners – all these non-verbal matters form an intrinsic part of the totally saturated experience, contributing to a totally saturated signification of politeness. They define the nature of a social occasion that circumscribes what verbal speech will be appropriate or out of place. So in LBSD, the linguistic politeness is an abstraction from the real-life totally saturated experience of politeness.

Now imagine that the banquet is 'attended' by way of net-conferencing or by reading a text. The experience of politeness would never be the same as the real-life one, even if the hostess makes more efforts in being polite to the guests. The three modes of experiencing politeness are contrasted graphically in Figure 1.

Figure 1 Three modes of experiencing politeness

In ABSD, as shown in Table 1, the interactants in the studio share the same type of experience as those in LBSD. In the air-borne mode, however, the air-borne projected persons (i.e. without physical bodies) and the audience, being physically separate and non-face-to-face, will make an anonymous, impersonalised indirect engagement in cases of radio and television. Politeness becomes one-sided. That is, the air-borne projected persons have to abide by politeness norms and values as those found in LBSD but the anonymous audience can become very rude to the persons being heard or watched. The social sanctions, if taking place, would come from the fellow audience sharing the same spatial-temporal setting.

In WBSD, on the other hand, the body and the person, in the state-of-the-art technology, are not counted as constituting a unique identity to be admitted into the networks. IP address and a password are used instead of the body-person. The separation of the real body and its social person from the web-identity recognition is total, although in net-conferencing, video chat etc., there is a projected person similar to that in ABSD. So in WBSD the engagement between interactants varies from being similar to that in LBSD (i.e. using net-conferencing technology, video chat) to that of total anonymity without any personal involvement (e.g. when using public access to the Internet, as found in an airport). Politeness varies correspondingly with the degrees of engagement and personal involvement.

Finally, regarding WWBD, this chapter, as argued above, holds that the face-to-face co-present verbal speech of im/politeness differs from written-text representation of it in experiential type: the former is a TSE, whereas the latter is not. The implication is that, given the same polite or rude message, the LBSD presentation will be more pleasing or harsh to the ear than the WWBD is to the mind.

3.4. Politeness and the regionalisation of activities

LBSD is patterned by human action on space and time. Natural habitats, villages, towns and modern cities form boundaries which can also be the spatial boundaries for LBSDs. A concept about politeness in one natural village (i.e. a village naturally formed by the physical landscape such as by a river, a valley and so on) can be quite different from that formed in the neighbouring village just across the valley. It can be literally true that a very polite remark in one village is interpreted as being very rude in another! (Note that what makes a remark polite or rude is decided by the underlying concept of politeness.) In my recent field work in Yunnan, Mr Yang, a Tibetan acting as my guide as well as my informant, demonstrated to us, while we were having stewed chicken, that in his hometown the chicken head is reserved for the most important guest. It must be first served to the God of Fire by displaying it at its Altar before it is served to the most important guest. There is nothing short of a ritual for the guest to eat the chicken head. Figure 2 is a series of screen shots from SCCSD showing the ritualistic stages of eating a chicken head in Tibetan culture.

This detailed sequence showing a VIP eating a chicken head demonstrates that the acceptance of a polite offer of food is not simply a matter of eating it. The guest needs to respond in a very respectful way. In a Han village, on the other hand, it is extremely impolite, if not insulting, to ask the most important guest to eat a chicken head!

3.5. Forces of diversity versus uniformity and the Internet challenge

The activity zones, villages, habitats, towns and cities as behaviour settings of LBSD are preserving forces that maintain the diversity of im/politeness concepts. Spatial mobility of migrant workers, however, undermines the diversity preservation. ABSD and the WWBD, on the

Figure 2 Ritualistic stages of eating a chicken head in Tibetan culture

other hand, are forces that promote uniformity and standardisation of politeness concepts. Furthermore, since education from ancient times to the present day has mainly relied on WWBD as means of content delivery, WWBD helps to iron out the diversities that are naturally formed within LBSD, as well as to impose the elite views of politeness, since WWBD authors represent an important section of the elite class. In fact, Gu's studies (1990, 1992) are mainly WWBD-based and the bias towards elite views of politeness is quite obvious.

WBSD presents a challenge to the status quo in two ways. First, as shown in Table 1, the text-based WBSD is mostly anonymous. Moreover, anybody who has access to the Internet is a potential information provider for the general public, the empowerment of which is absent from LBSD, ABSD and WWBD. So in the text-based WBSD the existing social hierarchy between the interactants fails to function: everyone is made equal with only a publicly available IP identity! Second, the equality resulting from anonymity undermines the pressure to exhibit deference derived from social hierarchy. Below is a BBS text writing about a celebrity's second marriage. Original names have been replaced by [...]:

Sender: Non (Donkey), mailbox: Boy Title: Re: [the name of celebrity deleted here]又结婚了(married again) Date: Sun Apr 14 11:49:28 1996

...

> > > 结不好瞎结呗.....:) (bad marriage last time, blind marriage this time) > > 和谁, 是 [another real name deleted here]吗? (married whom, is it [real name])?

> <<文汇报>>上登了两人的照片,介绍了那人,其是美国中产阶层一分子

> 长得不敢让人恭维,年龄大 [the celebrity name deleted here] 两岁,可看上去跟 [referring to the celebrity by her nursery name] 爹似的,大该属于 "心灵美"(兜里更美)那类. (The couple's photo was shown in the newspaper. That man was introduced. He is a middle class man in the USA. I can hardly make any comments on his looks. Though he is only two years older, he appears to be like her [her nursery name was actually used] grandpa. Probably it is a business of both beautiful heart plus beautiful purse.)

> 报上还说婚礼很"简单","只有几十位名人参加",比如 [real name deleted here]. (According to the newspaper the wedding ceremony was very simple. Only a dozen celebrities attended it, such as [real name deleted])

> 兄弟们,向美国冲啊!向美元冲啊!!冲啊..啊..啊. ... 啊..啊 (Brothers, let's march to America! March to US dollars! March! Ah ah ah ah)

> 然后就可静候祖国的亲人儿们向你扑来啦 ... (Then just wait for compatriots' relatives to embrace you.)

As it stands, the writer has not violated any existing laws. But has he or she violated the 'principle of politeness'? We would probably say 'yes'. This triggers a follow-up issue: if this is so, what about the same remarks being delivered in a private conversation behind the celebrity's back? Will they still be very rude? Think about this case. On 15 Sept 2009, my son made some rude remarks about his teacher over the dinner table. Both his mother and I found it inappropriate for him to say so. He was immediately told off by his mother. He wept and locked himself up in his own room. Compare this scenario with Jesse Jackson's microphone being live and catching him commenting that *Obama 'talks down to black people'*. Jackson had to make a public apology afterwards. But suppose that the microphone had been switched off. What would happen to him then? So should the experience of im/politeness be confined to the public domain? Is there a private experience of im/politeness? Where is the boundary of freedom of speech to be drawn? The exploration of these issues is no longer a pastime for academics and the legislators need to be informed on how to regulate Internet behaviour and im/polite behaviour in particular!

3.6. Spatial management and Chinese politeness

Spatial experience is no trivial matter in Chinese politeness. This can be demonstrated by the spatial management in the Centennial Anniversary Ceremony of Shanxi University, which Figure 3 illustrates.

The screen shot on the right top corner captures the overall scene of the ceremony locale, which is the University's converted football pitch. The ceremony was attended by more than two thousand people. One could well imagine the formidable task of spatial management for such a gathering. The graphical part of Figure 3 shows the spatial structure of the seating arrangement. The choice between onstage and offstage indexes the distinguished VIPs and the VIPs or plain alumni, respectively. The configuration of onstage, front row and the central seat index the most distinguished of all the VIPs. The politeness principle of spatial management in Chinese culture in case of the social situation of an institutional ceremony can be summarised as follows: the degree of prominence peaks at the front centre and decreases sidewise and row-wise.

4. Politeness as lived experience: theoretical implications and future research

Up to now we have outlined an ecological approach to the study of politeness in Chinese. The basic idea is that the Chinese language is

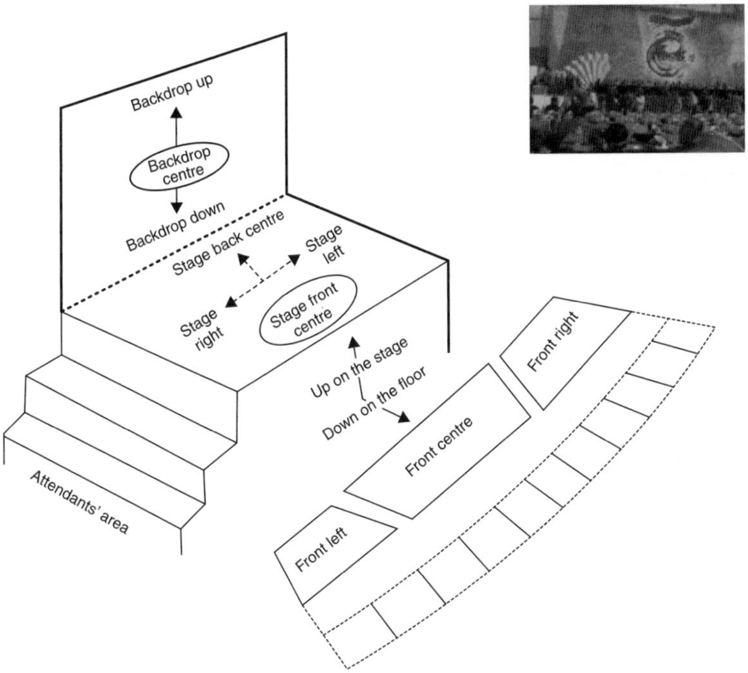

Figure 3 Spatial management in the Centennial Anniversary Ceremony of Shanxi University

like a multidimensional city currently comprising four modes of discourse, each of which constitutes its own domain and type of experience of politeness. Politeness phenomena and concepts of politeness can be found within each mode, but based on the differences between the four modes of discourse (recall the six analytic parameters listed in Section 3.2 above) they will differ and vary accordingly. Bearing in mind the multidimensional experiences of politeness, the assumption of universal politeness, even within a nation-state such as China, is difficult to maintain unless one aims at an extremely high level of abstraction. Note that it is not suggested here that high-level abstractions of politeness are useless. On the contrary, they can serve some theoretical as well as practical purposes. Leech's politeness and its maxims as part of general pragmatics regarded as high-level abstractions are still useful in providing an initial framework; a springboard for comparative or contrastive studies of politeness across different cultures. What is indeed suggested here is that one needs to make it clear from the outset that at what level of abstraction and at which dimension of discourse the research is being conducted.

As we know, the Gricean rationality of inference-making underpins both Brown and Levinson's and Leech's studies of politeness in linguistic communication. The speaker's formulation and hearer's interpretation of polite or impolite messages involve a highly rationalised process. In Brown and Levinson's case, for example, the 'model person' weighs various parameters (e.g. power, distance etc.) before reaching a rational choice of face-threatening strategy. Correspondingly, the hearer goes through varied, sometimes very elaborate steps in inference-making in order to interpret the message. In view of the proposal in this chapter to look at im/politeness as lived experience, the Gricean (1975) framework has left out one very important element of im/politeness, viz. affectivity. In other words, polite or impolite experience is emotionally charged. The current Gricean framework fails to accommodate the emotional side of im/politeness. The three types of im/politeness experience distinguished in Section 3 above and the notion of totally saturated experience have taken the emotional side of im/politeness as an intrinsic ingredient in theory-building. Im/politeness experience always has an emotional element which can simply be felt as 'that', and this 'that-experience' can resist verbal articulation or even go beyond it. A lot of research is needed to explore and develop this new direction (see Gu 2010 for a preliminary treatment).

Notes

1. It dates from 8000 BC to 7000 BC. It was already a well-organised society growing rice for its stable food. See《河姆渡》(Hemudu), DVD publication by Beijing Voice and Video for Science.
2. See Gaozi, Part II, Chapter 14, Mencius: 礼貌未衰, 言弗行也 (… polite demeanour of the prince remains the same…)
3. SCCSD stands for 'spoken Chinese corpus of situated discourse'. Visit www.multimodal.cn for details.
4. There are 21 real occurrences, plus one found in the index.
5. Only by the time the author had written this chapter did he come to know Scannell's work, hence the wording 'happens to share'.

References

Brown, P., and Levinson, S.C. (1978) 'Universals of Language Usage: Politeness Phenomena', in E. Goody (ed.), *Questions and Politeness*, Cambridge, Cambridge University Press, pp. 56–289.

Chen, R. (1996) 'Food-Plying and Chinese Politeness', *Journal of Asian Pacific Communication*, 7/3–4, pp. 143–155.
Duan, J. (段洁) (2007) *Canzhuo liyi yu koucai* 餐桌礼仪与口才 [*Dining Table Etiquette and Eloquence*], Beijing, Zhongguo jingqi chubanshe.
Fairbank, J.K. (1997) *China: A New History*, London, The Belknap Press of Harvard University Press.
Goffman, E. (1963) *Behavior in Public Places*, New York, Free Press.
Gou, C.y. (勾承益) (2002) *Xian-qin lixue* 先秦礼学 [*Li (Rite) Philosophies before the Qin Dynasty*], Chengdu, Ba-Shu shushe.
Grice, H.P. (1975) 'Logic and Conversation', in P. Cole and J.L. Morgan (eds), *Speech Acts, Syntax and Semantics, Vol. III: Speech Acts*, New York, Academic Press, pp. 41–58.
Gu, Y. (1985) 'Politeness Phenomena in Modern Chinese', M.A. dissertation, Lancaster University, UK.
Gu, Y. (1990) 'Politeness Phenomena in Modern Chinese', *Journal of Pragmatics*, 14/2, pp. 237–257.
Gu, Y.g (顾曰国) (1992) 'Limao, yuyong yu wenhua' 礼貌、语用与文化 [Politeness, Pragmatics and Culture], *Journal of Foreign Language Teaching and Research*, 4, pp. 10–17.
Gu, Y. (2002) 'Towards an Understanding of Workplace Discourse: A Pilot Study for Compiling a Spoken Chinese Corpus of Situated Discourse', in C. Candlin (ed.), *Research and Practice in Professional Discourse*, City University of Hong Kong Press, pp. 137–186.
Gu, Y. (2008) 'Collective Face, Public Image and Politeness', plenary speech at the 1st International Conference on Partnership in Action: Practice, Theory and Training, Hong Kong Polytechnic University and the City University of Hong Kong.
Gu, Y. (2009a) 'Four-Borne Discourses: Towards Language as an Ancient City of History', in L. Wei and V. Cook (eds), *Contemporary Applied Linguistics, Vol. 2: Language for the Real World*, London, Continuum, pp. 98–121.
Gu, Y. (2009b) 'From Real-Life Situated Discourse to Video Stream Data-Mining', *International Journal of Corpus Linguistics*, 14/4, pp. 433–466.
Gu, Y. (2010) '(Im)politeness as Lived Experience', invited paper submitted to the Pragmatics Conference, Lodz, Poland, 7–8 May.
Huang, S.p. (黄世平) (ed.) (1995) *Xiandai liyi xue* 现代礼仪学 [*Contemporary Etiquette Studies*], Wuhan, Cehui keji daxue chubanshe.
Jiang, T. (江涛) (2008) *Shagwu liyi* 商务礼仪 [*Commercial Etiquette*], Beijing, Huawen chubanshe.
Jin, Z.k. (金正昆) (2007) *Gong guan liyi* 公关礼仪 [*Etiquette in Public Relations*], Xi'an, Shaanxi shifan daxue chubanshe.
Jin, Z.k. (金正昆) (2008) *Zhichang liyi* 职场礼仪 [*Workplace Etiquette*], Beijing, Zhongguo renmin daxue chubanshe.
Kádár, D.Z. (2007) *Terms of (Im)politeness: A Study of the Communicational Properties of Traditional Chinese (Im)polite Terms of Address*, Budapest, Eötvös Loránd University Press.
Leech, G.N. (1983) *Principles of Pragmatics*, London, Longman.
Li, J.w. (李经伟) (2005 [1996]) 'Ying Han shuping zhong de limao celüe bijiao' 英汉书评中的礼貌策略比较 [A Comparative Analysis on the Politeness Strategies Used in English and Chinese Book Reviews], in C.s. Yan严辰松 and H. Gao高航

(eds), *Yuyongxue* 语用学 [*Pragmatics*], Shanghai, Shanghai waiyi jiaoyu chubanshe, pp. 392–404.

Li, W., and Li, Y. (1996) '"My Stupid Wife and Ugly Daughter": The Use of Pejorative References as a Politeness Strategy by Chinese Speakers', *Journal of Asian Pacific Communication*, 7/3–4, pp. 129–142.

Liao, C.-c. (1994) *A Study on the Strategies, Maxims, and Development of Refusal in Mandarin Chinese*, Taipei: Crane.

Pan, Y. (2000) *Politeness in Chinese Face-to-Face Interaction*, Stamford, Ablex.

Scannell, P. (1998) 'Media – Language – World', in A. Bell and P. Garrett (eds), *Approaches to Media Discourse*, Oxford, Blackwell Publishers, pp. 251–268.

Shu, D.f. 束定芳, and Wang Hong 王虹 (2001 [1993]) 'Yuyan jiaoji zhong de yang-sheng-yi-jiang yu limao yuanze' 言语交际中的扬升抑降与礼貌原则 [Complimenting and Self-Humbling Acts in Interpersonal Rhetoric and the Politeness Principle], in D. F. Shu束定芳 (ed.), *Zhongguo yuyongxue yanjiu lunwen jingxuan* 中国语用学研究论文精选 [*Selected Research Essays on Chinese Pragmatics*], Shanghai, Shanghai waiyu jiaoyu chubanshe, pp. 525–538.

Stewart, J. (1995) *Language as Articulate Contact: Toward a Post-Semiotic Philosophy of Communication*, Albany, State University of New York Press.

Stewart, J. (ed.) (1996) *Beyond the Symbol Model: Reflections on the Representational Nature of Language*, Albany, State University of New York Press.

Wang, J.h. 王景海, Chen, L.z. 陈劳志, Xing, S.J. 邢世杰, and Yang, D.H. 杨德宏 (eds) (1992) *Zhonghua liyi quanshu* 中华礼仪全书 [*An Anthology of Chinese Etiquette*], Changchun, Changchun chubanshe.

Wang, X.j. 王希杰 (1983) *Yuyan de mei he mei de yuyan* 语言的美和美的言语 [*The Beauty of Language and Beautiful Language*], Ji'nan, Shandong jiaoyu chubanshe.

Watts, R.J. (2003) *Politeness*, Cambridge, Cambridge University Press.

Watts, R.J. (2005) 'Linguistic Politeness Research: Quo Vadis?', in Watts et al. (2005), pp. xi–xlvii.

Watts, R.J., Ide, S., and Ehlich, K. (eds) (2005) *Politeness in Language: Studies in Its History, Theory and Practice*, 2nd edition, Berlin, Mouton de Gruyter.

Wittgenstein, L. (1997) *Philosophical Investigations*, 2nd edition (trans. G.E.M. Anscombe), Oxford, Blackwell Publishers.

Zhong, J.w. 钟敬文 (2001) *Zhongguo liyi quanshu* 中国礼仪全书 [*An Anthology of Etiquette in China*], Hefei, Anhui kexue-jishu chubanshe.

Zhu, W.f. 朱维芳 (1998) 'Shuxin yubian limao xianxiang diaocha' 书信语篇礼貌现象调查 [An analysis of politeness in letters], *Waiyi jiaoxue yu yanjiu* 外语教学与研究 [*Foreign Language Education and Research*], 1, pp. 15–20.

8

Modes of Address Between Female Staff in Georgian Professional Discourse: Medical and Academic Contexts

Manana Rusieshvili

1. Introduction

Very little has been published on linguistic politeness in the Georgian language or culture. Rukhadze (2002) focused on address forms, drawing mainly on the theories of Brown and Levinson (1987) and Scollon and Scollon (2001). She was interested largely in a comparative analysis of face-saving strategies in Georgian and English. Her work, however, has been published only in Georgian and is not accessible to the majority of researchers in the field of politeness research. While Rukhadze was innovative in her analysis of the use of conventional politeness strategies, she did not make use of natural language data in her work. Nevertheless, she points to the crucial significance of in-groups and out-groups as defining concepts in Georgian culture.

This chapter attempts to explore how in-groups and out-groups are initially defined by the use of address forms in two selected types of professional discourse, though they are often modified and redefined in these contexts in order to create working 'teams' of professionals. Based on the post-Brown and Levinson's approach to politeness theory, the chapter also explores how the variables of age, power/status and familiarity participate in the process of enacting and modifying the politeness norms in these types of professional discourse.

These modifications have several interesting theoretical implications:

(1) Brown and Levinson's concepts of positive and negative politeness strategies provided a convenient starting point but ultimately proved theoretically inadequate;

(2) Power is an important component in the use of address forms in professional contexts. Clearly, power in the workplace is not merely a 'given' which is stable, predictable and easily calculable. As Harris (2003) argues, not only do powerful people often use politeness/mitigation strategies but that power, status and age variables are often subject to a significant amount of negotiation in the discourse itself;
(3) Address forms in Georgian generally do not function independently but are used as introductory phases to communicative acts which are longer and more complex than a single utterance. Not only must linguistic politeness be approached as contextually dependent but also from a perspective which foregrounds discourse rather than lexical items or isolated speech acts (see, for example, Eelen 2001; Mills 2003; Watts 2003; Terkourafi 2005).

2. The Georgian language

Geographically, Georgia is a bridge between Europe and Asia and thus, has incorporated traditions of both. However, this cannot be applied to the Georgian language, which heads a group of Kartvelian languages of the Iberian-Caucasian family and is characterised by a complex paradigm of verbal and nominal systems. The Georgian verb paradigm which distinguishes between the categories of tense, aspect, voice, number and person possesses a higher number of morphological verb forms than those in European languages. Another typical feature of a Georgian verb is the insertion of inflexions denoting grammatical as well as honorific meaning into the verb itself. Thus the use of v/*t* forms of a personal pronoun is not mandatory. However, when used, normally only V forms are used with plural verb forms and *t* forms are used only with singular verb forms. However, in several cases discussed in this chapter, usage of 'mixed' address forms was observed which violated normative rules and could be defined by the pragmatic context of the interaction. For example, deferential address forms were used with involving singular verb forms, while involving address forms were followed by deferential plural verb forms.

It is also noteworthy that gender distinctions in Georgian are not expressed by personal pronouns but by lexical means.

3. Background: politeness theory and in-group/out-group distinction

Politeness research in the post-Brown and Levinson period often takes their model as a starting point, revealing two major trends of development (Terkourafi 2005). The first, classed as 'traditional' (Terkourafi 2005) or 'normative' (Harris 2007), shows the influence of Brown and Levinson's model but attempts to modify it in a more sophisticated form (Culpeper et al. 2003; Culpeper 2005). The second approach, referred to as 'post-modern' (Tekourafi 2005) or 'contestable' (Harris 2007), differs from Brown and Levinson's approach.

This chapter agrees with post-Brown and Levinson methodology for several reasons: firstly, it looks at politeness as a form of social practice which is deemed to be contested, with discourse participants making assessments as to what is polite or impolite (Eelen 2001; Mills 2003; Watts 2003). Secondly, politeness is looked at as contextually situated (enacted) within discourse. This means a shift of the focus of analysis from isolated lexical units or speech acts (Brown and Levinson approach) towards longer stretches of discourse including their prerequisites (Bousfield 2008).

Harris rightly considers that in order to explore the relationship between politeness and power, professional and institutional contexts must be taken into account along with informal situations depicting the linguistic behaviour of speakers as individuals. This certainly provides better insight into asymmetrical power relationships and differing levels of status which are formally embedded in such settings (Harris 2001, 2007). In addition, power, a significant component in Brown and Levinson's model, is regarded as being mainly stable, easily calculable and predictable. However, as Harris (2003) argues, not only do powerful people often make use of politeness/mitigation strategies but also that power, status and age variables are often subject to a significant amount of negotiation in the discourse itself.

In Georgian culture, a cross between Asian and European cultures, the distinction between in-group/out-group people acquires considerable importance. Georgia has often been invaded, which is partly responsible for the stability and importance of distinguishing 'insiders' from 'outsiders'. A Georgian in-group is a relatively small social group of people such as family (core and extended), close friends and members of an organisation or activity who interact and are friendly with each other without particularly welcoming outsiders. This stability is strengthened because Georgians tend not to change their place of residence or emigrate unless driven by circumstances. In addition, students who live in University towns generally study there preferring to live with their families.

Thus, Georgian culture differs from western cultures and is more like certain Asian cultures, which also find in-group/out-group distinction relevant to their life and mentality. For instance, Pan (2000) emphasises the Chinese tendency to treat people differently depending on whether they are inside or outside of the group; a Chinese in-group being formed by family members, close relatives, village friends or colleagues.

The distinction between in-group/out-group (*uchi/soto*) people is important also in Japan. Having studied relationships between in-group and out-group people in Japan and Turkey, Akdogan came to the conclusion that neither of these languages uses exalting honorific speech with either *uchi* or *soto* people. However, these cultures differ with regard to the extent of the in-group people (Akdogan 2007).

As argued by a number of authors (Sukle 1994; Makino 1996; Kamei 2007), the distinction between *uchi-soto* in Japan is linguistically expressed either by pronouns, signs or specific use of honorifics. Having analysed the relevant data, Kamei concludes that certain pronouns can serve as group indicators. For instance, the first person pronoun *uchi* is used as the indicator of the group the speaker belongs to. In addition, uchi/soto distinction (according to the author best realised through the Japanese honorific system in three categories – honorific, humble and polite) in Japan is directly connected with politeness (Kamei 2007).

In Georgian the distinction between in-group/out-group people may also be manifested through specific use of address forms and honorifics (Rukhadze 2002).

Goodenough (2003: 9) suggests that culture consists of what people within a community learn individually "in regard to the expectations their fellow members have of them in the context of living and working together".

From this viewpoint, the primacy of factors defining the creation of teams and in-groups at work (age, status and familiarity) and the modes of address and rules of interaction (including behavioural standards and rules of politeness) may differ from one type of professional discourse to another.

4. Theorising address forms

Previous studies of address forms explored the relationships between power, status and degree of familiarity among the participants of the communicative act. From this viewpoint Brown and Gilman (1960) showed that power and solidarity create reciprocal and non-reciprocal exchanges of address forms, while Brown and Ford (1961) revealed that familiarity over power in American culture results in moving TLN (title and last name) to FN (first name). Later, Scollon and Scollon (2001) stated that an expression of familiarity and acknowledgment of power differences through the use of address forms may be used to realise politeness strategies.

Studies of address forms in a crosscultural context concentrate on their relevance in crosscultural perspectives, especially in respect of maintaining 'face' while interacting (de Kadt 1998). Braun (1988), in a survey of address forms embracing several European and Asian languages, argues that in Asian languages familiarity does not override power (see also Ishikawa et al. 1981; Scollon and Scollon 2001). While discussing politeness and honorifics, Okamoto claims that even if all the relevant factors of the usage of honorifics are identified, their usage cannot easily be predicted. This can be explained, as the use of honorifics is defined by speakers acting as social agents and not by contextual features. In addition, different individuals may interpret and use honorifics differently relying on their experience and ideological beliefs (Okamoto 2004: 48, cited in Mills' 2011).

Ide rightly argues that politeness is important in acknowledging the social role of an individual. Moreover, by using a particular deferential form the speaker also acknowledges the importance of the social group (Ide 2006, cited in Mills' 2011).

Discussing conventional address forms used in Georgian, Rukhadze (2002) follows Scollon and Scollon's classification and puts forward two groups of address forms; those expressing involvement and those expressing independence. Her methodological approach is based on two types of data (personal observations and 'frozen' address forms and utterances from TV programmes or newspapers). Despite shortcomings, this work is important because, while analysing the data, she acknowledges the role of personal relationships for a Georgian. However, she prefers the terms 'familiar/not familiar' to 'in-group/out-group' employed in this chapter. Also, Rukhadze rightly points out that the crucial distinction between familiarity/non-familiarity may be shown through Georgian address forms and that familiar people are conventionally addressed with FN, endearment or kinship terms and singular verb forms. However, while communicating with unfamiliar people, honorifics and address forms expressing deference and distance such as *kalbatono* (lady) + FN and *batono* (sir) + FN are usually used. In professional discourse the use of titles is rare; for instance, doctors are sometimes addressed, mostly by middle-aged nurses, by the title *ekimo* (doctor) followed by FN and school teachers are usually addressed by FN + *mastsavlebelo (teacher)*. If these norms are violated the speakers violate politeness strategies and may be classed as impolite (Rukhadze 2002).

Rukhadze considers the use of solidarity/deference strategies as generally fixed (Rukhadze 2002). However, relying on my data from two types of professional discourse I argue that address forms do not always work in accordance with these conventional forms.

In addition, certain verbs in Georgian, classed as 'lexical honorifics' (Kikvidze 1999) have three register forms as defined by their semantics: impolite, neutral and distancing/deferential. Thus, in the first example

(Table 1) binary (singular/plural) oppositions of the paradigm of the distancing plural second-person verb *mibrdzandebit* are as follows: impolite (*mietrevi/ mietrevit*), neutral (*midixar/midixart*) and distancing (*mibrdzandebi/mibrdazandebit*). The use of the verb is defined by the context (Nikolaishvili 2000). Conversely, a system of involvement address forms which includes terms of family relationships, endearment or

Table 1 Conventional address forms expressing deference in Georgian

(To females) Honorific (*kalbatono*) + first name (FN)+ verbpl	*Kalbatono nino mibrdzandebit?* Lady Nino, are you (V form) going(verbpl)? **Mrs. Nino, are you leaving?**
(To males) Honorific (*batono*) + FN + verbpl	*batono davit, tkven rodis shemoxvalt?* Mr. David, when you (V form) will come (verbpl) in? **Mr. David, when will you come in?**
(Both sexes) FN + verbpl	*Nino, damirekavt xval?* Nino, will you (V form) call (verbpl) me tomorrow? **Nino, will you call me tomorrow?**
(Both sexes) FN + title + $\text{verb}_{\text{plral}}$ *ekimo* (doctor)	*Nino ekimo, gaamzadet sabutebi?* Nino doctor, have you (V form) prepared (verbpl) the documents? **Dr. Nino, have you prepared the documents?**
V form of the personal pronoun You (V form)	*Tkven, damitsadet, ra?* You (V form), wait for me, no? You, will you wait for me, please?

Table 2 Conventional address forms expressing involvement in Georgian

FN + $\text{verb}_{\text{sing}}$	*Keti, shen xom shemogviertdebi?* Katie, will you (*t* form) join in (verbsing)? **Katie, will you join in?**
Terms expressing family relationships (*deida* [aunt], *bidzia* [uncle]) + FN + verbsing	*Deida tina, rodis shemoxvedi?* Aunt Tina, when did you (*t* form) come (verbsing)? **Aunt Tina, when did you come in?**
Terms of endearment: (*dzvirpaso* [my dear]) + verbsing	*Dzvirpaso nana, shen ras aketeb?* Dear Nana, what are you (*t* form) doing (verbsing)? **Dear Nana, what are you doing?**
Words with informal forms of names: (*Niniko*) + verbsing	Niniko, momitsade, raa? Niniko, wait (verbsing) for me, no? **Niniko, wait for me please?**
t form of the personal pronoun (You [*t* form])	Shena, rodis dabrundebi? you (*t* form) when will you return (Verbsing)? **You, when will you return?**

informal forms of names followed by singular verb forms is usually used to denote informality of the occasion (Table 2).

5. Data and analysis

The data for this study were obtained from two typical professional contexts: medical and academic discourse. A multi-approach to data collection was adopted including recording, observing and conducting interviews. The medical data came from two sources, firstly a small private medical clinic at which 54 doctor/doctor or doctor/nurse interactions were recorded and analysed. Secondly, the National Hospital, which is a large multifunctional hospital consisting of ten departments. Fifty dialogues were recorded and analysed. In both institutions data were recorded using a tape recorder installed in the surgery and in selected medical sites involved in the study. The researcher was absent during the recordings.

Academic data were obtained from two universities in Tbilisi: 30 dialogues from a small private university and 30 from one of the largest universities in Georgia. Participants included teaching and administrative staff. The researcher was present when some of the recordings were made, though never as a participant. The final stage of the data collection was the interviews, which took place in the offices of the interviewees.

In every case full and prior permission to record and analyse data was obtained and all data presented are anonymous. With a single exception, data were obtained from female participants, which were a reflection of the availability of a predominantly female staff.

Since age, status and familiarity featured significantly in the analyses, these factors were taken into account when setting up the interviews. At the clinic seven doctors aged 30 to 45 and seven nurses between ages 20 and 40 were interviewed. At the National Hospital, seven doctors aged 35 to 55 and seven nurses between 25 and 60 were interviewed. Participants were engaged in discussion after listening to their recorded data and asked to evaluate and interpret them – specifically, to explain their choice of address forms and evaluate other participants' reactions with reference to politeness norms practised in their institutions. As the interviewees tended to link this to the concepts of in-group/out-group, they were asked to comment on in-group/out-group relationships and to discuss their perceptions of these relationships, the factors defining them and the manner of their manifestation in Georgian culture.

At the private university, five teachers between the ages of 25 and 60, along with four administrators between 30 and 60 were interviewed and at the large state university, 14 teachers aged 40 to 60 and four administrators between the ages of 30 and 50 were interviewed.

Initially, the purpose of this chapter was to examine the power, status and social distance variations of in-group/out-group relations. As the research unfolded it became obvious that the division between these two groups did not correspond to expectations and additionally, distinctions between an in-group and a team emerged. I argue that in the context of professional discourse, there are differences between teams and in-groups. A team is a group of people chosen to work together to do a specific job united by a common goal related to their job, whereas an in-group at work means a small group of people linked by some personal ties such as common friends, relatives or university background. Thus, members of an in-group tend to keep together at work and generally share a social life after work. If the members of the in-group are not members of the team, after having fulfilled their team duties, they prefer to spend time together. If they are members of the team then they are more loyal to each other than to other team members.

6. Modes of address in medical interaction

For these analyses several extracts have been chosen which display typical forms of address modes employed by staff members in both types of professional discourse.

The first example (Excerpt 1) was taken at one of the ten departments at the National Hospital. The department had nine wards with 16 doctors and 18 nurses, most of whom were female.

The participants of the first interaction are three doctors (Nino, 45, Head of Department; Tamuna, 35, a female doctor in charge of the ward and Merab, 37, a male doctor in charge of another ward) together with a nurse, Nelly, 56.

The extract is taken from the discussion at the routine meeting before morning rounds. Tamuna worked the previous night-shift and Nino was worried about one of the patients. Both Tamuna and Merab were equal, occupying a middle position of doctor in the department and had been in charge of two comparable wards for five years. At the interview Tamuna and Merab classed everyday meetings as semi-formal routine; their function was to report to the Head of the Department about the present state of patients.

Excerpt 1

1. Nino: *Tamuna, mexuteshi ra xdeba? patsienti rogor aris?*
   Tamuna, what is happening in the fifth (ward)? How is the patient?

2.	Tamuna:	*Kalbatono Nino, mdzimea kvlav, gushin gamis ganmavlobashi* Kalbatono Nino, serious again, during the night
3.		*daufiksirda magali sitskhe, gebineba, tkivili marjvena perdis* high temperature, vomiting and pain was observed in the area of
4.		*areshi, eem (-). shemdeg* the right side. erm (-), next
5.	Nino:	[*Tamuna*] [Tamuna]
6.	Merab:	[*Tamuna*] *mapatiet, gaagrzelet kalbatono Nino* [Tamuna] I am sorry, continue Kalbatono Nino
7.	Nino:	*Tamuna, dilit rogor iko, ra gvaria?* {(rustle of the paper)} How was he in the morning, what is his surname?
8.	Tamuna:	*dges dilit kvlav sitskhit, motentillia da kvlav sustad aris* This morning he's running a temperature again and is feeling weak
9.	Nino:	[*kargi*] [well]
10.	Merab:	[*Tamuna*] *Bodishi!* {(laughs)} [Tamuna] Sorry! {(laughs)}
11.	Nino:	*Merab, mapatiet tu sheidzleba. ra gindodat* ? Merab, I am so sorry. What did you want to say?
12.	Merab:	*diax kalbatono Nino kitxva mkonda. Tamuna, daazuste ra* Yes, kalbatono Nino. I had a query. Tamuna, will you specify
13.		*danishnuleba?* the treatment?
14.	Nino:	*ara. ar aris sachiro. axla (addresses the nurse) kalbatono Nelly,)* No, not important now, (addresses the nurse) kalbatono Nelly,
15.		*gauketda danishnuleba? Tkven ikavit ara morige?* has the treatment been followed? You were on duty, were you not?
16.	Nelly:	*Nino ekimo, ki me vikavi. rogorts Tamunam tkva, miuxedavad* Nino ekimo, yes I was. As Tamuna said, despite
17.		*danishnulebisa, maints ar moexsna simptomebi.* the treatment, symptoms are still there.
18.	Nino:	*kargi. vnaxot shemovlaze (-).* Alright. Let's see during the round (-).
19.		*kargi. davamtavrot, mashin. Nelly, momitsade* Good. Let's finish then. Nelly, wait for me
20.		*Nino ekimo, aqa var.* Doctor Nino, I am here.

Merab and Tamuna address Nino by *kalbatono Nino* followed by a plural verb form to show respect to their team leader (lines 2, 6, 12). Both interviewees confirmed that modes of address used were in accordance with the rules of politeness observed in Georgian culture and conditioned by Nino being middle-aged and occupying a higher position. In addition, neither of them knew her well. However, Merab addressed Tamuna by FN and Verbsing as they belonged to the same age group and had similar status (line 12).

There were interruptions in turn-taking and mitigating devices used by Nino who was interrupted twice (lines 6, 10). These were followed by instantaneous apologies from Merab (lines 6, 10). Nino continued without acknowledging the first interruption, thus exercising her power as team leader (line 7). Later, having finished her talk, Nino addressed Merab with FN + Verbpl, apologised and asked him to continue (line 11). This demonstrates that power is not always stable and 'given', but it is often negotiated in context. In this case, not only do less powerful interactants (Tamuna and Merab) use deferential forms while addressing Nino but she reciprocates to them (by using Verbpl and a mitigating expression *tu sheidzleba* [if it is possible]) (line 11). However, in this context the mitigating device as well as the plural form of the verb (at line 11) sound very formal because, as Nino explained at the interview, she was irritated by Merab interrupting her several times. Thus, in this case, hidden annoyance caused the change of address forms from a solidarity *t* form and Verbsing to a formal Verbpl. As stated by Merab at the interview, he considered the deferential strategy used by Nino as a warning to observe turn-taking in the interaction. Thus, it can be argued that, context permitting, deferential strategies are used for the reactivation of one's power over their interlocutors.

Tamuna continued her speech without acknowledging the interruption because not only did she not like to be interrupted but also it was the prerogative of the Chair (Nino) to intervene. On the other hand, Nino uses a deferential strategy (*kalbatono* Nelly, line 14) when addressing a nurse, who reciprocates by FN + title (Nino *ekimo*). It is worth noting that this is one of the exceptions when address forms denoting professional titles are used in professional discourse in Georgia. However, the nurse does not use this strategy while referring to Tamuna because of her age. Nino does not use honorifics *kalbatono/batono* while addressing younger doctors either because they were much younger than her, had been working in the hospital for a considerable time and could be considered as members of her team.

While addressing a nurse of her age Nino prefers FN followed by Verbsing and the latter reciprocates by FN + title (lines 19, 20), confirming again that in this institution, while addressing team members in semi-formal situations, status and age differences were important among team members and deferential strategies were used not only by less powerful participants but also by more powerful members of the team.

In Excerpt 2 participants engaging in small talk are recorded in the staff room of the National Hospital. The participants of the interaction are two female doctors: Maya, 40 and Katie, 38, with Tina, a female nurse who is 58 years old.

Maya and Tina have been working together for more than eight years. Katie works in another ward on the same shift.

Excerpt 2

1. Tina: *Maya, momatsode eg istoria raa*
   Maya, pass me that (patient's) history, please
2. Maya: *romeli? ai, Tina deida. (.) sxvata shoris, X gikitxat*
   Which one? Here it is, Aunt Tina (.) by the way, X asked about you
3. Tina: *Maya, gaarkvie, ra undoda, ra(-)*
   Maya, find out what he wanted, will you? (-)
4. *Ui,, gaikete eg samajuri? RA lamAAzia, tumtsa shen*
   Oh, are you wearing that bracelet? (it's) SO pretty ((laughs))
5. *kvalaferi gixdeba, chemo lamazo* ((laughs))
   Everything looks good on you though, my pretty one ((laughs))
6. Maya: *gmadlobt), deida Tina(.) tkven dzalian matamamebt*
   Thank you, aunt Tina (.) you always spoil me
7. *tkevni sityvebit {(laughs)}*
   with your words {(laughs)}
8. Maya: (addresses Katie) *Katie, xom mivdivart dres (-).*
   Katie, aren't we going there today (-)
9. Katie: *ki, dris bolos Malkhazi mova da gagvikvans*
   Yeah, at the end of the day Malkhaz will pick us up and drive us there.

Here, Maya, the more powerful participant, whilst addressing the less powerful nurse uses a mixed construction, an involvement address form denoting kinship *deida* (aunt) *Tina* followed by a plural verb form and V form of the pronoun (lines 2 and 6), which is a mixed strategy and aims at establishing distance between them. Maya used this strategy following politeness rules according to which older people are addressed by deferential strategies unless they are in-group members. However, when asked why she preferred the kinship term while addressing Tina, Maya claimed that in this way she wanted to acknowledge a higher degree of familiarity. It is worth noting that this mixed strategy violates the conventional rules according to which kinship terms are followed by singular verb forms. Tina reciprocates by address forms expressing involvement FN and Verbsing several times (lines 1, 3, 4). Furthermore, she addresses Maya by an endearment phrase *chemo lamazo* (my pretty one) (line 5), which is normally used to address very close people such as family members. In addition, Tina asks Maya directly to find out what a highly ranked officer wanted when he asked about her (line 3). This reveals asymmetrical relationships between these team members and suggests that in this institution status and power differences are neutralised by age and familiarity variables.

During the interviews, Maya, for the first time, differentiated between the team and in-group. She claimed that Tina is a member of her team whereas Katie was her friend from the university and belonged to her in-group. To the question of how they envisaged the difference between the in-group and the team, Katie and Maya pointed out that in the hospital, teams transformed into in-groups not only when the members got to know each other well but also shared common interests connected with their interpersonal and social lives. Arguably, the major factor that influenced transformation here is the degree of familiarity which, in its turn, is determined by the age and status variables of the participants and the length of their acquaintance, with the variable of age playing a definitive role. Maya also mentioned that Tina did not usually use endearment words while addressing her when they were tête-à-tête, though she still confirmed Tina usually addressed her by FN + Verbsing. Thus, the intimate address mode was used by Tina who was presumably trying to 'claim her place' in the presence of a more powerful in-group member of staff, Katie. This also suggests that, in certain contexts, involvement strategies are used as the means to set themselves inside the social system (in-group).

The dialogue in Excerpt 3 is at the smaller private clinic, which had a head, ten doctors and ten nurses working in shifts and occupying five consultancy rooms. One doctor (Irina, 37) and one nurse (Sopo, 25) make up a stable working team and they have been working together for five years.

Excerpt 3

1. Irina: Sopo, *damagvianda. ver gamovastsari da 'probkashi' movkevi.*
Sopo, I'm late. I was not able to leave earlier and got stuck in a traffic jam.
2. *moxda rame?*
anything happening?
3. Sopo: *ara, Irina. dabarabuli rom gkavda dges 9.30 iman dareka*
No, Irina. The man you asked to come at 9.30 has called and he's
4. *moval meore naxevarshio (.) samsacurshi ragats problema makvso*
coming in this afternoon (.) Said he had some problem at work
5. Irina: *Kai, ra vknat chemi dabadebis dgisatvis, tsavidet sadme?*
OK, what shall we do about my birthday, shall we go somewhere?
6. *haa (-) ras pikrob?*
Eh (-) what do you think?
7. Sopo: kii.(-) *ginda shardenze kafeshi, tan kviraa.*
Yeah (-) What about going to the cafe in Sharden? Anyway, it's Sunday.
8. *chvents tavisuflebi vart..*
Besides, we are free.
9. Irina: *itsi ra vknat (-) aqedan tsavidet shardenze da*
Let us (-) Let's go from here to Sharden and
10. *saxlshi kidev ragatsas movakerxeb natesavebisatvis (.) ras itkvi (-)*
I will arrange for something else at home for the relatives (.) How is this? (-)
11. Sopo: *tu maints unda gaaketo saxlshi, mashin chvents ik movalt (.)*
If you still plan to have a party at home, we could also come there (.)
12. *torem kvela shardenze rom dapatijo, gaikidebi*
If you invite us all to Sharden, it will cost you a fortune.
13. *kargi, chven tu tsavalt, chven tviton gadavixdit*
Anyway, if we go, we will pay for the party.
14. Irina: *ara-me* ((laughs)) *aqedan tsavidet chven Maya (.) Nini (.) Dato(.)*
No, I will ((laughs)) Let's go straight from here Maya (.) Nini (.) Dato (.)
15. *kidev vin (-)*
and who else (-)
16. Sopo: *Givis ar patijeb ?*
Aren't you inviting Givi?
17. Irina: *ara. marto chven tsavidet ra, axloblebi*
No. Let us, only close people, go.

This extract shows how address forms are modified when the 'borders' of the in-group and team coincide. In spite of power and status differences, in-group members Irina and Sopo address each other using solidarity strategies FN + Verbsing and the *t* form of the pronoun, thus status and power differences are neutralised by age and familiarity variables.

7. Modes of address in academic discourse

Excerpt 4 is taken from data collected in the office of the Coordinator of Western European Philology of a large state university. The participants are female members of staff: Assistant Professor Katie, 45, Full Professor, Tsisana, 60 and Coordinator Nana, 48.

Excerpt 4

1. Tsisana: *Katie, gamarjoba, rogora xart?* [*Naniko aris?*]
   Katie, Hello, how are you? [Is Naniko here?]
2. Katie: [*dila mshvidobisa] kalbatono Tsisana. ara, ar aris (.) kvemotaa*
   [Good morning] Kalbatono Tsisana. No, she is not (.)
3. *chasuli. amova male; davureko?*
   She is downstairs and will come back soon. Shall I call her?
4. Tisana: *ara, ara (.) davutsdi, xom sheidzleba?*
   No, no (.) I will wait, can I?
5. Katie: *ra tkma unda, kalbatono Tsisana, dabrdzandit*
   Of course, kalbatono Tsisana, take a seat, please.
6. Tsisana: *rogor tskhela, ara dres?! tskhela ar gvinda, tisva ar gvinda* ((laughs))
   How hot it is today?! When it's hot, we don't want it, when it's cold, we don't want it anyway ((laughs))
7. *Katie, es mitxarit raime xom ar*
   Katie, tell me, any news
8. *gagigiat konkursis shesaxeb*
   about the competition?
9. Katie: *diax (.) kalbatono Tsisana, Nanam itsis,*
   Yes (.) kalabtono Tsisana, Nana has found out something.
10. *rom amova, tviton getkvit*
    She will tell you herself when she comes (Nana enters)
11. Tsisana: *oh, ai movida kidets(.) Naniko, chemo sitsotskhlev (.) mitxari*
    Oh, here she comes (.) Naniko, my life (.) tell me,
12. *itsi reme axali konkursis shesaxeb ?*
    is there anything new about the competition?
13. Nana: *diax, vitsti, kabatono Tsisana (-) unda mibrdzandet XXXX...*
    Yes, kalbatono Tsisana (-) you should go to XXXX

It is obvious that in this context power and status differences are defined by the variables of familiarity and age. The most powerful participant, Nana, is addressed by Tsisana using an endearment form of her name, *t* form of the pronoun, Verbsing and the expression 'my life' (lines 1, 11). Normally the latter, according to the conventional norms of address in Georgia, is used in informal contexts, such as with close people and family members. In this case these address forms seem quite normal considering the fact that both Tsisana and Nana have known each other for a long time (Nana graduated from the university and was once Tsisana's students). Nevertheless, while addressing Tsisana, Nana still uses the deferential modes of address *kalbatono* + FN, followed by a Verbpl (line11) and also the verb form *unda mibrdzandet* ('you should go to'), which usually is considered the most respectful form of the semantic paradigm of this verb. At the beginning of the extract the third participant, Katie, also uses *kalbatono* FN + Verbpl (lines 2, 5) while addressing Tsisana, and is reciprocated by FN and Verbpl (lines 1, 7). Tsisana explained her choice of modes of address while talking to Katie as being due to Katie's younger age and a low degree of familiarity. At the interviews all participants were asked to comment on their choice of address forms in reference to in-group/team distinction. Tsisana considered Nana to be part of her in-group as Nana's mother had been a friend of hers irrespective of the difference in age. When commenting on the factors of transformation between in-group and team, she, like the participants from the medical discourse, stressed sharing small talk, socialising outside of work and common friends.

Excerpt 5 captures a conversation among members (all female) of the Department of English Language and Literature working at a small private university. The Vice-Dean (Baia), 60, discusses the departmental pre-final examination situation. Other participants are Nana, 43, a new teacher, Dali, Professor, 60 and Nino, Vice-Chancellor and Professor, 48.

Excerpt 5

1. Baia: *rogorts gitxarit, gramatikashi tseris biletebs sheadgens Dali.*
   As I told you, in Grammar the exam tickets will be compiled by Dali
2. (addresses Dali) *Dali, rodis momtsem biletebs?*
   (addresses Dali) Dali, when will you give me the tickets?
3. Dali: RA VKNA, *Baia(.) Ninom unda momtses tavisi natsili jer*
   WHAT CAN I DO, Baia, Nino has not sent me her part yet
4. Nino: *kalbatono Dali. dres gadmomigzavne sheni varianti, xolo me*
   Kalbatono Dali, send me your part today and I
5. *davamatebs chemsas, kargi? da isev gadmogigzavni. tu kargad*
   will add mine, OK and send it back to you. If all is well,

6.		*ikneba sakme, xval amovbechdav da mere mogtsem*
		tomorrow (I) will print it out and later, give it [to you]
7.	Nana:	*ME RAIME unda gavaketo? RAME ?*
		DO I HAVE TO DO anything yet? ANYTHING?
8.	Baia:	*Kalbatono Nana, tkven arts araferi*
		Kalbatono Nana, you are doing nothing this time
9.	Nino:	*Nana, tkven mxolod daestrebit..*
		Nana, you will only be an observer ....

This interaction reveals the address forms used in this University with out-group people (Nana) as well as those used by in-group (team) people. Out of the four participants, three (Nino, Baia and Dali) identified themselves as belonging to one team, whereas Nino and Baia belonged to the in-group as well. This is reflected in the use of address forms. Arguably, one and the same deferential form *Kalbatono* + FN in combination with a different number of verb forms can be used by team members as well as with the out-group people. In this interaction, Nino, the most powerful participant, uses this strategy followed by a Verbsing to address Dali (lines 4, 5) as Dali is older than Nino, whereas Dali refers to Nino by FN only (line 3). Baia still uses *kalbatono* + FN followed by V form of the pronoun while talking to a new member of the team (who is still classed by her as an out-group member) to mark the formality of relationship (line 8). At line 9 Nino addresses Nana by FN to soften the feeling of 'estrangement', indicating that she already considers Nana a member of the team though still preferring Verbpl to stress a low degree of familiarity (line 9), thus, in this case, following the conventional pattern of the usage of deferential address forms.

In the interview Nana mentioned that she felt 'silent hostility' coming from the other participants, hence her aggressiveness at the meeting. While reflecting on the reasons underlying this situation she reported that as the team was small, the members of staff being very friendly and a stable 'tight' in-group, that she felt they were reluctant to allow other prospective team members in.

8. Discussion and conclusion

The analysis of the data and interviews makes it possible to conclude the following:

(1) In-group/out-group distinction and its implications regarding issues connected with politeness in Georgian are manifested linguistically through the use of address modes in professional contexts.

(2) In Georgian, address forms are situation markers denoting the type of relationships (in-group/[team]/out-group), the status of the participants and power/age differences. For instance, as seen from the extracts provided, power differences are neutralised and negotiated by both working team members and in-group members. While doing so, connected politeness rules are also enacted and modified according to norms practised in the institutions selected for study. For instance, in Extracts 2, 4 and 5 more powerful participants address less powerful ones by deferential strategies acknowledging the difference in age. However, less powerful members of a team use involvement strategies successfully aiming at reducing the distance between themselves and more powerful members of the team. At the same time, the desire to 'show off' by a closer relationship with the direct supervisor in front of the others serves as an additional stimulus for using endearment terms (Extract 2). This, in other circumstances, would not be the preferred mode of address. In such a way, status and power differences are neutralised by age and familiarity variables.

(3) The powerful members, in order to mark 'boundaries' between in-group, team and out-group, use mixed strategies. Maia, for example, prefers such a strategy composed of a kinship term followed by a deferential plural verb form while addressing Tina to acknowledge the distance created by the interval in age and which, besides violating normative rules of the Georgian language, causes asymmetrical use of address forms (Extract 2). In Extract 5 Nino also applies a 'mixed' strategy while addressing a team-member Dali by a deferential address form *Kalbatono* + FN followed by an involvement Verbsing. However, she addresses Nana by an involving FN followed by a distancing polite Verbpl and corresponding V form. This shows that firstly, one and the same address form is used while addressing an out-group member (which follows the conventional use of the address forms) as well as a team or in-group member, the difference lying in the choice of verb form. Secondly, the choice of address forms from these data is situation – based and defined by the context, which can lead to violation of normative rules according to which V forms are used only with deferential address modes and plural verb forms and *t* forms are used only together with singular verb forms and address forms expressing involvement.

(4) In certain contexts, deferential strategies applied by powerful members of the interaction are used as a means of exercising power rather

than showing deference, for example, in Extract 1 Nino uses Vplural and a mitigation strategy to show irritation and keep the discussion focused.

(5) As suggested by the data, politeness rules are also modified together with the address forms as from the interviews all the participants, especially powerful ones, want to maintain polite relations with their staff members. However, as argued by the interviewees from all of the institutions studied, if the address modes together with the accompanying elements do not correspond to the situation, the speaker will face the danger of placing themselves outside of the social system of the institution.

(6) In spite of difference in power/status, a working team easily transforms into an in-group if the members belong to the same in-group (Extract 3).

(7) Age is a principal defining category during formation of in-groups at work, other factors being common background, status and socialising after work. The team members allow more variations in this respect which, as seen above, are mainly caused by differences in age, power and familiarity variables. Moreover, besides revealing asymmetrical relationships between the members of the team, status and power differences are neutralised by age and familiarity variables (Extract 2).

The above-mentioned points suggest that the conventional system of address forms is not fixed and unchanged as believed by Rukhadze (2002). In Georgian professional discourse the address forms build up a dynamic system foregrounding complex relationships between in-group/team and out-group people emerging in the interaction. In addition to this, contextual modification of address modes is directly connected to the assumption of being polite in the institution.

Transcription conventions

(.)	indicates a pause of two seconds or less
(-)	indicates a pause three seconds
[] []	closed brackets indicate simultaneous speech
WHAT DO I DO	capital letters indicate material was uttered loudly
XXX	indicates confidential information
((laughs))	material in double brackets indicates additional information.

References

Akdogan, P. (2007) 'A Contrastive Study of the Uchi-soto Relationship in Japanese and Turkish', *Hiroshima Daigaku Daigakuin Kyoukugaku Kenkyuka Kiyoo Bulletin of the Graduate School of Education, Hiroshima University. Part. II*, 56, Hiroshima, Japan, Hiroshima University Press, pp. 235–239.

Bousfield, D. (2008) *Impoliteness in Interaction*, Amsterdam, John Benjamins.

Braun, F. (1988) *Terms of Address: Problems of Patterns and Usage in Various Languages and Cultures*, Berlin, Mouton de Gruyter.

Brown, P., and Levinson, S.C. (1987) *Politeness: Some Universals in Language Usage*, Cambridge, Cambridge University Press.

Brown, R., and Ford, M. (1961) 'Address in American English', *Journal of Abnormal and Social Psychology*, 62, pp. 375–385.

Brown, R., and Gilman, A. (1960) 'The Pronouns of Power and Solidarity', in T.A. Sebeok (ed.), *Style in Language*, Cambridge, Cambridge University Press, pp. 253–276.

Culpeper, J. (2005) 'Impoliteness and Entertainment in the Television Quiz Show: The Weakest Link', *Journal of Politeness Research*, 1/1, pp. 35–72.

Culpeper, J., Bousfield, D., and Wichmann, A. (2003) 'Impoliteness Revisited: With Special Reference to Dynamic and Prosodic Aspects', *Journal of Pragmatics*, 35/10, pp. 1545–1579.

de Kadt, E. (1998) 'The Concept of Face and Its Applicability to the Zula Language', *Journal of Pragmatics*, 25, pp. 349–367.

Eelen, G. (2001) *A Critique of Politeness Theories*, Manchester, St. Jerome.

Goodenough, W.H. (2003) 'In Pursuit of Culture', *Annual Review of Anthropology*, 32, pp. xiv, 1–12.

Harris, S. (2001) 'Being Politically Impolite: Extending Politeness Theory to Adversarial Political Discourse', *Discourse and Society*, 12/4, pp. 451–472.

Harris, S. (2003) 'Politeness and Power: Making and Responding to "Requests" in Institutional Settings', *Text*, 23/1, pp. 27–52.

Harris, S. (2007) 'Politeness and Power', in C. Llamas, L. Mullany and P. Stockwell (eds), *The Routledge Companion to Sociolinguistics*, London, Routledge, pp. 122–129.

Ishikawa, A., Nogata, T., Miyaki, M., Nagao, A., and Iuzuka, H. (1981) 'Address-Forms in Modern Japanese: A Sociolinguistic Analysis', *Sophia Linguistica*, 3, pp. 19–41.

Kamei, Y. (2007) 'Uchi/Soto and Linguistic Expressions', *KGPS Review*, N7, October, pp. 67–80.

Kikvidze, Z. (1999) 'A Plural or an Honorific? Morpho-syntactic and Sociolinguistic Rules for Their Differentiation', paper presented at the Symposium 'Grammatik i fokus', Lund University, Sweden, 11–12 February.

Makino, S. (1996) *Uchi to soto no gengubunkagaku* [*The Study of Culture of In-Group and Out Group*], Tokyo, ALC.

Mills, S. (2003) *Gender and Politeness*, Cambridge, Cambridge University Press.

Mills, S. (2011) 'Discursive Approaches to Politeness and Impoliteness', in Linguistic Politeness Research Group (LPRG) (ed.), *Discursive Approaches to Politeness*, Berlin and New York, Mouton de Gruyter.

Nikolaishvili, M. (2000) *The Georgian Language*, Tbilisi, TSU Publishing House.

Okamoto, S. (2004) 'Ideology in Linguistic Practice and Analysis: Gender and Politeness in Japanese Revisited', in S. Okamoto and J. Shibamoto Smith (eds), *Japanese Language, Gender, and Ideology*, New York, Oxford University Press, pp. 38–56.

Pan, Y. (2000) *Politeness in Chinese Face-to-Face Interaction: Advances in Discourse Processes*, Stanford, Ablex.

Rukhadze, N. (2002) 'Face and Politeness While Expressing Solidarity in Present-Day English, Georgian and Russian', *Lingusitic Papers*, XII, pp. 221–230 (in Georgian).

Scollon, R., and Scollon, S.W. (2001) *Intercultural Communication*, Oxford, Blackwell Publishing.

Sukle, R. (1994) 'UCHI/SOTO: Choices in Directive Speech Acts in Japanese', in J. Bachnic and C. Quinn (eds), *Situated Meaning*, Princeton, Princeton University Press, pp. 118–121.

Terkourafi, M. (2005) 'Beyond the Micro Level in Politeness Research', *Journal of Politeness Research*, 1/2, pp. 237–262.

Watts, R. (2003) *Politeness*, Cambridge, Cambridge University Press.

Part III: Im/politeness and Face: Intercultural and Crosscultural Perspectives

9

Indirectness in Zimbabwean English: A Study of Intercultural Communication in the UK

Karen Grainger

1. Introduction

Indirectness in intercultural communication is an area that has received some considerable attention in intercultural pragmatics and in politeness studies, probably largely due to perceived cultural differences between different groups around the world and to the potential ambiguity and miscommunication that can result from this (Tannen 1984). This fact alone suggests that the notion of indirectness is an important one in intercultural pragmatics. However, the exact nature of indirectness, its relationship to politeness and to facework, and indeed whether it exists at all, is not agreed upon by scholars. Furthermore, since the work of Gumperz (1979, 1982) and Roberts et al. (1992) there has been very little work done on intercultural communication in the UK context and still less on the use of African English in the diaspora. Africans, including Zimbabweans fleeing the Mugabe regime, are a recent and growing immigrant group in the UK and so it would seem timely to re-visit questions of communication and intercultural relations.

The inspiration for this chapter came about because of my own experiences over a period of years of interacting with Zimbabwean (Ndebele)[1] immigrants whom I had come to know as part of a southern African singing group. Whilst at first communication seemed unproblematic (because on the whole Zimbabweans who make it over to the UK speak very good English), after some time I began to wonder why sometimes they took a long time to get to what I perceived to be 'the point' and why sometimes they did not 'say what they mean'. There seemed to be subtle but fundamental differences between my expectations of how to make meaning, and those of my Zimbabwean friends. It seems likely, then, that indirectness is an important, yet possibly unrecognised source of miscommunication between southern African[2] immigrants and British people.

Furthermore, the study of indirectness seems to get right to the core of some interesting methodological and theoretical questions in politeness theory. Perhaps the most fundamental question is what exactly politeness is and what we, as politeness scholars should be studying. As is now well known, Locher and Watts (2005) argued for a distinction between participant evaluations of politeness (first-order politeness) and the analyst's use of the term to mean 'facework' (second-order politeness). For them, it is only first-order politeness that should be the object of politeness research. I, along with Kádár and Culpeper (2010), regard second-order politeness as an important focus of politeness research. That is to say, the application of a 'technical' notion of politeness provides us with an empirical tool for examining interaction (O'Driscoll 2007). Utterances may not always be perceived by speakers as 'polite' but may nevertheless be conveyed using face-saving message construction, such as indirectness. In the context of intercultural communication, however, I must concede the relevance of participant evaluations for a meaningful account of indirectness. As I argue below, because indirectness relies heavily on speakers' shared understanding of the situation for its communicative value, participants' perceptions of what is polite behaviour become crucial. Thus, my viewpoint is now that studies of politeness should not be restricted to either first- or second-order politeness but should allow for a merger of both approaches.

In this chapter I investigate indirectness with reference to existing work in the area as well as to limited empirical data in the form of transcribed 'intercultural' interactions and conversation anecdotes. These serve as a springboard from which to explore and exemplify indirectness and its relationship to politeness and face management in intercultural encounters.

In keeping with the discursive turn in politeness studies (Haugh 2007; Mills forthcoming) which suggests that politeness is most fruitfully analysed for its construction in naturally occurring discourse, the examples of interaction I provide are all from naturally occurring encounters. They illustrate how:

(1) indirect meaning is managed (and sometimes misunderstood) between Zimbabwean and British English speakers. The analysis makes use of members' own categorisations of indirectness and politeness (through their meta-discourses) as well as the application

of technical (pragmatic and conversation analytic) categorisations and

(2) that the notion of indirectness, in Brown and Levinson's (1987) sense of going 'off record' is relevant and useful for the studies of intercultural pragmatics in general and for the study of Zimbabwean-British interaction in particular, but that Brown and Levinson and Blum Kulka's (1987) notion of 'conventional' indirectness is not a useful one; whether or not the relationship between linguistic form and intended meaning is 'conventional' is culturally specific.

I begin with a discussion of the existing debates around these subjects.

2. What do we mean by 'indirectness'?

2.1. Definitions

An examination of the literature on pragmatics and intercultural communication shows that 'indirectness' is variously and ambiguously defined. It is frequently assumed to be of crucial and fundamental importance in pragmatic meaning-making, however. For example, Leech states that: "General pragmatics relates the sense (or grammatical meaning) of an utterance to its pragmatics force. This relationship may be relatively direct or indirect" (1983: 30).

Many authors also characterise it in terms of the discrepancy between what is said and what is meant. For example, Holtgraves says that indirectness is "any communicative meaning that is not isomorphic with sentence meaning" (1997: 626) and Thomas describes it as "a mis-match between expressed meaning and implied meaning" (1995: 119). Tannen (2010) discusses it as inferred or implicit meaning, a way of putting meaning 'off record'. Bowe and Martin (2007) treat it as 'implied' or 'non-literal' meaning. According to Brown and Levinson, it is "any communicative behaviour ... that conveys something more than or different from what it literally means" (1987: 134).

There seem to be at least two problems with these definitions of indirectness. One problem is that the notion of 'literal' meaning is often taken for granted. However, Levinson (1983) argues that the notion of literal meaning is problematic. It assumes that illocutionary force is built in to sentence meaning, or rather that words and sentences have a 'natural' meaning independent of their usage. Clearly, these are decontextualised and static views of linguistic interaction that are not consistent with a discursive approach. They assume that 'literal meaning' is recoverable from surface features of the language alone. According to both Leech (1983) and Levinson (1983), if one assumes that literal meaning exists, almost all utterances would be indirect (Levinson 1983: 264), rendering indirectness as a fairly meaningless category which appears to become synonymous with 'implied meaning' (covered by implicatures) or 'polite' (tactful) formulations. Levinson goes on to argue that indirect requests (such as 'Do you have any torch batteries?') are better explained in structural, conversation analytic terms, as pre-requests (1983: 357). Silverstein (2010: 15) argues the notions of 'directness' and 'indirectness' are "descriptive and theoretical dead ends", particularly when one looks at crosscultural data, since there is so much cultural variation. Similarly, Wierzbicka (2003) suggests that the distinction between 'directness' and 'indirectness' should be abandoned on the grounds that there is no principled difference between imperatives ('Close the door') and conventionally indirect commands ('Would you close the door?').

Wierzbicka's point leads me to the second problem with the definitions mentioned above, which is that there is insufficient recognition that there may be different types of indirectness and that before we can have meaningful discussion about what we mean by the term, we must establish exactly which type of utterances we are counting as indirect. Authors such as Levinson (1983) and Leech (1983) seem to assume that indirectness refers mainly to 'polite' formulations such as what Brown and Levinson (1987) and Blum Kulka (1987) have called 'conventional indirectness' and what Wierzbicka (2003) calls 'whimperatives' (conventionally indirect imperatives). On the other hand, other authors cast the net of indirectness wide enough to include strategies that may in general be termed 'off record', such as hints (Pinker 2007), ventriloquising[3] (Tannen 2010), shared understanding (Tannen 1984; Wierzcicka 2003), ritual insults (Kiesling and Johnson 2010) and 'avoidance registers' (Nelson et al. 2002; Silverstein 2010).

In my view, the accounts of Brown and Levinson (1987) and Pinker (2007) betray a certain amount of confusion as to what indirectness refers to. Brown and Levinson attempt to include indirectness as part of negative politeness. Their discussion suggests that their notion of indirectness consists of 'conventional indirectness' alone, which they define as "the use of phrases and sentences that have contextually unambiguous meanings (by virtue of conventionalisation) which are different from their conventional meanings" (1987: 132). However, when one looks at their categorisations, it is difficult to see in what way indirectness differs from what they are calling negative politeness strategies. Thus, in their chart of negative politeness strategies (1987:

131) 'be indirect' is presented as being a sub-strategy of the super-strategy of 'don't coerce H' (H=Hearer) alongside 'don't assume', 'minimise threat' etc. Its only manifestation can be as 'conventional indirectness', which is a 'hybrid strategy' that allows the speaker to simultaneously 'be direct' and convey a desire not to coerce (be negatively polite). In other words, indirectness allows the speaker to say what they mean, but politely. Surely then, this is *the same as* negative politeness, not a special case of it? If this is taken to be the meaning of indirectness, I would agree with Wierzbicka (2003) that the notion is meaningless and is possibly better served by the term 'negative politeness', which is at least more clearly defined.

On the other hand, Brown and Levinson's (1987) account also suggests that indirectness extends beyond negative politeness, since it is also connected with the politeness strategy of going 'off record'. They define this as "A communicative act [that]...is done in such a way that it is not possible to attribute only one clear communicative intention to the act" (1987: 211). It is treated as a type of politeness that is distinct from negative or positive politeness (and thus, presumably, not oriented to either positive or negative face wants) but instead allows the speaker to not take responsibility for any potential face threats. It seems then, that for Brown and Levinson, indirectness is (somewhat shakily) *both* a specific part of negative politeness as well as being relevant to off-record strategies such as hinting, assuming, being ambiguous etc. Brown and Levinson may have been misled by the Anglo-American connotations of the term 'indirect'. They are using this first-order term to explain two different second-order phenomena. In fact, their model of politeness can already account for both types of 'indirectness' within the notions of negative politeness and off-record strategies.

Pinker (2007) treats indirectness in a similarly ambiguous way, although from the very different perspective of evolutionary psychology. He defines it as "the phenomenon in which a speaker says something he doesn't literally mean, knowing that the hearer will interpret it as intended" (2007: 437), which suggests that the intended meaning is non-negotiable and therefore is conventional indirectness. However, he subsequently states that the topic of his paper is the off-record indirect speech act (2007: 442) and that these sorts of utterances provide both the speaker and hearer with an 'out' in terms of how it is interpreted. Pinker, then, establishes that there are two types of indirectness: on-record indirectness is "off the shelf"(2007: 441), a cliché. Off-record indirectness is "freshly minted" (2007: 441) and thus much more open to interpretation.

This distinction can be equated to what other authors call 'conventional' indirectness (on record) and 'non-conventional' or implied meaning (off record) (Blum-Kulka 1987; Holtgraves 1997; Tannen 2010). However, as Pinker and others (Holtgraves 1997; Christie 2007; Tannen 2010; Kiesling and Johnson 2010) rightly point out, cultures differ as to what they consider to be the conventional or 'unmarked' (Kiesling and Johnson 2010) relationship between surface form and underlying meaning, therefore there seems to be little point in using either the term 'indirectness' or 'conventional' as a universal concept. A meaning that is 'off the shelf' in one community may be 'freshly minted' in another. Kiesling and Johnson (2010) argue that indirectness involves going a circuitous route to arrive at meaning, whereas directness involves meaning that requires no intermediary steps to arrive at meaning. However, whether or not a route to meaning is 'direct' or 'circuitous' is also a matter of perception, so this pseudo-cognitive definition does not lead to a satisfactory definition of second-order (technical) indirectness. Indeed, Wierzbicka (2003) and Silverstein (2010) argue that indirectness is impossible to define objectively and only exists 'in the ear of the beholder' or as a first-order phenomenon.

2.2. Indirectness on a scale

On the other hand, some scholars argue that the terms 'directness' and 'indirectness' do not work well as opposing categories. Leech suggests that, far from being a question of absolutes, "indirectness is a matter of degree" (1983: 38). He proposes a scale of indirectness that is related to degrees of 'optionality' and 'force'. Sperber and Wilson (1986, cited in Thomas 1995 and Christie 2007) propose a continuum of indirectness based on the amount of 'work' the hearer has to do in arriving at the meaning. These ideas also occur in Blum-Kulka's empirical work.

Blum-Kulka (1987) usefully categorises different *types* of speech act that can be placed on a directness scale according to native speaker (English and Hebrew) ratings. According to her research, there appears to be some broad agreement across the two language groups in that mood derivables (such as imperatives) were generally perceived to be most direct and hints were generally judged to be most indirect. In terms of judged politeness, however, she found that there is some cultural variability and that while indirectness itself may be on a scale, judgements as to how polite it is are not.

Blum-Kulka et al. (1989), looking at a broader range of languages, draw a clear qualitative distinction between 'direct strategies' (with five substrategies), 'conventionally indirect' strategies and 'nonconventionally indirect' strategies. Utterances are allocated to one of these categories on the basis of "the inferential process needed for identifying the utterance" (Blum-Kulka et al. 1989: 18). However, Wierzbicka (2003) and Christie (2007) both dispute the claim that expressions of these cultural values can be put on any sort of universal scale of indirectness or that the notion of 'inferential work' can be universally applied. Wierzbicka (2003) argues that the term 'indirectness' obscures the fact that different cultures are working with different cultural scripts or 'semantic formulae' which determine both how speakers express themselves and how hearers are likely to interpret indirect messages.

I would agree that there is a problem with using the term 'indirectness' to encompass a range of different communicative strategies that include hints as well as conventionalised meanings of negative politeness formulae (such as 'Can you pass the salt?'). Brown and Levinson (1987), Blum-Kulka et al. (1989), Pinker (2007), Kiesling and Johnson (2010) and others may be misled by the first-order usage of 'indirectness' which, confusingly, is often coterminous with polite (but on-record) formulations of speech acts. In my view, these formulations are better described as routine negative politeness, while hints and other strategies that are not explicitly expressed in language should be referred to as 'off record'. Whether or not they are also interpreted as 'polite' can then be treated as a separate, and culturally variable, issue.

2.3. Indirectness and politeness

Clearly the phenomena of indirectness and politeness are closely linked. Leech considers that there is a direct relationship between the two: "Indirect illocutions tend to be more polite (1) because they increase the degree of optionality, and (2) because the more indirect an illocution is, the more diminished and tentative its force tends to be" (Leech 1983: 108). Blum-Kulka (1987) is more explicit about the nature of the connection. She argues that they are 'parallel' dimensions but that there is no one-to-one relationship between them.

As we have discussed above, for Brown and Levinson (1987) conventional indirectness is a type of negative politeness, while off-record speech acts are considered to exhibit greater care over face needs and therefore are more polite. Thus for Brown and Levinson, indirectness is *part of* politeness. Elsewhere, however, it seems that authors consider the relationship to be the other way round. Thomas (1995) states that indirectness is only partly motivated by the desire to be polite, the other motivations being the desire to be interesting, the desire to increase the effectiveness of the message (by making the hearer work harder to uncover the meaning, and thereby having a greater investment in it) and a clash of speaker goals. Similarly, Pinker (2007) regards indirectness as the over-arching concept and places polite behaviour within it. These different applications of the terms 'indirect' and 'polite' seem to relate to the vexed and much-discussed question of what we mean by 'politeness'. For Brown and Levinson, 'politeness' is facework and overlaps with, but is not necessarily coterminous with the everyday usage of the term. On the other hand, for some recent scholars of politeness, speaker/hearer intentions and perceptions of polite interaction (first-order politeness) are the main object of study.

If we define indirectness only in terms of first-order politeness, then, it seems that indirectness (whether conventional or off record) is not always polite, since many authors acknowledge that certain forms of indirectness can be perceived as *im*polite and manipulative (Holtgraves 1997; Pinker 2007; Kiesling and Johnson 2010). However, it seems probable that, in terms of second-order politeness, indirectness is always to do with interactional facework, since it involves oblique meaning and avoidance behaviour. For example, Nelson et al. (2002: 47) define an indirect refusal as "containing a strategy that would soften the blow of the refusal" and Tannen (2010) suggests that indirectness is a way of giving meaning 'off record' and thereby saving face. Kiesling and Johnson (2010) point out that one can use indirectness to attack face in such a way that allows the insult to be deniable. In this way, one can save one's own face while attacking that of the addressee. Clearly then, indirectness that is perceived as manipulative or rude is not polite in the sense of first-order politeness. However, one could still maintain that it is 'technically' polite since it may still be doing facework (however disingenuously).

3. Indirectness across cultures

Many authors agree either explicitly or implicitly that indirectness in some form occurs universally in language-in-interaction (Brown and Levinson 1987; Thomas 1995; Pinker 2007; Kiesling and Johnson 2010). Others, as we have seen above, point out that the use and interpretation of indirectness varies across cultures. This is sometimes associated with geographical location or with global differences in value systems. Ogiermann (2009), for example, suggests that there is more likelihood of direct imperatives being used to make requests the further east one goes in Europe. Holtgraves (1997) claims that there is empirical support for the view that expressing meaning indirectly and seeking indirect meaning in others is associated more with collectivist cultures (such as Koreans) than with individualistic cultures (North Americans). In addition, Wierzbicka (2003) states that Greeks interact on the basis of a shared understanding whereas the Japanese notion of *enryo* is about restraint and the Javanese practice of *etok etok* ('dissimulation') is to do with concealing one's innermost wishes and thoughts. This collectivist orientation to avoidance behaviours has also been found in southern African styles of interaction, which are encapsulated in the concepts of *hlonipha* and *ubuntu* (de Kadt 1998; Grainger et al. forthcoming).[4]

The notion of 'culture' here needs to be problematised, however. In crosscultural and intercultural studies of politeness there can be a tendency to assume that language, nationality and culture are coterminous with one another and that they have homogeneous behaviours and practices (Mills and Kádár, forthcoming). This assumption carries many risks: the risk of overlooking variation, the risk of ignoring contested norms (Mills and Kádár, forthcoming), the risk of stereotyping and the risk of reducing participants' behaviour to essential differences in culture (Roberts and Sarangi 1993). And yet, if we do not attempt to talk about intercultural communication, how will we broach some of the problems of negative stereotyping and misunderstanding that can arise from ignorance and intolerance of difference? Some theorists have attempted to get round this by acknowledging that the notion of 'culture' can apply to groups of any size (e.g. Holliday 1999) and, importantly, many acknowledge that national culture is by no means the only variable in pragmatic strategies. Tannen (1984), Holtgraves (1997) and Nelson et al. (2002) all state that variation in indirectness is a matter of both individual and cultural 'style' such that in intercultural interaction it may be difficult to establish which aspects of style are down to personality and which are due to cultural background. Nelson et al. (2002) and Yeung (2000) both acknowledge that there are many intersecting factors that influence a speaker's use of indirectness. These factors include nationality, gender, status and – importantly – situation.

We need to be cautious, therefore, about what conclusions we draw about interactions between people of different nationalities. However, as Grainger et al. (forthcoming) also argue, I am convinced that people's interactional behaviour *is* connected to their experiences as members of various groups, including ethnic and national ones, and that this membership can at least in part explain common communication phenomena across people who share the same group memberships.

4. African indirectness

The limited literature of African politeness and face suggests that there are interesting parallels with so-called Eastern languages and their supposed collectivist orientation to communication (Holtgraves 1997; Ige 2007; Grainger et al. forthcoming). Nwoye (1992) states that the orientation to group face leads Igbo speakers to make requests directly (where speakers from more individualistic cultures might use conventional indirectness or negative politeness), since asking for help is not considered to be an imposition and is in fact a demonstration of one's group allegiance. De Kadt (1995) also finds that based on Discourse Completion Test (DCT) and role-play data, Zulu speakers are more likely to formulate requests and complaints directly than South African English (SAE) speakers (using the Blum-Kulka et al. 1989 scale of directness). Kasanga's (2003) DCT and interview data on the South African language of Sepedi also found that speakers preferred to use a direct locution than to use conventional indirectness (i.e. 'whimperatives') in making requests.

Kasanga (2003) claims that this tendency to directness may be due to pragmatic transfer from many of the African languages: "... it has become increasingly evident that African languages share broad socio-pragmatic and pragma-linguistic features" (Kasanga 2003: 215). However, paradoxically, there is also evidence that speakers of indigenous southern African languages also make extensive use of off-record indirectness. De Kadt (1992) reports that both Zulu and Sepedi speakers use a greater number of 'hints' than SAE speakers. Thus, Zulu request and directive strategies are described as 'polarised' (de Kadt 1995), in comparison with those of SAE speakers.

De Kadt (1992) argues that this is because in Zulu interaction indirectness does not inhere in the individual speech acts but instead emerges over a number of turns. This suggests that looking for indirectness in the sense of routinised formulations of speech acts (e.g. 'whimperatives') is not fruitful. To add to this, Kasanga (2006) states that 'indirectness' is an irrelevant notion for request strategies in Sepedi and that using the interrogative form ('Can you ... ?') does not in fact constitute polite behaviour for these speakers. Rather, explicit performatives and other tokens of mitigation (such as honorifics) signal politeness in Sepedi speakers of English.

Chick's (1989: 95) work focuses more squarely on intercultural interaction in South Africa. He notes that interaction between white South African English speakers and Zulu English speakers can be adversely affected by differences in listening, turn-taking and politeness practices.

As with Gumperz's (1982) intercultural work in the UK, Chick observes that such differences in conversational routines can lead to the formation of negative stereotypes on both sides. Since the Zimbabwean language of Ndebele (the mother tongue of my acquaintances) is closely related to Zulu, one might expect to find similarities between the findings of Chick, Kasanga, de Kadt and my own.

5. Data and methodological framework

In this section I examine various instances of intercultural exchanges between Zimbabwean English[5] speakers and British English speakers in various situations. My data are all from naturally occurring conversations between myself and several of my Zimbabwean acquaintances. These conversations occurred in the normal course of my daily life. On these occasions I, as simultaneous participant and observer, felt that I had to do inferential work over and above what I would normally have expected in that situation. Given my interest in the pragmatics of interaction, I realised that these incidents may have relevance for the topic of indirectness. I wrote them down immediately following the conversation (within minutes) so that accuracy of sequencing and content would be preserved. I subsequently obtained informed consent from each of the participants to use the material for the purposes of research. Their names and any other identifying details have been changed so as to ensure anonymity.

This is in keeping with an ethnographic approach to data gathering as it involves participant observation of naturally occurring meaning-making practices. I would argue that this 'incidental' type of data may be the best way of providing evidence of indirectness since, while on-record linguistic politeness strategies can be observed easily in discourse (positive politeness or deferential moves, for example), off-record indirectness, by definition, is not so easily predicted and observed from the outside. It often occurs in what is *not* said rather than what is said and so the participant perspective is a useful (though not the *only)* indicator of indirectness. Since the conversations were recorded from memory, without the use of audio-visual equipment, clearly some aspects (such as timing, tone of voice, hesitations) will be missed. As such, while my analysis does make reference to turn-taking and sequencing, these data are not suitable for a detailed conversation analysis approach.

The other advantage of being both participant and observer (analyst) in these interactions is that I have also had access to a 'meta-discourse' on how to interpret them. In two of the three examples, this consists of a discussion between the participants about the conversation they have just had. Locher and Watts (2005: 12) rightly point out that "politeness and related categories are discursively negotiated" and that it is "important to take native speaker assessments of politeness seriously and to make them the basis of a discursive, data-driven, bottom-up approach to politeness". Indeed, what Locher and Watts (2005:12) call the "discursive dispute" over politeness becomes of crucial importance in identifying potential sources of intercultural misunderstanding and their notion of 'first-order' politeness is therefore important for analysing these encounters.

In general, I would describe the method of analysis I use as closest to that of interactional sociolinguistics (IS). According to Gumperz, the aim of IS is "...to show how individuals participating in such exchanges use talk to achieve their communicative goals in real-life situations, by concentrating on the meaning-making processes and the taken-for-granted, background assumptions that underlie the negotiation of interpretations" (2003: 218). These background assumptions can be accessed partly through looking at the content and sequencing of interactional moves and partly via participants' meta-discourses and observations. As outlined elsewhere (Grainger et al. forthcoming), IS takes a constructivist view of discourse (that meaning is constructed and negotiated in talk), but maintains that in order to "illuminate the interrelation of language in use with culture" (Clyne 1994: 10) participants' interpretations have recourse to socio-cultural knowledge that is "associated with ideologies and principles of communicative conduct" (Gumperz 2003: 219).

6. Data analysis and discussion

This first example of intercultural indirectness involves a combination of face-to-face and mediated (mobile phone) communication between me and a Zimbabwean friend of mine at the end of an evening out with her and her husband. We have been to a pub in town. I live some distance from the town centre and have driven in, whereas the Zimbabwean couple live near the town centre and do not have a car. Just before we part, the following (face-to-face) exchange takes place between me[6] and my friend, Ellen:[7]

Example 1

Ellen: I think we will wait for a bus, I don't feel like walking home.
Karen: OK. Good night then.

At this point in the exchange, it is not at all clear that an off-record politeness strategy has occurred at all: there is no evidence in the discourse itself as to whether she *intended* to make a polite request (first-order politeness) and without this it is difficult to say whether a second-order off-record strategy is being used. However, we can say that Ellen's remark has more than one possible illocutionary force: the force of both an informative and a request (for a lift home) but that only the explicit one is taken up by the addressee. This, of course, is the 'pay off' (Pinker 2007) for going off record in any interaction (whether intercultural or not): by acting as if the off-record meaning is not present, both speaker and addressee have an 'out' (Brown and Levinson 1987: 211) and can save face. However, I would argue that the cultural background of the speakers affects the degree to which certain meanings are preferred by the participants in the conversation. In this particular incident, alternative interpretations occurred to me (as participant) later in the evening and I felt the need to respond to this, lest I should be thought selfish. I therefore sent a text message to my friend:

Karen: Sorry, should have offered you a lift home. Wasn't thinking straight.
Ellen: Its OK. We were just being lazy.

What is interesting here is that Ellen's response to my text ('We were just being lazy') suggests that her most accessible interpretation is that of a request for a lift. The other possible reading – that of informing me that she was waiting for a bus – is not offered by her as a face-saving 'out'. This suggests that the extent to which Ellen's original speech act ('I think we'll wait for a bus') can be regarded as 'off record' may be culturally bound. The force of it as a request seems to be obvious to Ellen, whereas it took me time to arrive at this interpretation. In other words, what may be conventional or routine indirectness for Ellen is off record for me. This seems to support the argument, made above, that the distinction between conventional 'off the peg' (Pinker 2007) indirectness (where the meaning is readily accessible) and off-record 'newly minted' (Pinker 2007) indirectness is not a useful one in intercultural communication.

On the basis of this one exchange alone, we cannot be sure that this difference in expectations is due to the different cultural backgrounds of the speakers. However, there have been enough of these types of experiences with this set of southern African acquaintances for me to strongly suspect that geographical and cultural origins are playing a part. Indeed, it was my previous interactional experiences with these friends that led me to question my own initial interpretation in the example above.

The next sample conversation provides further evidence of the use of off-record indirectness as politeness. This interaction took place between myself and another Zimbabwean friend.[8] We had previously arranged to meet up that evening for a meal and a film. To my surprise, he phoned me up about two hours before we were due to meet, ostensibly to confirm arrangements. Because of my interest in southern African politeness conventions, the conversation sparked a meta-discourse on that topic which gives access to our intentions and interpretations in this situation. This is how the phone conversation went:

Example 2

1.	Themba:	Just phoning to check we are still on for tonight
2.	Karen:	(thinking maybe he's phoning to cancel or delay) yes I am if you are
3.	Themba:	Yes, yes, I'm just leaving work now, I have to get the bus from R____ so I should be with you about 5.
4.	Karen:	OK that's fine.
5.	Themba:	Will you be very hungry?
6.	Karen:	I don't know. I might be by then.
7.	Themba:	Do you want to go somewhere for some food?
8.	Karen:	I thought we were going to S____ (name of café-bar)?
9.	Themba:	Yes we are. Will that be enough for you or will you be very hungry?
10.	Karen:	(Beginning to suspect that there is an off-record message) Erm we could go somewhere else if you like.
11.	Themba:	It's just that in my experience S____ does very small portions.
12.	Karen:	Oh do they? I only suggested there because it doesn't look too expensive.
13.	Themba:	It's not very good value for money.
14.	Karen:	We could go somewhere else. Do you have anywhere else in mind?
15.	Themba:	No, it's just that I think I will be VERY hungry by then. We could go to S____ for a bite before the film and then go somewhere else afterwards.
16.	Karen:	No let's go somewhere else. Why don't we talk about it when you get here.

17.	Themba:	OK.
18.	Karen:	(laughing) I wish I'd had that conversation on tape. It was a very good example of Zimbabwean indirectness.
19.	Themba:	(laughing) you mean I should just have said "I will be very hungry. Can we go somewhere else?"
20.	Karen:	Yes, you could have said that.
21.	Themba:	But I have to be polite don't I?

As with Example 1, this interaction shows that Themba's off-record meaning could be regarded as conventionally polite (i.e. routine and accessible) for him but not for me. Furthermore, what is often called 'conventional indirectness' in English (as in 'Can we go somewhere else?') does not appear to signal politeness to him in this situation.

According to Brown and Levinson (1987: 211), for an interlocutor to realise that meaning should be accessed through inference, there has to be a 'trigger', which may be the violation of a Gricean maxim (Grice 1975) and there has to be a 'clue' as to how to derive what is meant from what is said. In this case, the initial trigger for me (as participant) is the fact that Themba has phoned at all, which could be taken as a violation of the quantity maxim (this of course could be a culturally specific value – it may be perfectly normal behaviour to re-confirm arrangements in some cultures or even in some relationships). As far as I was concerned, the arrangements for meeting up had already been finalised the previous evening so this triggers the implicature that there must be some other reason for phoning – perhaps to cancel the arrangement or change some aspect of it. Line 3 suggests that no such change is being proposed (5 pm was the original meeting time) and as far as I was concerned provides no clue so I was still searching for the intended meaning. Line 5 is perhaps the first 'clue' that the reason for ringing may be something to do with the proposed meal. However, whether or not this is *recognised* as a clue may be very culture-dependent. I have argued elsewhere (Grainger et al. forthcoming) that the southern African concept of 'face' tends to foreground the needs of the group (or in this case, the other) over the needs of the individual self, whereas middle-class British norms often promote the needs of efficiency and the individual. In that case, we can hypothesise that a reference to *my* state of hunger may be somewhat puzzling for a British person, but for a southern African (operating within a similar interpretation framework as Themba) could act as a cue that the intended meaning has something to do with the speaker's own desires.

At line 6, I do not take up any meaning other than the literal one, and respond directly to his question about my likely state of hunger. At line 7, Grice's maxim of quantity (and possibly manner) is flouted (Grice 1975) as Themba asks for information which I think has already been provided the previous day. My response in line 8 indicates my slight confusion. Themba agrees – superficially – that there is already a prearranged plan ('yes we are') but then provides an additional clue that relates more specifically to the amount of food that the restaurant is likely to serve. It is at this point that I infer that the restaurant I had suggested is not to Themba's liking and guess Themba's intended meaning. In this case, although the process may have been somewhat laborious (to someone working within a more individualistic framework), Themba and I did eventually arrive at a mutually acceptable meaning. In Brown and Levinson's terms the 'pay off' was that Themba gave me the opportunity to be seen to care for the speaker; I was able to give a 'gift' to the speaker (Brown and Levinson 1987: 71) in the form of an offer to go elsewhere. In this way, the speaker achieves his aim without threatening his own or the addressee's positive face needs. However, one can see the potential for misunderstanding. If the indirectness (in the form of off-record speech acts) were not identified as a first-order politeness strategy within an interpretation framework of the southern African philosophy of *ubuntu*, it would have been difficult to arrive at an interpretation that was mutually satisfying. If I did not already have some knowledge of the interactional style of southern Africans in general, and of my friend in particular, I may have concluded that the only inferences I could make were unflattering ones, such as, Themba is irritatingly vague, unnecessarily solicitous, forgetful or just a bit strange. As with example 1, if he had assumed that his motives were fairly obvious (conventional) but his polite request strategy was not responded to, he might have concluded that I was stubborn and cared more about my own needs than his. In intercultural communication, then, the danger is that indirectness will not be spotted as such, or if it is, it may not be recognised as an attempt to *be polite,* in the 'first-order' sense of the term. The very benefits that speakers may reap by going off record (to allow for alternative readings) can also lead to serious misunderstanding where interlocutors are not working from the same 'principles of communicative conduct' (Gumperz 2003: 219).

In this case, somewhat unusually, Themba makes his intended meaning explicit at the end of the encounter. When I mention 'indirectness' (line 18), he seems to know exactly what I am talking about and re-phrases his request/suggestion in what he must regard as a more direct (to me) and less polite (to him) way. Clearly to him, to phrase it in what to the British ear is 'conventional indirectness' ('Can we go somewhere else?') makes his request more explicit but would not be polite.

In my third and final example, there is no meta-discourse but the intended meaning emerges as the interaction progresses. This encounter is between myself and a Zimbabwean woman whom I paid to clean the house.[9] She has recently obtained refugee status, which means that she can now look for work elsewhere. This is how she informs me that she can no longer work for me:

Example 3

1.	Karen:	Congratulations on getting your papers
2.	Lizzie:	Yes I was very happy
3.	Karen:	So you'll be looking for a job now?
4.	Lizzie:	Yes I'm looking for accommodation at the moment
5.	Karen:	Oh do you have to move out?
6.	Lizzie:	Yes on the 13th. That's why I want to move to L
7.	Karen:	Oh do you have someone you can stay with there?
8.	Lizzie:	Yes my brother
9.	Karen:	We'll miss you if you go
10.	Lizzie:	Thank you for everything you've done for me. You have helped me a lot.
11.	Karen:	You've helped us too
12.	Lizzie:	Next week I'll be coming on Wednesday
13.	Karen:	Ok that's OK. And will you be coming the week after that?
14.	Lizzie:	No. Next week is my last week.

This is a potentially face-threatening encounter for both participants and there is a measure of off-record indirectness on both sides. In my own interpretation of the situation, as participant, I had neither the right nor the obligation (Thomas 1995) to ask Lizzie what her intentions were. To do this explicitly would threaten her negative face wants. Hence, my veiled enquiries at lines 3, 5 and 9, which leave the way open for her to tell me her plans. This she does, but in a less clear and direct way than I might have expected. Her utterance, 'that's why I want to move to L___' is ambiguous to me. For Lizzie, however, it is likely that this was a conventionally indirect way of telling me her news. In other words, what to me sounds like uncertainty is polite certainty for Lizzie, triggered by the inference that if she is in a different town she will not be able to travel to my house for work. My use of a conditional formulation at line 9 ('*if* you go') reflects my uncertainty but Lizzie responds to this as if we have come to the end of our arrangement ('thank you for everything you've done for me'). At this point she has succeeded in conveying that she will not be able to work for me much longer, without (as far as I am concerned) actually saying so. Notice that her next utterance in line 12 is quite direct and not open to multiple interpretations, presumably because informing me that she will be coming one more time is much less face-threatening. Finally, she tells me explicitly that 'next week is my last week', but only after I have prompted her with a direct question (line 13).

From my point of view, this was a reasonably successful interaction, in which we arrived at mutual understanding through a process of negotiation. I hope that Lizzie felt this too, though I do not know. (Perhaps she thought that I was rather too direct or somewhat obtuse.) However, this happy outcome was perhaps only achievable because I was already aware of the possibility of off-record indirectness in my interactions with Zimbabweans. As with the other two examples, another British interlocutor could have interpreted Lizzie's indirectness as evasiveness or cowardice. Far from cueing a politeness evaluation, her indirectness may have signalled rudeness. If there were several such encounters between British employers and Zimbabwean employees (or vice versa), the potential for negative stereotyping and deteriorating relations is easy to see.

7. Conclusion

This chapter has been an exploration of the phenomenon of indirectness in intercultural encounters between myself as a British English speaker and some of my English speaking Zimbabwean acquaintances. It has looked at how we can define indirectness, and indeed whether it can be said to exist at all. It has also dealt with the relationship between indirectness and politeness, and in particular how this relationship is interpreted and analysed in intercultural interactions.

The distinction between conventional indirectness and off-record indirectness turns out to be an important one for intercultural understanding. My enquiries into intercultural indirectness between Zimbabwean English speakers and British English speakers lead me to conclude that notions of *both* first-order and second-order politeness are simultaneously relevant and valuable. I have argued that those politeness strategies in British English that are sometimes called 'conventional indirectness' are probably best accounted for under Brown and Levinson's second-order notion of negative politeness, since the perception of what is both 'conventional' and 'indirect' is culturally relative and there is no principled or technical way of distinguishing between deferential/distancing forms of language and conventional indirectness.

It may be best then, to restrict the study of indirectness as a second-order politeness phenomenon to what Brown and Levinson (1987) call 'off-record' strategies. These can be defined as strategies which allow for more than one interpretation, where at least one meaning has to be arrived at through inference. As Pinker (2007) maintains, this type of indirectness may be a universal strategy: all speakers may have going off record as a resource. It may even be a universal second-order politeness strategy. However, it is not always *perceived* as politeness: the relationship between indirectness and first-order politeness depends on the interpretation frameworks of the speakers. Methodologically, where participants' interpretive resources do not match, it is useful to have access to participants' intentions and interpretations. To this end, I have examined both participants' discourse as well as their meta-discourses on their conversational behaviour. Without such 'insider' insights (which are unusual in everyday interaction) off-record politeness strategies could go completely unrecognised by both participants *and* analyst. In terms of second-order politeness, this would mean that face-management strategies are overlooked by the analyst and valuable insights about intercultural pragmatics are lost. In terms of first-order politeness, the situations for which going off record is expected and evaluated as 'polite' depends on the interpretation framework of the participants. From a southern African perspective, it seems that going off record can in some face-threatening circumstances be a fairly conventional (routine) form of politeness. Just *how* conventional it is for other Zimbabweans requires further investigation, but this same strategy from a British perspective could constitute a hint or no politeness at all. As we have seen, where the participants do not share the same interpretation frameworks misunderstanding or misattribution of intention may result. There is great potential for the recipient of 'indirectness' to misinterpret it as vagueness, weakness or rudeness and ultimately, for the deterioration of intercultural relations.

Notes

I would like to thank Sara Mills and three anonymous reviewers for their constructive comments on earlier drafts of this chapter. I also thank my Zimbabwean friends for allowing me to reproduce some of our conversations in the interests of intercultural harmony.

1. The Ndebele 'tribe' or 'nation' is the smaller of the two major ethnic groups in Zimbabwe. They are geographically, linguistically and culturally distinct from the dominant group: the Shona.
2. Although all the interactions on which I have based this chapter were with people of Zimbabwean nationality, it should be remembered that the country of Zimbabwe is a British colonial creation. Many linguistic, social and cultural practices may be shared with peoples throughout the southern African region. The interactional behaviour in question is therefore not restricted to one social, tribal or national group, but neither is it necessarily generalisable to all southern Africans, who are themselves a diverse multicultural group.
3. Tannen (2010: 310) defines ventriloquising as "instances in which speakers frame their utterances as representing others' voices".
4. The concept of *ubuntu* is sometimes translated as 'humanity' (de Kadt 1998). It is an ethical system concerned with the connectedness of each human being to others; a recognition that we could not exist without each other and therefore others must be respected as if they were part of you (Kamwangamalu 1999; Tutu 1999; Bonn 2007). *Hlonipha* is described by de Kadt (1998: 182) as "the central concept in [Zulu] societal interaction". It can be translated as 'to pay respect' through a system of verbal and non-verbal avoidance.
5. Although Zimbabwean English is, of course, a type of southern African English, I am assuming here that its usage is more akin to the Zulu English discussed in de Kadt's (1995) study, than to SAE. De Kadt does not specify who her speakers of SAE are, but one assumes that their background and culture is more European in style than that of Zulu English speakers.
6. I (Karen) am a highly educated, white British English speaking woman, in my 50s. I have spent most of my life in the UK but have also lived abroad for periods of up to four years. My social networks include British people, Zimbabweans and people of other nationalities.
7. 'Ellen' (pseudonym) is a highly educated Ndebele speaking woman aged between 25 and 40. She is originally from the rural areas of Matabeleland, Zimbabwe but has spent a substantial part of her adult life in Harare. At the time of this conversation, she has been living in the UK approximately one year. Her social networks include both white British people as well as other Zimbabweans.
8. 'Themba' (pseudonym) is a moderately well educated Ndebele speaking man aged between 25 and 40. He is originally from the townships of Bulawayo but lived and worked in Harare before coming to the UK approximately eight years ago. His social networks include white British people as well as other Zimbabweans.
9. 'Lizzie' (pseudonym) is an Ndebele speaking woman aged between 25 and 40. She has completed compulsory education in Zimbabwe. She grew up and worked as a primary teacher in rural Matabeleland. She has lived in the UK for approximately eight years but her social networks do not tend to include indigenous British people.

References

Blum-Kulka, S. (1987) 'Indirectness and Politeness in Requests: Same or Different?', *Journal of Pragmatics*, 11, pp. 131–146.

Blum-Kulka, S., House, J., and Kasper, G. (1989) *Cross-Cultural Pragmatics*, Norwood, Ablex.
Bonn, M. (2007) 'Children's Understanding of "Ubuntu"', *Early Child Development and Care*, 177/8, pp. 863–873.
Bowe, H., and Martin, K. (2007) *Communication across Cultures*, Cambridge, Cambridge University Press.
Brown, P., and Levinson, S.C. (1987) *Politeness: Some Universals in Language Use*, Cambridge, Cambridge University Press.
Chick, K. (1989) 'Intercultural Communication as a Source of Friction in the Workplace and in Educational Settings in South Africa', in O. Garcia and R. Otheguy (eds), *English across Cultures: Cultures across English*, Berlin, Mouton de Gruyter, pp. 130–160.
Christie, C. (2007) 'Relevance Theory and Politeness', *Journal of Politeness Research*, 3/2, pp. 269–294.
Clyne, M. (1994) *Inter-Cultural Communication at Work: Cultural Values in Discourse*, Cambridge, Cambridge University Press.
de Kadt, E. (1992) 'Requests as Speech Acts in Zulu', *South African Journal of African Languages*, 12/3, pp. 101–106.
de Kadt, E. (1995) 'The Cross-Cultural Study of Directives: Zulu as a Non-Typical Language', *South African Journal of Linguistics*, Supplement 27, pp. 45–72.
deKadt, E. (1998) 'The Concept of Face and Its Applicability to the Zulu Language', *Journal of Pragmatics*, 29, pp. 173–191.
Grainger, K., Mills, S., and Sibanda, M. (forthcoming) ' "Just Tell Us What to Do": Southern African Face and Its Relevance to Intercultural Communication', *Journal of Pragmatics*.
Grice, H.P. (1975) 'Logic and Conversation', in P. Cole and J. Morgan (eds), *Syntax and Semantics 3: Speech Acts*, New York, Academic Press, pp. 41–58.
Gumperz, J. (1979) 'Cross-Cultural Communication', in R. Harris and B. Hampton (eds), *The Language, Ethnicity and Race Reader*, London, Routledge, pp. 267–275. (Originally published in J. Gumperz, T. Jupp and C. Roberts (eds), *Crosstalk*, London, BBC.)
Gumperz, J. (1982) *Discourse Strategies*, Cambridge, Cambridge University Press.
Gumperz, J. (2003) 'Interactional Sociolinguistics: A Personal Perspective', in D. Schiffrin, D. Tannen and H. Hamilton (eds), *The Handbook of Discourse Analysis*, Oxford, Blackwell, pp. 215–228.
Haugh, M. (2007) 'The Discursive Challenge to Politeness Research: An Interactional Alternative', *Journal of Politeness Research*, 3/2, pp. 295–317.
Holliday, A.R. (1999) 'Small Cultures', *Applied Linguistics*, 20/2, pp. 237–264.
Holtgraves, T. (1997) 'Styles of Language Use: Individual and Cultural Variability in Conversational Indirectness', *Journal of Personality and Social Psychology*, 73/3, pp. 624–637.
Ige, B.O. (2007) 'Impoliteness in Context: Impoliteness, Gender and Construction of Identities as a South African University', PhD thesis, University of Kwa-Zulu Natal.
Kádár, D.Z., and Culpeper, J. (2010) 'Historical (Im)politeness: An Introduction', in J. Culpeper and D.Z. Kádár (eds), *Historical (Im)politeness*, Berne, Peter Lang, pp. 9–36.

Kamwangamulu, N. (1999) 'Ubuntu in South Africa: A Sociolinguistic Perspective to a Pan-African Concept', *Critical Arts*, 13/2, pp. 24–41.
Kasanga, L. (2003) '"I Am Asking for a Pen": Framing of Requests in Black South African English', in K. Jaszczolt and K. Turner (eds), *Meaning through Language Contrast*, Amsterdam and Philadelphia, John Benjamins, pp. 213–235.
Kasanga, L.A. (2006). 'Requests in a South African Variety of English', *World Englishes*, 25/1, pp. 65–89.
Kiesling, S.F., and Johnson, E.G. (2010) 'Four Forms of Interactional Indirection', *Journal of Pragmatics*, 42/2, pp. 292–306.
Leech, G.N. (1983) *Principles of Pragmatics*, London, Longman.
Levinson, S.C. (1983) *Pragmatics*, Cambridge, Cambridge University Press.
Locher, M., and Watts, R.J. (2005) 'Politeness Theory and Relational Work', *Journal of Politeness Research*, 1/1, pp. 9–33.
Linguistic Politeness Research Group (LPRG) (2011) *Discursive Approaches to Politeness and Impoliteness*. Berlin and Philadelphia: Mouton de Gruyter
Mills, S., and Kádár, D.Z. (forthcoming) 'Politeness and Culture', in S.Mills and D.Z. Kádár (eds), *Politeness in East Asia*, Cambridge, Cambridge University Press.
Nelson, G., Al Batal, M., and El Bakary, W. (2002) 'Directness vs. Indirectness: Egyptian Arabic and US English Communication Style', *International Journal of Intercultural Relations*, 26, pp. 39–57.
Nwoye, O. (1992) 'Linguistic Politeness and Socio-cultural Variations of the Notion of Face', *Journal of Pragmatics*, 18, pp. 309–328.
O'Driscoll, J. (2007) 'Brown and Levinson's Face: How It Can – and Can't – Help Us to Understand Interaction across Cultures', *Intercultural Pragmatics*, 4/4, pp. 463–492.
Ogiermann, E. (2009) 'Politeness and In-directness across Cultures: A Comparison of English, German, Polish and Russian Requests', *Journal of Politeness Research*, 5/2, pp. 189–216.
Pinker, S. (2007) 'The Evolutionary Social Psychology of Off-Record Indirect Speech Acts', *Intercultural Pragmatics*, 4/4, pp. 437–461.
Roberts, C., and Sarangi, S. (1993) '"Culture" Revisited in Intercultural Communication', in T. Boswood, R. Hoffman and P. Tung (eds), *Perspectives on English for International Communication*, Hong Kong, Hong Kong City Polytechnic, pp. 97–102.
Roberts, C., Davies, E., and Jupp, T. (1992) *Language and Discrimination*, London and New York, Longman.
Silverstein, M. (2010) '"Direct" and "Indirect" Communicative Acts in Semiotic Perspective', *Journal of Pragmatics*, 24/2, pp. 337–353.
Sperber, D., and Wilson, D. (1986) *Relevance: Communication and Cognition*, Oxford, Blackwell.
Tannen, D. (1984) 'The Pragmatics of Cross-Cultural Communication', *Applied Linguistics*, 5, pp. 189–195.
Tannen, D. (2010) 'Abduction and Identity in Family Interaction: Ventriloquizing as Indirectness', *Journal of Pragmatics*, 42/2, pp. 307–316.
Thomas, J. (1995) *Meaning in Interaction*, London, Longman.

Tutu, D. (1999) *No Future Without Forgiveness*, Random House, London.
Wierzbicka, A. (2003) *Cross-Cultural Pragmatics*, Berlin, Mouton de Gruyter.
Yeung, L.N.-T. (2000) 'The Question of Chinese Indirectness: A Comparison of Chinese and English Participative Decision-Making Discourse', *Multilingua*, 19/3, pp. 221–264.

10
On Im/politeness Behind the Iron Curtain

Eva Ogiermann and Małgorzata Suszczyńska

1. Introduction

This chapter examines culture-specific conceptualisations of Polish and Hungarian im/politeness, the influence of political and societal changes on im/politeness and the differences between the developments in Poland and Hungary before and after the fall of the Iron Curtain. The analysis is based on narratives revealing perceptions of im/polite behaviour and metapragmatic terms referring to im/politeness elicited with the help of semi-structured episodic interviews.

2. Theoretical background

In our chapter we draw on recent contributions to politeness theory in that we take into consideration the full spectrum of behaviour from polite to impolite and recognise the evaluative and discursive nature of politeness (Mills 2003; Watts 2003; Haugh 2007). We agree that a theory of politeness can only be developed on the basis of first-order perceptions of politeness (Eelen 2001; Watts 2003), which are subject to diachronic and synchronic variability and change (Ehlich 2005). We therefore stress the importance of participants' own understanding of im/politeness, their evaluations of im/polite behaviour and their use of metapragmatic terms referring to im/politeness.

We assume that the perception of what constitutes im/politeness is culture-specific in that values rooted in various cultural traditions of a community persist despite changes brought about by political or economic factors. At the same time, the enactment and perception of im/politeness are always 'situated' in a particular socio-political and economic system (Marcjanik 2007: 157), and as the system changes, so does im/politeness.

Although cultures cannot be conceptualised as homogeneous entities (Eelen 2001) that determine their members' language usage in a particular way, they can be expected to share cultural assumptions that facilitate intracultural communication (Ogiermann 2009a: 24). For politeness to arise there needs to be some degree of consensus about social norms and conventions and the linguistic forms representing them (Haugh 2003: 400), which lay members are able to reach "by interacting with other members of the culture in different situations throughout their lives" (Janney and Arndt 1992: 30).

While Brown and Levinson's (1987) distinction between positive and negative politeness has been criticised by the proponents of the discursive framework, it has also been taken up by several researchers who reformulate it as 'connection' and 'separation' (Arundale 2006) or 'approach' and 'withdrawal' (Terkourafi 2007). Although we focus on first-order politeness, we do not dismiss Brown and Levinson's framework as an ethnocentric theory of second-order politeness, while regarding their dichotomy as exceedingly useful for analysis linking im/politeness with culture and societal change.

3. Previous research

While there is a growing body of literature on politeness in various cultures, little is known about politeness in Eastern Europe. Although linguistic politeness has been studied in these countries, for many years the research focused on questions of linguistic etiquette, appropriateness and norms of usage (e.g. Zgółkowie 1992; Kiss 1995), with address forms being in focus in both Polish (e.g. Lubecka 1993; Huszcza 2005) and Hungarian (e.g. Nyomárkay 1998; Bence 2005) politeness research. In recent years, sociopragmatic approaches to politeness in Hungarian (Reményi 2001; Domonkosi 2002; Szili 2004; Suszczyńska 2005) and Polish (Suszczyńska 1999; Lubecka 2000; Jakubowska 2003; Ogiermann 2009a, 2009b) have also gained ground.

Studies attempting to explain politeness in terms of underlying culture-specific 'values' and 'attitudes' are scarce. Wierzbicka (1985, 1991) argues that the Polish concept of politeness differs from the Anglo-Saxon one in that it is characterised by straightforwardness, interpersonal warmth, cordiality, emotionality and spontaneity. Hungarian politeness literature of the *nyelvmüvelés* ('cultivation of language') tradition (see Kontra 2003 and Minya 2005 for reviews) uses the term *(nyelvi) tiszteletadás* ('linguistic respect paying') as a synonym of *nyelvi udvariasság* ('linguistic politeness'). In Hungarian studies *nyelvi tiszteletadási formák* ('forms of paying respect') include both honorifics and endearments. Although lay native Hungarians may not consider endearments as part of *nyelvi tiszteletadási formák*, our data suggest that in Hungarian *udvariasság* respect is compatible with displays of warmth and closeness.

When analysing politeness in Eastern European countries, one needs to bear in mind the complex political and social changes these countries have been undergoing in the past century. The enforcement of 'communism' led to an imposition of a collectivist mentality and the assumed values of the 'proletariat'. In addition, political oppression and permanent shortages of basic goods led to new power constellations affecting public face-to-face communication, particularly in service encounters and in interactions between representatives of state institutions and citizens.

However, it is important to remember that the countries forming the Soviet Bloc were never culturally homogeneous. As a result of the political compromise following the dramatic uprising of 1956, Hungary experienced relative political and economic stability from the mid-1960s, while Poland was afflicted by numerous political and economic crises (Hankiss 1990; Rotschild and Wingfield 2000). As these countries were subject to ideological assimilation, some similarities in language use were bound to develop (e.g. the introduction of 'comrade' as a new form of address in official situations: *towarzysz* in Polish, *elvtárs* in Hungarian). At the same time, the political, economic, societal and cultural changes affected Polish and Hungarian citizens' communicative styles in different ways.

Cultures are regarded as "large-scale outcome[s] of people interacting over time" (Eelen 2001: 246–247) – and of various socio-historical processes. Contemporary Polish culture has been described as an amalgam of three different historical, political and social traditions: Poland's national heritage, the values introduced by the communist regime and the values resulting from an increasing assimilation to western lifestyle since the fall of the Iron Curtain (Lubecka 2000: 32). The market economy and 'western values' have equally influenced Hungarian culture. The Hungarian *elvtárs* ('comrade') was officially in use until 1989 and then disappeared from one day to the next. While the deferential forms *Úr* ('Mr') or *Asszony* ('Madam') returned to everyday language use, the use of *t* forms has also increased (Bence 2005: 241–246). Likewise, Polish linguists report a decrease in the use of titles and a stronger tendency to reduce social distance and formality when addressing others (Marcjanik 2007: 26–34).

4. First-order politeness

Eelen distinguishes two different aspects of first-order politeness: the action-related side and the conceptual side (2001: 32). In discursive politeness studies the focus has been on the action-related side, namely on how politeness arises and is evaluated in ongoing conversation, simultaneously leading to an emphasis on the heterogeneous nature of politeness and culture. In order to be able to arrive at culture-specific concepts of politeness, however, one needs to focus on the conceptual side of first-order politeness, with lay members' judgments providing an insight into the concept of politeness in their own culture.

Previous research has demonstrated the usefulness of etymological and semantic analysis of lexemes denoting politeness in obtaining insights into the culture-specific first-order meanings of politeness (Watts 2003: 34) as well as into their historical relativity (ibid.: 45). The most common Polish adjectives denoting politeness are *uprzejmy* and *grzeczny*. Etymologically, the word *uprzejmy* goes back to the Old Church Slavonic **prěm-*, meaning *szczery* ('honest') and *otwarty* ('open') (Brückner 1970: 594). The word *grzeczny*, on the other hand, has been derived from *k rzeczy* (ibid.: 162), which can be translated as 'to the matter'. Berger (2006) argues that the concept of *uprzejmy* reflects the upright behaviour characteristic of Polish gentry, while *grzeczny* depicts situation-appropriate behaviour.

In Hungarian the adjective denoting politeness is *udvarias* ('polite', 'courteous'), its root, *udvar*, meaning 'court'. According to Tótfalusi (2002) *udvar* is of Slavonic origin (*dvor*, originally 'yard') while *udvarias* was derived from *udvar* after the German pattern: *Hof-höflich* > *udvar-udvarias*. Early studies on Hungarian politeness define *udvariasság* as *tiszteletadás* ('paying respect'), *társadalmi távolság* ('social distance'), *illendőség* ('propriety', 'decency') or 'appreciation' (*megbecsülés*) (e.g. Simonyi 1911, in Domonkosi 2002: 21).

5. Methodology

Since the period of our interest lies in the past, we derived our data from interviews with Poles and Hungarians who remember the communist times. Interviews have proved "particularly useful as a research method for accessing individuals' attitudes and values" (Byrne 2004: 182). Previous politeness research based on interviews tended to focus on the informants' metapragmatic knowledge. However, what is problematic about asking lay members to provide metapragmatic information on politeness is that they "tend to evoke normative descriptions of the phenomenon" (Blum-Kulka 1992: 257). In order to avoid such a bias, potentially leading to an overemphasis on formal politeness, we have used the so-called episodic interview (Flick 2009). It is based on the assumption that "subjects' experiences of a certain domain are stored and remembered in forms of narrative-episodic and semantic knowledge" (Flick 2009: 185), and consist of a "combination of narratives oriented to situational or episodic contexts and argumentation that peel off such contexts in favour of conceptual and rule-oriented knowledge" (Flick 2009: 186).

In the first part of the interview, we asked our participants to share with us their memories of interactions with other Poles/Hungarians before and after the fall of the Iron Curtain in various settings: private and public, with family, friends, acquaintances and strangers. In their narratives, the informants spontaneously used a range of lexemes referring to im/politeness without consciously reflecting on what constitutes im/politeness, thus allowing us to tap into their concepts of first-order politeness. In the second part of the interview we asked them to provide definitions of politeness and impoliteness, which provided additional insights into their normative knowledge.

The chapter presents the results of ten interviews conducted with Poles living in Germany and nine interviews with Hungarians living in Hungary. Although these groups are not fully comparable in that one of them consists of immigrants, both have first-hand experience of living in their countries during communist times and they perceive the differences in im/politeness after the change of regime from that perspective. The Polish participants visit Poland on a regular basis, thus having an opportunity to experience changes in politeness phenomena in their culture.

The interviews vary in length between 35 minutes and 1 hour 14 minutes. The Polish interviewees were aged between 25 and 63, with the average age being 44. There were six females and four males, six participants had secondary and four had higher education. The Hungarian interviewees were aged between 37 and 60, with the average equalling 53. Six of them were female and three male, and all of them graduated from university.

6. Analysis

6.1. Polish data: politeness

Watts argues that the concept of first-order politeness is reflected in the various terms a language offers to refer to polite behaviour, and he names 'considerate', 'thoughtful' and 'well-mannered' (2003: 35) as synonyms of the English 'polite' and 'courteous'. As the Polish informants were describing interpersonal encounters in various settings that they experienced before and after the fall of the Iron Curtain, they used a number of adjectives other than *uprzejmy* and *grzeczny*. The most frequent among them was the word *miły* ('nice', 'pleasant'), which was often used synonymously with *uprzejmy*, suggesting that the type of politeness depicted by the word *uprzejmy* refers to maintaining a pleasant atmosphere.

The remaining adjectives used by the Polish informants can be subdivided into those defining people in terms of their attitude to others and those focusing on the person they describe. The former generally reflect the concepts of approach and connectedness, while the latter focus on non-imposition and display of good manners. Most of the adjectives used to refer to polite behaviour were related to the concepts of approach and connectedness, namely *otwarty* ('open'), *emocjonalny* ('emotional'), *serdeczny* ('cordial'), *wylewny* ('effusive'), *życzliwy* ('kind'), *uczynny* and *pomocny* ('helpful'). While these adjectives can be classified as oriented towards positive face, the nouns *szacunek* ('esteem') and *respekt* ('respect') reflect distance and negative politeness. Interestingly, these two nouns were used almost exclusively when referring to teachers, priests, women, the elderly and people in higher positions.

The definitions of politeness that were provided differ greatly from those found in the Hungarian data, in that they contain hardly any reference to verbal politeness. Only one respondent indicated that he takes it as a form of politeness if somebody says 'thank you' and smiles at him – provided that the smile is 'not forced' (*nie wymuszony*). In the following definition, the concepts of approach and connectedness dominate the interviewee's understanding of politeness:

> *Uprzejmość* to jest dla mnie (1) wychodzenie na przeciw drugiej osobie i (2) próby wczulenia się w drugą osobę na tyle, aby rozpoznać, co ta osoba w danym momencie ode mnie chce.
>
> (Politeness for me is (1) meeting somebody half way (2) attempts to feel with the other person to an extent that allows me to recognise what that person wants from me in a given moment.)
>
> (female, 27)

Several respondents explained that there are different types and degrees of politeness and recognised the necessity to always maintain some degree of politeness. As the following two quotations show, lay members exhibit awareness of the distinction between politic and polite behaviour (Watts 2003):

> Generalnie wychodzę z założenia, że trzeba być *grzecznym*. Natomiast to, jak daleko się w tej *grzeczności* posunę zależy po prostu od sytuacji.
>
> (Generally I think that one has to be polite. But the extent to which I'm polite depends simply on the situation.)
>
> (female, 35)

> Termin *uprzejmość* ma dla mnie dwa wymiary. Jeden z nich to jest właśnie taka *uprzejmość*, która mi się kojarzy z neutralnością. Nie masz nic przeciwko tej osobie... *Uprzejmość* kojarzy mi się też z taką chęcią pomocy, może nie tyle altruistyczną – gdzie ty nie masz żadnej korzyści a komuś w czymś jesteś chętna pomóc.
>
> (For me the term politeness has two dimensions. One of them is politeness that I associate with being neutral. You don't have anything against that person... I also associate politeness with willingness to help, not necessarily altruistic – where you don't profit from it but are willing to help somebody with something.)
>
> (female, 25)

The neutral type of politeness in the second definition seems to denote unmarked politic behaviour. What is striking about this and the remaining definitions in the Polish interviews is the central role assigned to being helpful to others.

Although the two most common terms *uprzejmy* and *grzeczny* were used interchangeably most of the time, some of the interviewees made interesting distinctions between them:

> ...*uprzejmość* to ja to kojarzę tak, że jest to związane z wzajemnością. *Grzeczność* nie, *grzeczność* jest jednostronna, dla mnie – chcesz być dobrym człowiekiem, to pomóż bliźniemu, a *uprzejmość* to jest taka, byłoby *chamstwem*, jak ktoś jest *uprzejmy* być *nieuprzejmym* dla niego, nie?
>
> (... *uprzejmość*, my association is that it's reciprocal. *Grzeczność* not, *grzeczność* goes one way, for me – if you want to be a good human, help your next, while *uprzejmość* is such that it would be *chamstwo* if somebody is *uprzejmy*, not to be *uprzejmy* to him, no?)
>
> (male, 49)

One of the interviewees suggested that a person who is *uprzejmy* merely tries to be nice and helpful, while somebody who is *grzeczny* is nice and helpful by nature. Another treated *grzeczność* like a character trait, which comes from the heart, while describing *uprzejmość* as something that needs to be acquired. The following respondent further portrays *życzliwość* ('kindness', 'benevolence') and *grzeczność* as related concepts, distinct from *uprzejmość*:

> *Uprzejmość* to jest dla mnie właśnie taka rzecz, która jest bardziej wyszkolona (...) a *grzeczność*, albo *życzliwość* to przychodzi z serca, wydaje mi się. *Życzliwość* to jest wręcz cecha charakteru, można by powiedzieć. Natomiast *uprzejmość* nie.
>
> (*Uprzejmość* for me is the thing that's more trained (...) while *grzeczność* or *życzliwość* comes from the heart, it seems. *Życzliwość* that's even a character trait, one could say. *Uprzejmość*, on the other hand, is not.
>
> (female, 39)

Finally, several respondents described *uprzejmość* as more formal than *grzeczność*, on the whole suggesting that *uprzejmość* has more features of negative politeness than *grzeczność*.

6.2. Polish data: impoliteness

The lexemes used to refer to impoliteness included, apart from the negated forms *nieuprzejmy*, *niegrzeczny* and *niemiły*, the noun *chamstwo* and the corresponding adjective *chamowaty*, which were described as depicting a higher degree of impoliteness than the other terms. For our participants *chamstwo* consists in behaving impolitely to those who are being polite, disregarding others and using vulgar language. Other terms used to refer to impoliteness were *niekulturalny* ('lacking culture'), *niewychowany* ('lacking breeding'), *nachalny* ('impudent', 'pushy') and *bezczelny* ('insolent'), the first two suggesting lack of manners and the latter two a disregard for the other's right to non-distraction. Hence, these terms clearly depict lack of negative politeness.

The adjectives *chamowaty* and *bezczelny* mainly appear in accounts of encounters with salespersons during communist times. The adjectives *niekulturalny* and *niewychowany*, in contrast, were used to refer to today's young people, who are different from the older generation in that they show no *szacunek* ('esteem', 'respect'), especially for older people.

As the negated forms of many of these terms suggests, impoliteness is generally viewed as the opposite of politeness, and this is also how it was conceptualised by the Polish interviewees. However, while the definitions of politeness are clearly based on the concept of approach and connectedness, those of impoliteness centre on the lack of manners and restraint, characteristic of negative impoliteness.

6.3. The changing nature of Polish politeness

When describing the changes in conversational styles after the fall of the Iron Curtain, the Polish respondents tended to link them with the changes occurring in Poland's economic and political systems.

Communist Poland was characterised by power constellations dividing its citizens into those sympathising with the government and those rejecting the system and distrusting people in authority (Richmond 1995: 23), which resulted in an opposition of *my* ('us') versus *oni* ('them') (Ronowicz 1995: 19). Basically, anybody wearing a uniform was marked as a member of the *oni* group. Paradoxically, the desolate economic situation allowed even people such as salespersons to take on a superior status. It seemed that those in power felt entitled to behave in an impolite manner and they often did. The Polish respondents all agreed that service encounters during communist times were characterised by a great degree of impoliteness.

In smaller communities, an unequal use of im/politeness was often encountered; with politeness prevailing in the conversational styles of the customers and impoliteness in that of the 'powerful' salespersons. One interviewee explained that the customers were

> ...pokorni i spokojni (...) żeby nie obrazić panią ekspedientkę, bo na drugi raz nic nie dostałbyś.
>
> (... humble and quiet (...) so as not to insult the salesperson, because next time you wouldn't get anything.)
>
> (male, 56)

In bigger cities, impoliteness was more likely to be reciprocal. Some customers became pushy when new supplies arrived and it was obvious that they would not suffice for everyone in the queue. Others did not tolerate the bossy behaviour of the salespersons and the situation escalated.

Not surprisingly, all Polish interviewees reported an increase of politeness in service encounters after the fall of the Iron Curtain as the changes in this domain are most readily observable and have resulted directly from the change of the economic system. Many linked it with the well-filled shelves in the shops, competition on the market and the requirement of keeping both the client and the management satisfied. Although this new politeness was appreciated, it was also viewed critically and described as: *neutralna* ('neutral'), *pozorna* ('apparent'), *sztuczna* ('artificial'), *nieszczera* ('insincere'), *udawana* ('faked'), *wymagana* ('required') and *szkolona* ('trained'). Several informants commented that it is only *uprzejmość* and there is nothing behind it.

> Taka wyciśnięta uprzejmość jest w sklepie, na przykład, sprzedawczyni musi być uprzejma do klienta mimo, że on jest gburem i tam ją objeżdża. To to nie jest uprzejmość, tylko to jest po prostu walka o ten job, który ma.
>
> (Such squeezed out politeness can be found in a shop, for instance, the saleswoman has to be polite to the customer, even if he's a churl and puts her down. That's not politeness, but simply the struggle to keep the job she has.)
>
> (male, 49)

Changes in the relations among status-equals that occurred since the fall of the Iron Curtain were portrayed negatively. Many informants recognised that a positive by-product of the supply shortages during communist times was that money had little value and people depended on one another. Living in a country whose government they could not rely on to provide them with the most basic goods and services and who they did not trust, they managed to make ends meet by building networks of reciprocal help, which reduced social distance and formality and created a feeling of solidarity.

> Duża serdeczność była, dlatego że była bieda i tam była wartość załatwiania. Ja byłem taki, mogłem coś załatwić i byłem ceniony w rodzinie, na przykład. I taki człowiek, który niezaradny był też był przyjmowany przez rodzinę, a bo on niezaradny, trzeba mu pomóc.
>
> (There was a lot of cordiality because people were poor and organising things had a value. I was such a guy, I could arrange something and I was valued in the family, for example. And such a person who was clumsy was also accepted by the family as he's so clumsy he needs help.)
>
> (male, 56)

Accordingly, salespersons could manipulate the supplies and use them as favours to people within their network and as a means of extending their network. Likewise, officials could speed up the procedure (e.g. of issuing a passport) upon reference to a common or influential acquaintance or when bribed. Since 1989, the sheer possibility of losing one's job, full shelves in the shops as well as political and administrative changes have deprived these people of their power (see Galasiński 2009: 217).

The descriptions of interactional styles which emerged after 1989, provided by our informants, generally indicate an increase of social distance and decrease of positive politeness. Most of them stated that people do not help each other that much anymore, they do not have time since they are busy making money and there is more competition and envy.

> Dzisiaj jak porównuję te czasy i tamte – dzisiaj nikt nie ma czasu dla ciebie, bo wszystko jest przeliczone na pieniądz. A kiedyś się liczyło zdobyć zaufanie drugiego człowieka.
>
> (Today when I'm comparing those and the present times – today nobody has time for you, because everything's converted into money. What counted back then was to gain another person's trust.)
>
> (male, 56)

At the same time, many of our informants lamented the decrease of negative politeness among young people:

> ... było kiedyś więcej uprzejmości, na przykład w środkach komunikacyjnych, że młodzież ustępowała osobom starszym miejsca.
>
> (... there was more politeness, for instance in public transport, where youngsters gave up their seats for older people.)
>
> (female, 47)
>
> A dzisiaj idź do autobusu, stara babcia może zemdleć przy tobie i nikt nie ustąpi miejsca.
>
> (And today go take a bus, an old grandmother can faint next to you and nobody will offer her a seat.)
>
> (male, 56)

These changes were blamed on the influence of the west, mostly western TV programs but also 'more tolerant' attitudes towards childrearing practices and education. On the whole, the described changes result in a stronger emphasis on the concept of withdrawal not only among strangers but, with the decreasing importance of social networks, also among people who are socially close. At the same time, the possibility of getting on in life without the help of networks has led to a greater social distance and a decrease of positive politeness.

6.4. Hungarian data: politeness

Hungarian participants associated politeness with *illemtudás* ('etiquette', 'good manners'), which should be acquired through proper upbringing and education, mainly in the family. *Illemtudás* included a wide range of verbal and non-verbal behaviours, such as appropriate forms of greetings and address, not interrupting others, observing table manners or appropriate dress on social occasions. Importantly, some participants stressed that good manners should be practiced not for their own sake but as a way of showing respect for others.

The concept that occupies a central place in the Hungarian politeness definitions is *tisztelet* ('respect'). Seven out of nine Hungarian participants used this lexeme in their definitions:

> Udvarias vagyok, amikor megtisztelem az embereket.
>
> (I am polite when I honour people.)
>
> (female, 57)

> Az alap és a lényeg a másik embernek a tisztelete és, ami megnyilvánul a viselkedésben és a verbális kommunikációban, a másik ember figyelemben vétele, előre engedem, türelmes vagyok, meghallgatom, a szavaim elfogathatóak, nem durvák, szépek, mert ő neki mondom.
>
> (The basis and the essence is respect for another human being, which reveals itself in behaviour and in communication, taking others into consideration, I allow the other to pass ahead of me, I'm patient, I listen to the other, my words are acceptable, they are not coarse, they are gentle, because I say them to that person.)
>
> (female, 60)

All Hungarian participants paid special attention to polite language use, including the use of polite formulae, as a way of paying respect to others:

> Szép hangon beszélek, megadom a tiszteletet másaknak.
>
> (I speak in a gentle voice, I give respect to others.)
>
> (female, 57)

> Szép szavakat használok, például légy szíves.
>
> (I use gentle/friendly words, for instance would you please.)
>
> (female, 57)

In another definition, the rapport-enhancing function of politeness was highlighted:

> [...] mind két fél számára jobb közérzetet biztosító dolog, kölcsönösen jó hangulatot kelt: bennem is egy kölcsönös kis öröm van, hogy a másik embernek örömet szereztem.
>
> ([...] it secures a better disposition for both parties, it mutually brings about good mood: I also experience some reciprocal joy that I have made another man/human happy.)
>
> (male, 60)

Other linguistic expressions that were given to describe *udvariasság* ('politeness') included the following:

Megbecsülés – esteem, appreciation
Előzékenység – consideration, courtesy, civility
Figyelmesség – attentiveness/considerateness
Odafigyelés – listening to, paying attention to others
Barátságosság – friendliness
Kedvesség – kindness
Készségesség – helpfulness
Közvetlenség (de nem túlzott, mert az udvariatlan) –informality (but without exaggeration, because it is impolite)
Egyenrangúság – equality

The concept of Hungarian politeness emerging from the presented definitions is difficult to classify as representative of either positive or negative politeness. It seems that *udvariasság* can be best described as an expression of deference, combining regard for others with an appropriate amount of attentiveness and involvement, the proportions being defined by the context.

6.5. Hungarian data: impoliteness

Six Hungarian participants emphasised the cultural importance of social background and upbringing in passing on politeness conventions, which is well expressed in a conventionalised Hungarian expression *Nem volt gyerek szobája* ('S/he didn't have a nursery room'), used by a Hungarian female (age 56) in her interview, and which implies that the lack of proper social background results in lack of manners. Ill-mannered behaviour could be unintentional, still, it was considered impolite and in need of commentary. For instance, a female participant (aged 60) received a very inappropriately formulated e-mail request from a student. She concluded that the student did not know any better and in her response she instructed the student how to write a polite e-mail letter to a teacher.

Impoliteness also concerned using bad language, which was *trágár* ('obscene', 'indecent', 'dirty'), *durva* ('coarse', 'rough') and *csúnya* ('ugly', 'bad'), and full of *orditozás, ordibálás* ('bawling', 'shouting') and *káromkodás, anyázás* ('swearing', 'cursing'). An impolite person was most often described as *bunkó* ('boor') and *goromba* ('rough', 'rude', 'boorish'), but also as *faragatlan* ('unpolished', 'rough'), *paraszt* ('boorish fellow', 'lout', lit. 'peasant', 'countryman') or *tahó* ('boor', 'blout').

A couple of participants defined an impolite person as being *gőgös* ('arrogant'), *törtet* ('pushy'), *rideg* ('cold', 'unfriendly'), *visszautasító* ('rejecting'), *elhárító* ('unwelcoming'), *türelmetlen* ('impatient'), *megalázó* ('humiliating') and *lenézü* ('disdainful').

Some participants attempted longer and more complex definitions:

> Goromba, érezteti a magasabb beosztását, utasít parancsokat, nem tesz hozza hogy kérem szépen, köszönöm szépen, megalázza a másikat csúnya szavakkal, gorombán, káromkodva.
>
> ([S/he's] boorish, makes you conscious of his/her position, gives orders, doesn't add 'please' and 'thank you', humiliates the other with bad language, rudely, swearing.)
>
> (male, 60)

> Nem tartja be azokat a szabályokat, mint előre engedek, nem vágok a szavadba, nem tolakszom, szép szavakat használok.
>
> ([S/he] doesn't keep such rules as allowing the other to go ahead, not interrupting, not pushing one's way forward, using gentle words.)
>
> (female, 60)

The Hungarian participants defined impoliteness (both as a form of behaviour and as a set of personal attributes) in a complex way, focusing on lacking good manners, culture or civility and displaying disrespectful behaviour towards others. Again, the role of language in generating impoliteness was very prominent.

6.6. The changing nature of Hungarian politeness

For the Hungarian participants language use in the socialist regime meant first of all the use of the politically and ideologically informed address form *elvtárs/nő* ('comrade'), which was used mainly to party members and *kartárs/nö* ('colleague', 'fellow worker'). There was also the form *pajtás* ('mate', 'pal', 'buddy'), mainly used to address pioneers – schoolchildren enrolled in the Pioneer Movement.

The use of *elvtárs/nő* and *kartárs/nő* represented a new communist etiquette, which was introduced by the communist system in order to substitute traditional ideologically alien forms like *Úr* ('Sir') or *Asszony* ('Madam'), which nevertheless continued to be used. The Hungarian participants described them as formal, but never as polite. Politeness was associated exclusively with the traditional system of address and V forms (*önözés, magázás, tetszikelés*). Many Hungarian participants reported that in the communist regime there was a decrease in the use of Hungarian V forms, which they experienced as a decrease in linguistic politeness.

The two address systems functioned simultaneously, although in different contexts. The address terms *elvtárs/nő* and *kartárs/nö* were used in many workplace and institutional settings, mainly on more official occasions and towards superiors. One of the female interviewees recollected that a school headmaster was addressed as *Igazgató elvtárs/nő*, 'Comrade Headmaster/mistress', and a director of a company was *Fekete kortárs'* colleague Fekete', instead of *igazgató úr* 'Mr director'. Those new forms of address were constant reminders of the dominant political and ideological context. The participants considered them as alien and accepted them as a necessary evil. In some workplaces, like many university departments, they were not used at all.

The simultaneous presence of the traditional and the communist system of address resulted in a struggle over language use, with the attempts to discredit the other party's linguistic behaviour and the value system behind it. For instance, one of the female participants related that one of her primary school teachers showed his disdainful attitude to the communist etiquette jokingly addressing them in class as *elvtársak és elvtársnők* 'comrades'. At the time this kind of public irony was quite risky and they, as children, realised that.

The conflict over traditional politeness forms could emerge in face-to-face interaction. A female participant who worked as a university librarian asked her superior's permission to leave earlier, using the polite V construction, *tetszikelés*: *El tetszik engedni?* ('Would [he] be kind to let me go?'). She explained that her superior's inappropriate mocking response *Eltetszem* ('I would be kind') not only ridiculed her attempt to be polite but also her middle-class background, which in the communist regime was often held up to ridicule.

Being politically on the 'right' side gave plenty of interactional power. A female participant, a researcher, reported that her subordinate technician made a teasing comment on her work. She did not react because she suspected that the technician belonged to the party nomenclature (while she did not) and thus felt free to ignore workplace hierarchy. Some other interviewees mentioned similar cases.

Three Hungarian participants reported interactions with the secret police, who used politeness and impoliteness instrumentally to intimidate the interrogated individuals and force them to become informants. This is how an interviewee describes the police officers' behaviour, who met her in a hotel lobby in 1979:

> Nem voltak udvariatlanak, sőt, azt kell mondjam, hogy akarták, hogy cigarettára gyűjtsek rá, igyak egy pohár drágább konyakot, mindenre meghívtak, hát, azt szerették volna, hogy időről időre beszélgessek velük a Jugoszláviai tanítványaimról és a munkatársaimról.
>
> (They weren't impolite, what's more, I have to say that they wanted me to light a cigarette, to drink a glass of more expensive brandy, they invited me to everything, well, what they would have liked, was that from time to time I would talk to them about my Yugoslavian students and about my colleagues.)
>
> (female, 60)

When she refused, they switched from politeness to impoliteness and threatened her that they would reveal private details of her life to her superior. When that did not work they let her go, but for years they tapped her phone.

A similar story was told by a woman who was met by the secret police in the mid-1960s. She also reported that they spoke very kindly, they smiled and showed interest. She realised it was all manipulation but acted as if she did not realise. In both cases the participants and their police interviewers were aware they were playing a game. Politeness was used strategically and genuine considerateness or respect were not expected by either side.

Interestingly, the party elites made some attempts to change their behaviour over time in order to win the acceptance of Hungarian society, mainly the Hungarian intelligentsia. As one of the male interviewees remarked: *csiszolódni kényszerültek* ('they had no choice but to improve their manners'). Although he was not a party member they recognised his professional status and they were kind and polite: *nem elvtársaztak de uraztak* ('they didn't address me as Comrade but Mr'). At the end of the interview he commented:

> A polgári vonásokat beépítették a vezetőknek a fegyvertárába.
>
> (They built middle-class features into the [party] leaders' strategic resources.)
>
> (male, 60)

The Hungarian participants reported some instances of impoliteness in service encounters. Although in Hungary the deficit economy was least noticeable, there were occasional shortages of various goods (like oranges, bananas, TV sets, washing machines) and shop assistants had control over their distribution. The choice was scarce and clients' complaints were impolitely retorted:

> Ez van, más nincs! Ha nem tetszik, menjen be a másik üzletbe, de ott is ugyan ezt kapja!
>
> (This is what we have, there's nothing else! If you don't like it, go to another store, but you will get the same there!)
>
> (female, 57)

All participants agreed that at the time of communism people sought refuge in friendships. Interpersonal relationships were considered to be deeper and much more informal than after the political change, giving many opportunities to celebrate 'solidarity' politeness. Sharing common experiences and a critical attitude towards the communist regime consolidated people and developed a feeling of togetherness that not only generated politeness but helped people jointly come out against the communist regime and bring about the long-awaited change.

The change of political regime had an impact on Hungarian politeness. The communist address terms disappeared completely and there was a return to former politeness forms such as *uram, asszonyom, hölgyem*. '(My) Sir, (My) Madam, (My) Lady', and also to *tetszikelés*.

Some participants found that shop assistants, waiters or bank clerks became much more helpful, kind and polite. They used polite formulae rarely met in the communist times such as *Miben segíthetek?* ('Can I help you') or *Mit tetszik kérni?* ('What can I do for you?'). They really wanted to make a customer feel important, so that s/he would come back another time. Still, the majority of participants felt that politeness in services was often unnatural, trained and too servile. The staff were polite mainly because there were cameras and they wanted to keep their jobs.

The interviewees also noticed the spread of informality and *t* forms in addressing and greetings (e.g. *Heló! Szevasz!*), which they often assessed as inappropriate and disrespectful. Many interviewees observed that customers became more impolite and impatient if they did not get what they wanted. It was also noticed that new rich elites were impolite, demanding and used rude, humiliating language because they believed that money put them in a privileged position. As one of the female interviewees concluded, people misunderstood democracy: they thought it was all about individual rights and forgot about obligations.

Although interpersonal relationships at work became less formal (people often used reciprocal *t* forms, even with their superiors) it did not presuppose interpersonal closeness and did not generate a feeling of security. People were no longer respected for their age and experience because the only thing that mattered was profit. One of the male participants admitted that in the old system he felt honoured at work while now he was at the mercy of a young and ruthless manager.

Politeness has also changed in the private domains of life. Many interviewees complained that friendships had become superficial and shallow as people no longer had time to cultivate relationships. Individuals had become more isolated and distant, and group ties had weakened in comparison to communist times. As one of the interviewees concluded, the tyranny of the political system was replaced by the tyranny of money.

7. Conclusion

Our study has revealed some interesting differences between Polish and Hungarian concepts of im/politeness and provided some insights into the changes concerning the understanding and use of politeness in these two countries resulting from the change of political and economic systems.

The Polish data illustrate the distinction between the concepts of positive and negative politeness and a clear preference for the former. For Polish people politeness seems to be closely linked with interest in other, in particular with willingness to help. There was hardly any reference to the use of linguistic politeness formulae in the Polish interviews. Many informants, however, stressed the importance of authenticity, while asserting that real politeness 'comes from the heart'. It should not be forced, trained or instrumental. The need for negative politeness was linked with certain sociological variables, such as age, gender and profession. Interestingly, impoliteness was associated with lack of manners, that is with lack of negative politeness. Lack of the features used to define a person's behaviour as polite, on the other hand, would rather classify him or her as inconsiderate, selfish and having a deficient character rather than manners. Nonetheless, the politeness associated with 'separateness' or 'negative politeness' has become more salient since 1989 in Poland.

The picture arising from the Hungarian data is somewhat different. The Hungarian definitions of politeness centre on the concept of respect, defined in terms of etiquette and deference as well as attentiveness and friendliness. Theoretically, the Hungarian politeness seems to combine 'withdrawal' and 'approach' orientations (Terkourafi 2007), with more prominence being given to the former. Both the definitions and the narratives of the participants' experiences emphasised the importance of polite language, particularly the use of address terms and polite formulae. Language was also essential in defining impoliteness, which, as in the Polish data, was interpreted mainly as lack of manners. The participants' narratives also threw some light on im/politeness phenomena before and after the change of regime. While certain polite language forms successfully returned to language use, the economic changes brought about the rise of superficial politeness, mainly in services, and the experience of distance in interpersonal relationships.

While the different conceptualisations of politeness in the Polish and Hungarian data are situated in a broader cultural and historical context, our participants' narratives illustrate the differences in the communist systems in the two countries. The more acute economic problems in communist Poland are reflected in the numerous narratives reporting impoliteness in service encounters in the Polish data.

Our study has also revealed the great potential of the episodic interview as a method accessing first-order concepts of politeness. It has proved very useful in eliciting the participants' metapragmatic knowledge, their experiences and assessments and in exploring crosscultural and historical differences in the understanding of im/politeness.

On the one hand, the data show a great degree of awareness of distinctions such as polite and politic behaviour (Watts 2003). On the other, they show that lay members of certain cultures, in particular Polish culture, attach little attention to verbal politeness and the use of routine formulae. Indeed, these manifestations of 'politeness' (constituting the focus of previous politeness research) are rejected if they do not come across as sincere or if they appear to be instrumental or forced.

The interviews helped to access not only aspects of im/politeness discussed in theories of politeness but also those that have been largely overlooked. Our analysis of the influence of economic factors on interactional styles seems to validate the parallel between money and politeness drawn by Werkhofer (1992). Both are viewed as symbolic media deriving their functions from values; and both were subject to devaluation in the former communist countries. The changes after the fall of the Iron Curtain made the citizens of these countries strongly aware of the relation between money and politeness, which is why the increasingly polite style characterising present service encounters is often evaluated critically as not sincere. However, most customers still prefer this superficial politeness to the authoritarian conversational styles of those who acquired them during communist times and continue using them up to the present day.

Although the small number of participants we have interviewed so far calls for some caution in drawing conclusions, our study has addressed contextual features situating politeness (and power) that have been largely neglected in previous theorising about politeness, and our data suggest that the broader socio-political context redefines cultural values and has a deep impact on politeness-related concepts and behaviour.

References

Arundale, R. (2006) 'Face as Relational and Interactional: A Communication Framework for Research on Face, Facework, and Politeness', *Journal of Politeness Research*, 2, pp. 193–216.

Bence, L. (2005) 'Politeness in Hungary: Uncertainty in a Changing Society', in L. Hickey and M. Stewart (eds), *Politeness in Europe*, Clevedon, Multilingual Matters, pp. 218–234.

Berger, T. (2006) 'Sprachliche Konzepte von "Höflichkeit" in den slavischen Sprachen im Vergleich mit ihren westeuropäischen Äquivalenten', paper read at the University of Tübingen, 12–13 May.

Blum-Kulka, S. (1992) 'The Metapragmatics of Politeness in Israeli Society', in R.J. Watts, S. Ide and K. Ehlich (eds), *Politeness in Language: Studies in History, Theory and Practice*, Berlin, Mouton de Gruyter, pp. 255–280.

Brown, P., and Levinson, S.C. (1987) *Politeness: Some Universals in Language Usage*, Cambridge, Cambridge University Press.

Brückner, A. (1970) *Słownik Etymologiczny Języka Polskiego* [*An Etymological Dictionary of the Polish Language*], Warszawa, Wiedza Powszechna.

Byrne, B. (2004) 'Qualitative Interviewing', in C. Seale (ed.), *Researching Society and Culture*, London, Sage, pp. 179–192.

Domonkosi, Á. (2002) 'Megszólítások és beszédpartnerre utaló elemek nyelvhasználatunkban' [Address Forms and Elements Referring to the Interlocutor in Hungarian Language Use], Debrecen, A debreceni Egyetem

Magyar Nyelvtudományi Intézetének Kiadványai, accessed on 10 August 2009 from: http://mek.niif.hu/01700/01715/01715.doc.
Eelen, G. (2001) *A Critique of Politeness Theories*, Manchester, St. Jerome.
Ehlich, K. (2005) 'On the Historicity of Politeness', in R.J. Watts, S. Ide and K. Ehlich (eds), *Politeness in Language: Studies in History, Theory and Practice*, Berlin, Mouton de Gruyter, pp. 71–108.
Flick, U. (2009) *An Introduction to Qualitative Research*, London, Sage.
Galasiński, D. (2009) 'Narratives of Disenfranchised Self in the Polish Post-Communist Reality', in A. Galasińska and M. Krzyżanowski (eds), *Discourse and Transformation in Central and Eastern Europe*, Basingstoke, Palgrave, pp. 204–217.
Hankiss, E. (1990) *East European Alternatives*, Oxford, Clarendon Press.
Haugh, M. (2003) 'Anticipated versus Inferred Politeness', *Multilingua*, 22, pp. 397–413.
Haugh, M. (2007) 'The Discursive Challenge to Politeness Research: An Interactional Alternative', *Journal of Politeness Research*, 3, pp. 295–317.
Huszcza, R. (2005) 'Politeness in Poland: From "Titlemania" to Grammaticalised Honorifics', in L. Hickey and M. Stewart (eds), *Politeness in Europe*, Clevedon, Multilingual Matters, pp. 218–233.
Jakubowska, E. (2003) 'Everyday Rituals in Polish and English', in K. Jaszczolt and K. Turner (eds), *Meaning through Language Contrast II*, Amsterdam, Benjamins, pp. 331–343.
Janney, R.W., and Arndt, H. (1992) 'Intracultural Tact versus Intercultural Tact', in R.J. Watts, S. Ide and K. Ehlich (eds), *Politeness in Language: Studies in History, Theory and Practice*, Berlin, Mouton de Gruyter, 21–41.
Kiss, J. (1995) *Nyelvhasználat és társadalom: Szociolingvisztikai alapfogalmak* [*Society and Parlance: Sociolinguistic Terms*], Budapest, Nemzeti Tankönyvkiadó.
Kontra M. (ed.) (2003) *Nyelv és társadalom a rendszerváltáskori Magyarországon* [*Language and Society in Hungary at the Fall of Communism*], Budapest, Osiris.
Lubecka, A. (1993) *Forms of Address in English, French and Polish: A Sociolinguistic Approach*, Kraków, SUI.
Lubecka, A. (2000) *Requests, Invitations, Apologies and Compliments in American English and Polish: A Cross-Cultural Communication Perspective*, Kraków, Księgarnia Akademicka.
Marcjanik, M. (2007) *Grzeczność w Komunikacji Językowej* [*Politeness in Linguistic Communication*], Warszawa, PWN.
Mills, S. (2003) *Gender and Politeness*, Cambridge, Cambridge University Press.
Minya, K. (2005) *Rendszerváltás – normaváltás: A magyar nyelvművelés története, elvei és vitái 1989-től napjainkig* [*A Change of Regime – A Change of Norms: The History, Principles and Disputes over Language Cultivation in Hungary from 1989 to This Day*], Budapest, Tinta Könyvkiadó.
Nyomárkay, I. (1998) 'A nyelvhasználat udvariassági stratégiái' [Politeness Strategies in Language Use], *Magyar Nyelvőr*, 122, pp. 277–284.
Ogiermann, E. (2009a) *On Apologising in Negative and Positive Politeness Cultures*, Amsterdam, Benjamins.
Ogiermann, E. (2009b) 'Politeness and In-directness across Cultures: A Comparison of English, German, Polish and Russian Requests', *Journal of Politeness Research*, 5, pp. 189–216.

Reményi, A.Á. (2001) 'Language Use and Hierarchy: A Dyadic Analysis of Address in Workplace Groups', *Review of Sociology*, 7, pp. 49–65.
Richmond, Y. (1995) *From Da to Yes. Understanding the East Europeans*, Yarmouth, Maine, Intercultural Press.
Ronowicz, E. (1995) *Poland: A Handbook in Intercultural Communication*, Sydney, Macquarie University.
Rotschild, J., and Wingfield, N.M. (2000) *Return to Diversity: A Political History of East-Central Europe Since WW2*, Oxford, Oxford University Press.
Simonyi, Z. (1911) 'Az udvariasság nyelvéről' [On the Language of Politeness], *Magyar Nyelvőr*, 40/1–8, pp. 149–155.
Suszczyńska, M. (1999) 'Apologizing in English, Polish and Hungarian: Different Languages, Different Strategies', *Journal of Pragmatics*, 31, pp. 1053–1065.
Suszczyńska, M. (2005) 'Apology Routine Formulae in Hungarian', *Acta Linguistica Hungarica*, 52, pp. 77–116.
Szili, K. (2004) *Tetté vált szavak* [*Words Turned Acts*], Budapest, Tinta Konyvkiado.
Terkourafi, M. (2007) 'Toward a Universal Notion of Face for a Universal Notion of Cooperation', in I. Kecskes and L.R. Horn (eds), *Explorations in Pragmatics*, Berlin, Mouton de Gruyter, pp. 313–344.
Tótfalusi I. (2002) *Szó-tár-lat: Szótárak és lexikonok* [*Electronic Dictionaries and Lexicons*], Budapest, Arcanum Adatbázis Kft.
Watts, R.J. (2003) *Politeness*, Cambridge, Cambridge University Press.
Werkhofer, K. (1992) 'Traditional and Modern Views: The Social Constitution and the Power of Politeness', in R. Watts, S. Ide and K. Ehlich (eds), *Politeness in Language: Studies in Its History, Theory and Practice*, Berlin, Mouton de Gruyter, pp. 155–199.
Wierzbicka, A. (1985) 'Different Cultures, Different Languages, Different Speech Acts: Polish vs. English', *Journal of Pragmatics*, 9, pp. 145–178.
Wierzbicka, A. (1991) *Cross-Cultural Pragmatics: The Semantics of Human Interaction*, Berlin, Mouton de Gruyter.
Zgółkowie, H., and Zgółkowie, T. (1992) *Językowy Savoir-Vivre* [*The Linguistic Savoir-Vivre*], Poznań, SAWW.

11
Conflict, Culture and Face

Yasuhisa Watanabe

1. Introduction

Research has shown that there are variations in what is being claimed as one's face, that is, 'positive social value' (Goffman 1967), and how the claims are made, between cultures (Brown and Levinson 1987; Ide 1989; O'Driscoll 1996). When participants from different cultural backgrounds communicate with each other, their different interactional rules must be negotiated so that potential threats to face can be avoided. Because the judgement of face threat and/or im/politeness usually lies with the receiver of such actions (Spencer-Oatey 2005), failure to observe what is 'appropriate' in the receiver's culture can threaten face (e.g. Spencer-Oatey and Xing 2003). Thus, a new set of interactional norms, which combines the different norms that participants bring to the interaction, may emerge within a group of people from different cultural backgrounds who are involved in a continuous relationship (Sunaoshi 2005).

When the relationship between participants extends over time, it is highly probable that the face claims being made in the past are accumulated and carried over by each participant to the subsequent interactions. Without such a process taking place, it is difficult to contend that one's perception of others is used to guide subsequent interactions (e.g. Fraser 1990; Arundale 2006). However, many of the current theories of face appear to be short-sighted in this regard as they only treat face as a phenomenon that becomes apparent in a single interaction (Goffman 1967; Brown and Levinson 1987; cf. Ho 1994; Mao 1994; Spencer-Oatey 2005). Furthermore, the role that third parties, namely side-participants and bystanders (Verschueren 1999), may take in upholding the face of the speaker(s) is not considered, although our actions and thoughts in real life are often influenced by those who do not participate in the interaction directly. A longitudinal analytical perspective is necessary to account for the unfolding of face in a multi-party long-term relationship. It may also provide a key to moving from the individualistic model of face to a more socially oriented one (Ervin-Tripp et al. 1995; Bargiela-Chiappini 2003).

In this chapter, Japanese–English bilingual interactional data gathered from a meeting in a Japanese company in Australia will be analysed. The interaction involves four native speakers and two non-native speakers of Japanese who hold different positions in the company. Conversation analysis and ethnographic methods are used to analyse how participants' faces are claimed and upheld in the multi-party interaction. Through this approach, the chapter will argue that (1) there are multiple methods that one can use to claim face in interaction; and (2) the responsibility for upholding face does not only rest upon direct participants interacting with each other, but on everyone present at the scene of the interaction. The following section will firstly review relevant literature, followed by the analysis of three excerpts that illustrate the perspective advocated above.

2. Background

2.1. Contrasting face in Japanese and Australian cultures

The current conceptualisation of face appears to agree that one's face is constructed through interaction by interlocutors claiming their positive social values and others ratifying such claims (Goffman 1967; Spencer-Oatey 2000; Haugh and Hinze 2003; Haugh 2009). It is widely accepted, however, that such positive social values vary between cultures. For example, showing independence is highly valued in Anglo-Saxon cultures (Bargiela-Chiappini 2003; Yabuuchi 2004; Ide 2006), while showing conformity to the group and acknowledging one's position in society seems to be more important in many Asian cultures, including in Japan (Matsumoto 1988; Ide 1989; Mao 1994; Spencer-Oatey and Xing 2003; Haugh 2005).

In Japanese–Australian intercultural communication, interlocutors need to understand these differing social values between cultures when attempting to claim face, otherwise the claim may not be ratified by other interlocutors. One may have to carefully choose which values can be used to claim face when interacting with interlocutors from different cultural backgrounds.

These various social values involved in claiming face can be identified by applying Schwartz's framework of value constructs (Schwartz 1992). Schwartz (1992) lists 11 value constructs that motivate people to behave in certain ways: self-direction, stimulation, hedonism, achievement, power, security, conformity, tradition, spirituality, benevolence and universalism (see Table 1). Spencer-Oatey (2005, 2007) argues that these value constructs may help identify which of the attributes are more likely to cause face threat when contrasted with projected positive image of self. Likewise, the framework can also be used to analyse which value constructs are deemed as more influential in a given culture and are strategically deployed to claim face and/or avoid loss of face in a given situation. For example, in Japanese culture people are usually expected to know their place and act accordingly (Ide 1989, 2006; Haugh 2005, 2007). Observing this tradition and conforming to it may be valued more highly than showing one's superior ability to achieve something independently. Thus, when attempting to claim face with Japanese audiences, one may strategically try not to act 'out of line' rather than actively appeal to one's achievements.

Table 1 Schwartz's value constructs and their associated qualities (based on Schwartz 1992)

Value construct	Explanation
Self-direction	Independent thought and action – choosing, creating, exploring
Stimulation	Excitement, novelty and challenge in life
Hedonism	Pleasure and sensuous gratification for oneself
Achievement	Personal success through demonstrating competence according to social standards
Power	Attainment of social status and prestige, control or dominance over people and resources
Security	Safety, harmony and stability of society, relationship and self
Conformity	Restraint of actions, inclinations and impulses likely to upset or harm others and violate social expectations or norms
Tradition	Respect, commitment and acceptance of the customs and ideas that one's culture or religion imposes on the individual
Spirituality	Meaning and inner harmony through the transcendence of everyday reality
Benevolence	Preservation and enhancement of the welfare of people with whom one is in frequent personal contact
Universalism	Understanding, appreciation, tolerance and protection for the welfare of *all* people and for nature

Even though only one value construct may be claimed as one's face at any given time, many face claims in respect of different value constructs can be accumulated over time. As the relationship between two interlocutors extends over time, they may establish an idea of what the other interlocutor is like and interact accordingly within the bounds of what they feel comfortable with (Arundale 2006). According to empirical findings discussed in Haugh and Hinze (2003), it is also conceivable that interlocutors ratify how much of other attributes, such as benevolence and universalism (Schwartz 1992), the other party has through observation over time, and uphold such face in subsequent interactions.[1] Although much research is limited to the analysis of single instances of interaction, analysis should be extended over a longer period of time to account for 'accumulation of face' and its effect on potential face threat (Spencer-Oatey 2005).

2.2. Considering the role of third parties

By extending this line of argument to the role that third parties play in a multi-party interaction, we must also consider the way they influence, and are influenced by it.

Firstly, a side-participant can still ratify the face claim made by one of the participants although he/she may not verbally express such ratification. As argued by Clark and Carlson (1982), when a speaker requests someone to 'come to the other room' with the speaker, the utterance is not only relevant to the direct addressee but also to the side-participants to the interaction. This is because side-participants understand that they are not invited (Clark and Carlson 1982). Likewise, it can be hypothesised that side-participants understand what the speaker claims as his/her face and use it to establish interactional norms in subsequent interactions.

Secondly, the course of interaction can be influenced by the actions, or by the mere presence, of side-participants. This is evident when an interaction is suddenly 'overshadowed' by a bystander. For example, it is often observed that school-age children may talk with friends freely until they notice their parents are listening in to their interaction. The children may change the topic of interaction in order to avoid parents finding out something that they have done. By doing so, children may avoid potential loss of their face by preventing their parents thinking less of them (Haugh and Hinze 2003) and potential punishment they may receive in subsequent interactions.[2]

Despite such possibilities, research on face has tended to ignore the role of third parties in an interaction. The analysis in this chapter attempts to explore third-party influences evident in a multi-party interaction.

3. Setting the (cultural) scene

The group under study in this chapter is a company in Australia, called company S. It is established and owned by a Japanese president and employs both Japanese workers, two males and six females, and two male non-Japanese workers; one in a management position and another his subordinate. Because company S operates in Australia, the Japanese informants from the company reported that the interactional norms in the company are influenced more by the Australian than the Japanese norms. However, both non-Japanese informants reported that the interactional norms in the company are more Japanese compared to those of other Australian companies. From my observation it seems that they have developed their own norms of interaction that are different from either purely Japanese or Australian ones.

The term 'culture' is used in this chapter to refer to a common set of meanings, values and practices shared by a group of people, not necessarily identified by national or geographical boundaries. There are subgroups within the group bounded by geography, who may share more of the same meanings and values than others (Takiura 2008). For example, a group of people working for the same company may share more common culture among them, which may emerge as a 'corporate culture'. If a subgroup involves people of different nationalities and/or upbringings it can arguably create an intercultural communication situation. When individuals in such groups interact with each other over an extended period of time they may start to develop their own rules of communication, which can be classified as 'the third place'; a set of communication rules that are neither their own (first place) nor of the interlocutors' (second place) (Lo Bianco et al. 1999). The third place is not in the figurative middle between first and second place, but may inherit more of one culture than the other in terms of language choice and sociolinguistic features. It may even include an enhancement of what the interlocutors share as their common knowledge in order to better accomplish communicative tasks within the group. The result of the creation of the third place can, ethnographically speaking, be defined as a 'culture'. In the group under study, the language of interaction switched between Japanese and English frequently depending on the intended goal of the utterances and language ability of the interlocutors. This phenomenon is not commonly observed in either mono-cultural Japanese or Australian interactions.

In many corporate cultures, that is intra-company business communication situations, there are interlocutors who occupy various positions within the company, such as president and manager, or play various roles, such as organising the production of goods and managing financial matters. It can be argued that these positions and roles are the result of face being claimed in past interactions among them because one must fulfil certain criteria to be promoted. Therefore such positions and roles and faces being accumulated through long-term relationships may overlap and are reflected in the interactions between the employees of a company. For example, a superior must act appropriately in order to uphold the face being claimed in the past. The subordinates may need to respect the face their superior claimed in the past and behave accordingly. Spencer-Oatey's labels 'social identity face' and 'behavioural expectation' (Spencer-Oatey 2005) may not be enough to account fully for actions adopted by subordinates in a multi-party interaction. In the presence of the third party subordinates need to show that they understand their positions in the culture (Ide 2006) and if necessary, sacrifice their own face, that is project themselves as less than they are capable of, in order not to interfere with the face of the superior (*kao wo tsubusanai*, 'not to crumble the other's face') (Haugh and Watanabe 2009). Although the act of 'face sacrifice' is common in some Asian cultures (e.g. Ervin-Tripp et al. 1995), it is yet to be noted in interactional data being studied in face and politeness research. By analysing a multi-party interaction, this chapter attempts to show the need for considering the influence of a third party on the faces of the participants which are being negotiated in the interaction.

4. Methodology

The data for this study was collected in 2004 over a ten-month period as part of a larger study on business communication in Japanese by non-native speakers of Japanese. The interaction data used in this chapter was recorded at a presentation meeting held at company S. Ethnographic observation and follow-up interviews with each of the key participants will also be used in the analysis.

The company exports processed food items to Japan. In order to produce a new product the company must (1) research the market for competition, (2) obtain the raw materials and process them, (3) package and label the product, (4) create an appropriate advertising and promotional package, and (5) ship the finished product to Japan. The meeting described in this chapter is what the participants call a 'first-stage' meeting, where the draft concept for all of the above process is developed (comparing the competitors' products, outlining the ideas for marketing, label and packaging ideas and costing) and presented to the rest of the company to seek approval from the company president. Once the 'first stage' is complete, the product moves on to the 'second stage', where the outcome of the first stage is further developed and fine-tuned, for example designing the actual marketing materials to be used by the Japanese importer and organising shipping processes.

There were six members of the company present at the meeting, of whom two were non-native speakers of Japanese. The key participants to the meeting were Carl (Australian of Indonesian origin who spoke English as his second language, responsible for the first stage), Takashi (President of the company, responsible for approving the work done in the first stage), Matthew (Australian, direct superior of Carl, responsible for the second stage), Ken (direct superior of Matthew and Carl, responsible for Carl's work currently presented) and Naoko (General Manager).[3] The purpose of the meeting was for Carl to (1) update everyone in the company on the development of marketing and production plans for the prune juice product and to attain the approval of the President, Takashi, and (2) introduce the new propolis product that the company will be selling in the near future. Therefore, most of the interaction in the meeting was held between Carl and Takashi. The meeting went on for one and a half hours. Although the meeting started with Carl's presentation in English, the questions that followed were asked and answered mainly in Japanese. The tenor of the meeting, such as the preconceived notion of interaction, was Japanese, although Japanese participants accommodated towards the language proficiency of non-native speakers.

The meeting, held in July 2004, was recorded by a video camera and several microphones placed within the room where the meeting was held to capture the verbal interaction as well as non-verbal aspects. During this process the researcher was not present in order to eliminate the effects of his physical presence in the room. After the meeting, follow-up interviews were organised with the participants during which the video recording of the meeting was used to elicit their reactions to the interaction.

Three excerpts from the meeting will be used in the next section to illustrate how a subordinate attempts to claim his face, how a superior's face is interactionally upheld and how side-participants contribute to the interaction. Conversation analysis is applied to identify various face negotiation features (cf. facework) as projected and perceived by interlocutors in terms of various value constructs of face (Schwartz 1992;

Spencer-Oatey 2007). Multi-modal transcription is used to include non-verbal aspects of the interaction (see conventions in Appendix 1).

5. Data analysis and discussion

Interviews with participants to the study revealed that in doing business the tasks given to each employee must be completed to a satisfactory level or the company may fail to survive in the business environment. Thus, if a junior member of the company fails to complete his/her tasks appropriately, his/her superior may impose required standards by asking for the tasks to be redone in a satisfactory manner. This can be perceived as a threat to the subordinate's face because his/her attempts to claim face on his/her achievement is denied. In such circumstances, it appears that subordinates may attempt to claim face on other value constructs, as presented by Schwartz (1982), in order to maintain the level of face already attained.

One such example is analysed in Excerpt 1. In this excerpt, Carl attempts to show the audience that he is capable of doing his tasks satisfactorily, thus claiming his face based on the value construct 'achievement' (Schwartz 1992). However, the company President, Takashi, blocks this attempt by commenting that his work 'missed the point'. Upon hearing this, Carl changes his strategy and shows obedience to the President by listening to his instruction carefully, thus enhancing his face according to the value constructs 'conformity' and 'security' (Schwartz 1992).

Excerpt 1. Presentation meeting: 0:22:00~

Carl is responding to a question from Ken to clarify the difference between the proposed new product and a French prune juice already on the Japanese market. He goes on to point out that the competitor's claim that it is 100 % juice is actually incorrect.

216	C:	okay (.) this is like the back label samples (0.7)	((Pulls out a photocopy of the back label of the competing product and places it on the table for others to see)) ((T and M lean over to see the photocopied label))
217		<this is like just black and white> ((quick & quietly))	((M straightens up, arms crossed, still looking at the label))

218	and in here they mention that	((T leans back))
219	*sutoreeto hyaku paasento juusu desu* 'It is 100 percent straight juice'	((C points to the label with his left index finger as he reads from the label))
220	in here	((C stands up straight, looks around and right hand is swishing pencil downwards))
221	I will mention that it is (0.5)	((C looks down to his notebook on his right))
222	wrong?	((C swishes pencil downward, looks up to T, both hands lift up))
223	'cause like (.) you can't get 100 per cent straight juice,	((picks up the competitor's bottle with right hand, left hand moves towards the bottle while talking to the audience))
224	out of the prunes,	((left hand swished twice, turns face to left)) ((T puts down his pen, eyes off C and sits back on his chair))
225	like you have to add waters,	((bottle to left hand, looks around, straight posture, right hand swished numerous times for emphasis))
226	because prune itself is very thick,	((holding right hand up in front, fingers closed together, looks around at the audience and swishes hands numerous times))
227	it only contains 20 percent of moisture	
228	and I did asked them (.) to the manufacturer (.)	((both hands tumble in front, then right hand points up with pencil))
229	to the ((Company)) V (.)	((puts his hand on the bottle))
230	like whether do you know	((lifts the sample bottle up with left hand and looks at it))

231		((Product)) E,	(looks up to the audience))
232		what about the manufacturing process chart and everything,	((bottle to the right hand, moves it and his left hand in front of his chest))
233	T:	hmm::	((T nods once))
234	C:	and they said no, they are all the same,	((C starts to smile a little))
235	T:	hmm	((T starts to nod))
236	C:	and they can't claim the straight juice=	((C arms opened))
237	T:	=any other point	((C looks at T, stunned, mouth opened, holding the bottle with both hands))
238	C:	ah::::m other point from that	((looks up, hand movement becomes bigger)),
239		they are using the hybrids (.) prunes, so they have	((looks at T))
240		selected (.) the prunes	((right hand swishes once))
241	T:	hmm	((T nods once))
242	C:	no- no- not any other, not any prunes	((shakes head left-right))
243		(2.0)	((C stops all movements))
244	T:	you missed the point (1.2)	((looks at C, tilts head))
245		you have to compare the (.) fibre	((lift his right hand to left side))
246	C:	um hm?=	((stays still))
247	T:	=and fib[re,	((moves right hand from left to right))
248	C:	[un ummm	
249	T:	and (.) the sodium, s[odium	((moves right hand from left to right))

250	C:	[ah ok	
251	T:	they are the nutritions	((puts hand down))
252	C:	ah, ok=	((puts bottle down, picks up notes))
253	T:	=did you?= [did you do that?	
254	C:	=ah [no, no I didn't [I-	((looking at T, arranging bottles on the table with mouth opened))
255	T:	[*sore* important point *da ro Caaru* 'That is an important point, Carl'	
256	C:	ah (.) *sou des-*, ye= 'Ah righ-, ye-'	((looks down))
257	T:	=*U::::n* 'Yeah'	

During the interview, Carl said that he wanted to prove to the rest of the company that he could do his job well. The way he presents himself in lines 216–232 seem to reflect that desire. He points out that the competitor's claim is inaccurate and company S can use it to its advantage, citing scientific evidence to support their case. By explaining this, Carl is trying to claim his face on achievement, that he has done his job by finding a point that the company can use to market the new prune juice. Even when Takashi responds by asking whether he has any other points to make (line 237), Carl manages to come up with another comment in an attempt to maintain his face claim on achievement. However, his face claim is nullified by Takashi's comment in line 244, 'you missed the point'. As a result of this comment, Carl looks stunned and sits still, possibly feeling that his attempt to claim face on achievement has failed.

The interaction continues between Takashi and Carl in lines 245–252 to jointly establish what Carl should have done as a part of his task, which is to find out the nutritional content of the prune juice. Takashi then asks Carl what he has done (line 253), to which Carl responds negatively (line 254), further damaging his face claim on achievement. However, Carl agrees with what he is told to do (line 256) and even picks up his notebook and starts taking notes (line 252). In the interview he confirmed that he did so because he realised it was necessary to become a part of the company. This change of strategy might not have been a conscious decision, but by showing his obedience to Takashi, Carl claimed his face on value constructs 'conformity' and 'security' (Schwartz 1992).[4] Interviews with his superiors confirmed that his taking notes assured them that Carl will do what he was told to do, thus ratifying his adherence to the aforementioned value constructs. Despite losing his face as a competent achiever, Carl has managed to gain face in other value areas.

A similar strategy was observed when a subordinate's face claim almost caused his/her superior to lose face. Excerpt 2 below illustrates the instance when the President failed to identify the taste of the new product to be introduced to the market. Because the President had established the company by exporting food items to Japan, his *kao* in Japanese culture involves superior knowledge of the items he exports (Haugh 2005). Therefore, not being able to identify his own product can damage his *kao*, thus losing face in front of his employees. To avoid this, Carl sacrifices his own face so that Takashi's face continues to occupy a higher position than Carl's face.

Excerpt 2. Presentation meeting: 0:59:20~

Carl introduces to Takashi a new propolis product that the company is going to sell and invites him to taste it.

1066	C:	ah, and the taste, this is too little but,	((lifts the cup and shakes it a little))
1067		*chotto nonde mitai desu ka.* 'do you want to try it?'	((straightens his back and offers the cup to T))
1068		(0.5)	((T leans over and reaches for the cup with left hand))
1069	C:	do you like propolis?	((C pulls the cup back to himself))
1070		(.)	((T tries to take the cup from C))
1071	K:	*kore zehi nonde mite kudasai* 'I would really like you to try this.'	((off screen))

1072	C:	*a: zehi nonde mite kudasai* 'Ah, I would really like you to try this.'	((C lets go of the cup))
1073		(8.0)	((T tries to take a sip, but moves the cup away from his mouth slightly and smells it, then takes a sip slowly)) ((after taking a sip, moves the cup away from his mouth and squints his eyes several times. Makes no verbal response))
1074	C:	*are?* 'Huh?'	((shrugs his head, then smiles))
1075		(4.0)	
1076	T:	*ama:i* 'It's swee:::t.'	((slowly faces others and smiles))
1077	All:	*hhhhhh=*	((laughter))
1078	T:	*=uso* 'I lied.'	((shakes his head))
1079		*iya nannimo aji shinai* (.) no taste= 'No I don't taste anything. No taste.'	((turns to C))
1080	C:	=↑no↓ taste (.) not even wate- not not even propolis	((T takes another sip)) ((C points at the bottle))
1081		oh ↑may↓be too much water	((lighter tone))
1082		(2.0)	((T long shrug))
1083	T:	*<anmari aji ga shinai ne>* 'It doesn't taste much.'	((to C, quickly))
1084	C:	ah maybe too much water but (.) ah (.)	((right hand trying to reach for the cup, then shrugs))
1085		*<chotto shippai shita>=* '[I] made a mistake.'	((quickly))

1086	T:	=*shi(h)ppai shita*:?= '[You] made a mistake?'	((laughingly))
1087	All:	=*hhhh* ((laughter))	

Prior to this excerpt, Carl has been demonstrating that the new product dissolves in water quicker than other products on the market by lining up four cups in front of him and dropping a few drops of each product in separate cups. Carl first offers Takashi to taste the propolis dissolved in water (line 1066–1067), because the taste of the product itself is another sales point that Carl is going to discuss. Takashi tastes what he is offered (line 1073) but is not able to identify the flavour of the product. As a result, he employs humour in an attempt to mitigate the impact of the failure (line 1076). He turns to the others and jokingly says *ama:i* ('it's sweet') (line 1076). This is received with laughter (line 1077), indicating that everyone present took this utterance as humorous (Holmes 2000). Takashi seems to minimise damage to his face in the area of achievement and gain in the area of hedonism and universalism (Schwartz 1992) by using humour to maintain harmony in the group.

Takashi's real answer comes in line 1079 when he turns to Carl and declares that he failed to taste the flavour of the product. Even after the second attempt at tasting Takashi returns a negative response (line 1083). This can be a potentially face-threatening situation for Takashi as he fails to uphold his face as the President.

However, when Takashi's loss of face becomes dangerously salient, Carl immediately offers a reason for Takashi not being able to taste the product – that he has put 'too much water' in (lines 1081 and 1084) and that he has made a mistake. By taking the blame for it, Carl actively sacrificed his 'positive social value' as a competent individual. However, as a result, he avoided further loss of his boss's face in front of his employees (*kao o tsubusanai*), thus maintaining the social hierarchy within the group (Haugh 2005).

What must be considered in this situation is the role that the third party to this interaction plays. If there were no side-participants to this interaction, both Carl and Takashi would not have needed to adopt a strategy to mitigate the loss of their faces. Takashi could have told Carl that he had failed to do his task satisfactorily and Carl could have maintained that he had done nothing wrong. On the contrary, doing so before an audience could imply that they were not performing the roles demanded by the 'culture' they operated in: Takashi as the President and

Carl as a subordinate. To avoid such perception by the third party, displaying discernment (or *wakimae*) to maintain or sacrifice face was necessary (Ide 2006).

When the side-participants are included in the equation, although on the surface it appears that Carl has lost his face because he admitted to making a mistake, in the side-participants' eyes, Carl has gained face in other value constructs, namely conformity and benevolence (Schwartz 1992). The fact that his admission is received with laughter (lines 1086–87) also shows that it was intended as a means of building solidarity within the group (e.g. Holmes 2000), which includes side-participants. This attests to the success of Carl's strategy in maintaining his face with the side-participants. It also leaves the interaction open for Takashi to reclaim his face with the side-participants by trying to taste the product again. In fact, two turns later, Takashi asks Carl to add more propolis to his cup so that he can taste it.

Side-participants are also called upon when upholding the faces of the direct interlocutors. Excerpt 3 illustrates two such situations, where Takashi asks for help from a third party when he struggles to come up with a word while explaining to Carl what he expects from him.

Excerpt 3. Presentation meeting: 0:28:30~

Takashi tells Carl what information is to be included in the promotional package.

382	T:	*soreto*: PR *pointo de ore ga zettai tsukete hoshii no wa* 'And, what I really want you to include in your PR point is,'	((looking down to his notes))
383		*ano* region, where the prunes from 'ahm, the region, where the prune is from.'	((looks at C)) ((C blinks))
384		*kore wa* biggest (.) one of biggest sales point *desho* 'This is the biggest, one of the biggest sales points, isn't it?'	((a nod to emphasise 'biggest')) ((C nods and starts taking notes))
385	C:	*un* 'Yeah'	

386	T:	*furansu kara kimashita*(.) 'It came from France.'	((gazes at C))
387		*<shikamo>* furansu *no doko dakke kore a-* [*agen* 'And where is this in France, Agen?'	((looks at M))
388	C:	[*agen* 'Agen'	((looks up to T))
389	T:	*agen da yo ne,* 'It is Agen, isn't it?'	((nods to M))
390		*agen kara kita* 'It came from Agen.'	((faces C))
391		*what agen* 'What is Agen?'	((opens his arms, shakes his body))
392	C:	*un* 'Yeah'	((nods))
393	T:	Japanese people *sono hou ga ureshiku nai?* 'Don't Japanese people feel happy that way?'	((arms come around to the front of his chest))
394		*age*[*n tte nani?* 'What is Agen?'	((big nods twice as he starts))
395	C:	[*a*: *a*: *a*: 'Ah, ah, ah'	((smiles, nods as he speaks))
396	T:	*<soshitara> agen tte iu no wa sa*, if you research about Agen, 'Then Agen is, if you research about Agen,'	((shifts his body to left, right hand starts to move in a circular motion from the lower end))
397	C:	*un* 'Yeah'	((nods numerous times))
398	T:	*soshitara mou agen tte iu no wa sa* 'Then it is, the place called Agen is,'	((keeps drawing a circle in the air, stops at the top of the circle))

399		*e:to* English *de nante iu? chokkei -tte* 'How do we say "chokkei" (diameter) in English?'	((faces M, both arms opens wide to show 'diameter'))
400	M:	region?	((facial expression of uncertainty))
401	T:	*chokkei* ((articulates clearer)) for *en no=* ' "chokkei" (diameter), of a circle'	((maintains the same posture, then draws a circle in the air with his right arm))
402	N:	=*a::* diameter 'Ah, diameter'	((from off screen. M, T, C all face N's direction))
403	T:	dia[meter	((turns to C, arms still opened wide))
404	C:	[diameter ((very softly))	((Turns to T))
405	M:	*a:::* diameter *ne* 'Ah:::, you mean diameter.'	((mouth opened, blank face))
406	T:	*no* thirty *kiromeetoru* by 'of 30 kilometres by'	((both arms opened wide horizontally from the centre))
407		thirty *kiromeetoru,* '30 kilometres,'	((both arms move vertically from the centre))
408		*kore ga ze::nbu* prune tree *nan da yo* 'that is a::ll prune tree.'	((draws a circle again with right arm, then puts the hand down at the end of the utterance))
409	C:	*sou nan desu ka* 'Is that right…'	((nods several times))

The company's website as well as other marketing and promotional materials for other products that company S sells, gathered as a part of the ethnographic study, reveals that the information on the origins of the ingredient for their products is an important branding factor. While Takashi attempts to tell Carl that such information must be included in the promotional materials, he struggles a little in recalling where the prunes are produced. He foresees the problem in line 387 and, from his non-verbal cues, he seems to be asking Matthew for the information on which region of France the prunes come from. This call for help is answered by Carl in line 388, which comes at the same time as Takashi's own recollection. Then in line 389, Takashi confirms the information with Matthew, despite hearing the repair from Carl.

Takashi then goes on to make his point to Carl on why such information should be included in the promotional package using rhetorical questions (lines 391 and 394) and explaining the value of such information to the Japanese consumers (line 393). In the process, Takashi comes across another term that he does not know. He starts to make his point in line 396 while drawing a circle in the air, but repeats the same utterance in line 398, suggesting he is not able to come up with the term in English. Takashi then asks Matthew for the term in English (line 399). In response to this, Matthew provides a translation ('region', line 400), but this is rejected by Takashi in line 401 when he repeats the same word *chokkei* with a clearer pronunciation, giving Matthew another chance to supply an alternative translation. Naoko takes the floor in line 402 to come up with the correct translation. Upon hearing this, Takashi, Carl and Matthew all focus their attention on Naoko and repeat the word (lines 403–405). After receiving this information, Takashi continues with his explanation as to why this information should be included (lines 406–408) by adding that the whole area is covered with prune trees, as if the previous requests for information had not been made.

What appears to be important in this excerpt is that side-participants are also responsible for upholding the face of the direct interlocutors. It is obvious from the non-verbal behaviour of Takashi that he wanted to be helped by side-participants, namely Matthew and Naoko, rather than Carl (lines 387, 389, 399 and 401). This is especially evident in line 389 when Takashi deliberately backchannels Matthew even when the information is supplied by Carl. Although Takashi did not comment on this incident when interviewed, one possible explanation is that if Takashi accepted the information supplied by Carl, it could indicate that the subordinate knows more than President, thus potentially causing Carl to think less of Takashi (Haugh and Hinze 2003). Because this could be a threat to his face, Takashi deliberately avoided help from Carl while eliciting it from side-participants. As the side-participants did not object to being called upon they arguably supported Takashi's face by not emphasising his weakness.

6. Conclusion

The analysis in this chapter highlights two aspects of face in interaction that previous research had neglected, namely the strategies that the interlocutors can adopt to enhance their face in interaction and the need to include third parties in the analysis of face in a multi-party interaction. As shown through the first and second excerpts, there are various 'positive social values' that one can claim depending on the context and underlying culture of the group. Schwartz's (1992) framework of value constructs can be useful in identifying which value construct is being emphasised to claim one's face in different situations. The perspectives of the side-participants can also explain why one chooses to enhance and/or sacrifice one's face in order to save that of another interlocutor. As shown through the second and third excerpt, even when it appears that one has lost one's face, side-participants may take it as a display of benevolence and ratify it as one's face on the basis of conformity to cultural norms. This advantage can then be used in the evaluation of face in subsequent interactions.

In shifting the understanding of face as located within a group of people rather than between two interlocutors, the perspectives of participant third-parties must be included.

Appendix 1: Transcription Conventions

[	overlap
=	latching
(0.0)	elapsed time in silence by tenth of seconds
(.)	a short 'gap' within or between utterances
word	stress, via a pitch and/or amplitude
::	prolongation of the immediately prior sound; multiple colons indicate a more prolonged sound
-	a cut-off
.	a stopping fall in tone
,	a continuing intonation
?	a rising intonation
↑↓	marked shifts into higher or lower pitch in the utterance
<>	an utterance or utterance-part indicate speeding up
w(h)ord	breathiness, as in laughter, crying, etc.
(( ))	transcriber's description, including non-verbal aspects of the interaction

Translations of Japanese utterances are marked with 'single-quotation marks'.

In the translation, some words may be inserted in English due to the differences in syntactic structures between Japanese and English. Such words are marked with [square brackets].

Notes

1. Such accumulation of ratified face that other people have is almost synonymous to the Japanese emic notion of face, *kao* or 'place one stands' (Haugh 2005).
2. Such influences have been explained as a result of power held by the parent over children (Raven 1993), but no connection to face research has been made outside of Asian culture.
3. Pseudonyms are used for all the participants, as well as for the names of other firms and products mentioned in the course of the meeting.
4. Other value constructs such as 'self-direction' and 'tradition' may have been claimed as well.

References

Arundale, R. (2006) 'Face as Relational and Interactional: A Communication Framework for Research on Face, Facework, and Politeness', *Journal of Politeness Research*, 2/2, pp. 193–216.

Bargiela-Chiappini, F. (2003) 'Face and Politeness: New (Insights) for (Old) Concepts', *Journal of Pragmatics*, 35/10–11, pp. 1453–1469.

Brown, P., and Levinson, S. (1987) *Politeness: Some Universals in Language Usage*, Cambridge, Cambridge University Press.

Clark, H.H., and Carlson, T.B. (1982) 'Hearers and Speech Acts', *Language*, 58/2, pp. 332–373.

Ervin-Tripp, S., Nakamura, K., and Guo, J. (1995) 'Shifting Face from Asia to Europe', in M. Shibatani and S. Thompson (eds), *Essays in Semantics and Pragmatics: Essays in Honour of Charles J. Fillmore*, Amsterdam, John Benjamins, pp. 43–71.

Fraser, B. (1990) 'Perspectives on Politeness', *Journal of Pragmatics*, 14, pp. 219–236.

Goffman, E. (1967) *Interaction Ritual: Essays on Face-to-Face Behavior*, New York, Pantheon Books.

Haugh, M. (2005) 'The Importance of "Place" in Japanese Politeness: Implications for Cross-Cultural and Intercultural Analyses', *Intercultural Pragmatics*, 2/1, pp. 41–68.

Haugh, M. (2007) 'Emic Conceptualisations of (Im)politeness and Face in Japanese: Implications for the Discursive Negotiation of Second Language Learner Identities', *Journal of Pragmatics*, 39/4, pp. 657–680.

Haugh, M. (2009) 'Face and Interaction', in F. Bargiela-Chiappini and M. Haugh (eds), *Face, Communication and Social Interaction*, London, Equinox, pp. 1–30.

Haugh, M., and Hinze, C. (2003) 'A Metalinguistic Approach to Deconstructing the Concepts of "Face" and "Politeness" in Chinese, English and Japanese', *Journal of Pragmatics*, 35/10–11, pp. 1581–1611.

Haugh, M., and Watanabe, Y. (2009) 'Analysing Japanese Face-in-Interaction', in F. Bargiela-Chiappini and M. Haugh (eds), *Face, Communication and Social Interaction*, London, Equinox, pp. 78–95.

Ho, D.Y.-F. (1994) 'Face Dynamics: From Conceptualization to Measurement', in S. Ting-Toomey (ed.), *The Challenge of Facework*, New York, State University of New York Press, pp. 269–286.

Holmes, J. (2000) 'Politeness, Power and Provocation: How Humour Functions in the Workplace', *Discourse Studies*, 2, pp. 159–185.

Ide, S. (1989) 'Formal Forms and Discernment: Two Neglected Aspects of Universals of Linguistic Politeness', *Multilingua*, 8/2–3, pp. 223–248.

Ide, S. (2006) *Wakimae no goyoron* [*The Pragmatics of Wakimae*], Tokyo, Taishukan shoten.

Lo Bianco, J., Liddicoat, A., and Crozet, C. (1999) *Striving for the Third Place*, Melbourne, Language Australia.

Mao, L. (1994) 'Beyond Politeness Theory: "Face" Revisited and Renewed', *Journal of Pragmatics*, 21, pp. 451–486.

Matsumoto, Y. (1988) 'Reexamination of the Universality of Face: Politeness Phenomena in Japanese', *Journal of Pragmatics*, 12, pp. 403–426.

O'Driscoll, J. (1996) 'About Face: A Defence and Elaboration of Universal Dualism', *Journal of Pragmatics*, 25/1, pp. 1–32.

Raven, B.H. (1993) 'The Bases of Power: Origins and Recent Development', *Journal of Social Issues*, 49/4, pp. 227–251.

Schwartz, S.H. (1992) 'Universals in the Content and Structure of Values: Theoretical Advances and Empirical Tests in 20 Countries', *Advances in Experimental Social Psychology*, 25, pp. 1–65.

Spencer-Oatey, H. (2000) 'Rapport Management: A Framework for Analysis', in H. Spencer-Oatey (ed.), *Culturally Speaking: Managing Rapport through Talk across Cultures*, London, Continuum, pp. 11–46.

Spencer-Oatey, H. (2005) '(Im)politeness, Face and Perceptions of Rapport: Unpackaging Their Bases and Interrelationships' *Journal of Politeness Research*, 1/1, pp. 95–120.

Spencer-Oatey, H. (2007) 'Theories of Identity and the Analysis of Face', *Journal of Pragmatics*, 39/4, pp. 639–656.

Spencer-Oatey, H., and Xing, J. (2003) 'Managing Rapport in Intercultural Business Interactions: A Comparison of Two Chinese-British Welcome Meetings', *Journal of Intercultural Studies*, 24/1, pp. 33–46.

Sunaoshi, Y. (2005) 'Historical Context and Intercultural Communication: Interactions between Japanese and American Factory Workers in the American South', *Language in Society*, 34/2, pp. 185–217.

Takiura, M. (2008) *Poraitonesu Nyuumon* [*Introduction to Politeness*], Tokyo, Kenkyusha.

Verschueren, J. (1999) *Understanding Pragmatics*, London, Arnold.

Yabuuchi, A. (2004) 'Face in Chinese, Japanese, and U.S. American Cultures', *Journal of Asian Pacific Communication*, 14/2, pp. 261–297.

12
Cultural Variability in Face Interpretation and Management

Ewa Bogdanowska-Jakubowska

1. Introduction

Face is a sociocultural construct. It is created by the participation of other people during social interaction and shaped in terms of social values (Goffman 1967; Lim 1994). Goffman (1967: 5) defines face as "the positive social value a person effectively claims for himself" and "an image of self delineated in terms of approved social attributes". In other words, face is a complex image of self which is socially constructed and determined by a system of cultural values. In a similar vein, Bargiela-Chiappini describes face in the *Encyclopedia of Languages and Linguistics* (2006: 423):

> as a bridging concept between interpersonal interaction and social order in the sense that face, at the micro-level of verbal and nonverbal behaviour, encapsulates and dynamically displays the manifestations of (macro-level) cultural values.

Thus, although public self-image (face) and the social need to orient oneself to it in interaction are universal, face also has culture-specific constituents. The basic universal desire inherent in human nature "for a 'good' face acquires different interpretations in different cultures, because the constituents of 'good' are culturally determined" (O'Driscoll 1996: 4); thus there are differences in the content of face (Mao 1994). Moral rules, hierarchies of values and social organization are specific to particular cultures and as a consequence, the image of self created on their basis must also differ.

In this chapter I am going to present a model of face which seeks to explain the cultural variability of face in its interpretation and management. According to this model, face is a multi-faceted construct which can be analysed at different interrelated levels.

2. Face and interaction

Goffman claims that there is a close relationship between the process of creation of the self and the context of interaction. Depending on the context, individuals try to create and maintain their face, adjusting their behaviour to the roles they play and to the expectations of the other people they are interacting with. During social interaction an individual presents an image of self which is intended to be supported by the judgements of other participants. Thus, face is determined by the participation of others and earned through social interaction (Goffman 1967; Ho 1994; Mao 1994).

For Goffman, face is a public property. It is not part of the person's body, but something that is "located in the flow of events in the encounter" (1967: 7). As such it is only on loan to the person from society (see also the Chinese conceptualisation of face in Hu 1944). Face is at the centre of interaction. It can be key to understanding why interactants behave in one way and not another. The whole interactional activity is focused on the management of the individual's face. In Goffman's world of social encounters, "maintenance of face is a condition of interaction" (Goffman 1967: 12). To be able to interact with others successfully, or at all, the person has to maintain his/her own face and the face of the other (cf. Holtgraves 1992). So what is at issue is the interactional order, although individual psychology also matters in social encounters and facework also involves self-presentation (Bargiela-Chiappini 2003).

The interactional character of face can be looked at from different perspectives. Its meanings and actions emerge during social interaction in the same way as other 'interpretings' formed by participants using language do (Arundale 2006). Though he does not deny its interactional character, Arundale sees face differently from Goffman. For him, it is "an emergent property of relationships" rather than a social psychological phenomenon (2006: 201). According to Spencer-Oatey (2007: 643): "face entails making claims about one's attributes that in turn entail the appraisal of others, so in this sense the notion of face cannot be divorced from social interaction".

Face, however, is not only constituted in interaction as the result of self-presentation and a property of relationships emerging during interaction; it is also 'constitutive of interaction', constraining language use (Haugh 2009) and imposing on the interactants certain patterns of behaviour. Undeniably, face is an integral element of social interaction, and it has an impact on what happens between interactants. Individuals entering into interaction with others become, as Arundale (2006) claims, "persons-in-relationship-to-other-persons". However, while assuming certain social identities and performing certain social roles, they do not stop being individuals. Therefore, face cannot be said to be exclusively the property of the emergent relationship between interactants. It is also a property specific to the individuals involved.

3. Face as a property of the individual

Spencer-Oatey (2007: 648) suggests that analysing face only in interaction is comparable to studying just one side of a coin: "face, like identity, is both social (interactional) and cognitive in nature [...] there are cognitive underpinnings that influence (but do not determine) how face unfolds in interaction". These cognitive underpinnings are values and expectations. Individuals have different personal value constructs which influence their judgements of their own attributes and of those of the others. These can have a strong impact on their face claims and sensitivities (ibid.). And so can expectations, which derive from a wide range of sources, for example, different conventions of communicative activities, different conceptualisations of role relationships (ibid.) and different personality characteristics (cf. 'idiocentric' and 'allocentric' types of personality in Triandis et al. 1988).

One of the most important elements of communicative behaviour is 'self-presentation', which can occur exclusively during social interaction and whose end result is the image of the individual self. Creating a self-image is a matter of self-presentation only insofar as it is concerned with establishing the image of oneself in the minds of others (Baumeister 1982). However, the individual's 'true', 'real' or 'private' self is constructed through his/her choices and performances (Cooley 1902; Mead 1934), which also contribute to the creation of his/her self-image. Self-presentation is a complex activity that is shaped by "a combination of personality, situational, and audience factors", such as an expression of self, a role-played response to situational pressures and conformity to the identity expectations of salient others (Schlenker 2003: 498). And equally complex is its end result – the self-image (face), which can tell us something about its owner: a set of positive attributes the individual wants to be associated with and characterized by. These attributes vary with respect to the interpersonal relations between individuals, the social situations in which they interact and the culture they belong to.

4. Face and culture

It is widely accepted that "culture affects the development of an individual's psychological makeup, which, in turn, affects communication behavior" (Singelis and Brown 1995: 355). There is a relational sequence of culture, its individual members and the different behaviour patterns they follow. Culture, by influencing the psychological make-up of individuals, shapes their behaviour. Apart from affecting people's value constructs and ways of thinking, cultural experience also conditions the formation of the self (Marsella 1985). As a consequence, face, which has a central role in interpersonal communication and is a major contributor to behaviour, is also strongly influenced by cultural norms and values (Markus and Kitayama 1991). As Ruhi and Işik-Güler (2007: 681) claim, "cultures may foreground different aspects of self toward which people show sensitivity in relational work". Face and related concepts of self are "value-laden conceptual and social frames, evoked in evaluative judgements of self and/or others" (2007: 682). Values provide guidance for human activities. Different understandings of face across cultures result from differences in cultural values, communication styles and conceptualisations of self (Chu 1985; Lim 1994). Members of different cultures are 'face sensitive' to a wide variety of attributes related to different hierarchies of values (Spencer-Oatey 2007).

Social norms "influence our expectations about behavioural responsibilities so that failure to fulfil these expectations may be perceived as 'negatively eventful' occurrence, and the result may be face threat and/or face loss" (Spencer-Oatey 2007: 652). Thus, the perception of some act as a face threat depends also on people's conceptions of rights and obligations, of role relationships and interpretations of face-related values (Spencer-Oatey 2007: 652). Social norms which are specific to a given culture constitute the social order expressed in interpersonal and inter-group encounters (Bargiela-Chiappini 2003). All these elements of culture combine in shaping self and face.

As already mentioned, face is a complex construct. First, it includes an implicit concept of moral judgement (cf. Goffman 1967; Penman 1994; Earley 1997). Second, it depends on a person's achievements and position in a social hierarchy (Earley 1997). Third, as social beings, we cannot function without other people and we only have face in their presence. Therefore, face also includes a concept of interpersonal relations. Thus, face is the image of self created on the basis of judgements concerning a person's adherence to moral rules of conduct, his/her position within a given social structure and the interpersonal relations he/she creates with others. Moral rules, social organization and interpersonal relations are specific to a particular culture; thus, the image of self created on their basis must also differ across cultures.

5. The cultural face model

In order to account for all cultural differences shaping the content of face, I suggest a 'cultural face model'. The conceptualization of face stems from the idea of multiple selves (James 1890; Mead 1934; Showers and Zeigler-Hill 2003). Multiplicity of selves refers to a self-concept which is represented as a set of self-aspects involving distinct roles, contexts, relationships, activities, traits and states. By analogy to the concept of multiple selves, we can refer to the 'multiple faces' of a person, though not referring exclusively to his/her distinct social roles. Multiplicity of face refers instead to different aspects of the person's self-image, related to his/her moral integrity, social position and relations with others.

In the cultural face model, face has two dimensions: social and individual. The social dimension of face involves those attributes of the individual's self-image that are socially relevant (Bogdanowska-Jakubowska, 2010). According to Ho (1994: 276), the following attributes relevant to face judgements are valid across cultural contexts:

(1) moral integrity (moral, for example, skill-related or task-oriented aspects of social performance; moral character, judged on the basis of personal conduct; freedom from stigmata),
(2) biographical variables (e.g. age, sex) and relational attributes (e.g. blood or marriage ties),
(3) social status indicators: (a) based on personal effort or achievement (e.g. educational attainments, occupational status and income; social connections and influence; membership in clubs, associations and/or other organizations; or formal title, position or rank acquired through personal effort); (b) not based on personal effort or achievement (e.g. wealth and/or social connections acquired through marriage; or formal title, position or rank acquired through ascription).

In addition to the attributes mentioned above, there are also other attributes called upon in face judgements – interpersonal aspects of social performance. They include interpersonal skills and 'facework competence', which can be characterized in terms of three dimensions

(Ting-Toomey and Kurogi 1998: 200):

(1) cultural knowledge which would help the individual understand other people's cultural perspectives;
(2) mindfulness in simultaneous attendance to one's own and the other's assumptions, cognitions and emotions;
(3) 'communication skills in managing self's and other's face-related concerns', such as identity- and relational-management issues.

An individual competent in facework can be evaluated as behaving appropriately and effectively and as being able to adapt to problematic interpersonal situations. The relative value of all these attributes varies across cultures and depends on the hierarchy of values, social norms and social organisation existing in a given culture.

The social dimension of face includes:

- 'Moral face' – face tied to moral conduct (cf. the Chinese concept of *lian*; Goffman 1967; Earley 1997);
- 'Prestige face' – face as a position in a social setting (cf. the Chinese concept of *mianzi;* Earley 1997);
- 'Relational face' – face tied to interpersonal skills and facework competence, and emerging from the relationship between interactants (cf. Arundale 2006).

The three constituents of the social dimension of face form a culture-general construct. This can be treated as an empty container which, when filled with some specific cultural content, comes to represent the face specific of a given culture.

Face cannot be considered as either exclusively monadic (see Goffman 1967) or as exclusively relational (Arundale 2006). Spencer-Oatey (2007: 654) claims that "face belongs to individuals and to collectives, and yet it also applies to interpersonal relations". It is both a result of self-presentation and purposeful impression management as well as of other types of behaviour (moral face and prestige face) and a property of an emerging relationship (relational face), which is formed during social interaction.

To make this face model truly culture-general, it is necessary to distinguish between situation-specific face (cf. Goffman's [1967] conception of face) and pan-situational face (cf. the Chinese conception of face; Ho 1994; Spencer-Oatey 2005). Moral face can be both situation-specific and pan-situational, as it involves a self-image created in a particular social interaction and a 'largely consistent over time' image of self concerned with moral character and ability to function within a community. Prestige face is a pan-situational self-image concerned with social status, rank and prestige. Relational face is situation-specific, as it appears as a result of the interaction between individuals establishing a certain kind of relationship.

Every human being has several basic wants and desires, the desires for proximity and inclusion and for distance, independence and individuation among them. These two sets of desires are socially relevant. The fulfilment of the desires contributes to the maintenance of an individual's face; disregard for the desires results in his/her face damage or loss. By analogy to the two sets of desires, the individual dimension of face consists of two complementary elements:

(1) 'Solidarity face', resulting from the desire for proximity and inclusion – cf. Durkheim's (2001 [1912]) positive rites; Goffman's (1967) presentational rituals; Brown and Levinson's (1987) positive face;
(2) 'Autonomy face', resulting from the desire for distance, independence and individuation – cf. Durkheim's (2001) negative rites; Goffman's (1967) avoidance rituals; Brown and Levinson's (1987) negative face.

Solidarity face and autonomy face are culture-general concepts; they are not based on any emic concept of face (cf. culture-general dialectic of connection face and separation face in Arundale [2006]). The two desires 'for proximity and belonging' and 'for distance and individuation' are inherently present in every individual, in every culture; the crosscultural difference is only measured in their intensity (O'Driscoll 1996: 4; Terkourafi 2007). Whether one prevails over the other depends on culture, the context of a situation and the individual characteristics of a person (cf. Mao's [1994] 'relative face orientation'; Markus and Kitayama's [1991] 'independent' and 'interdependent self-construals').

According to the cultural face model, both dimensions of face and all their constituent elements are culture-general. What makes particular emic concepts of face different from one another is the content of face which depends on cultural context (social organization, social norms, moral rules and a hierarchy of social values).

6. The applicability of the cultural face model

To test the applicability of the cultural face model I present two emic concepts: Anglo-American face and Polish face (*twarz*), which differ in their interpretation and management. The two concepts are discussed against a cultural background which is presented mainly in terms of the individualism–collectivism dimension. The choice of this dimension is motivated by changes that the Polish culture has been undergoing since 1989. Social transformations which involved the opening to modern western culture, American culture in particular, and the borrowing of individualistic values, for example, success, independence, freedom of choice and mobility.

In mainstream American culture, equated with the predominant white middle class, value orientations emphasize the individual and individuality (Spindler and Spindler 1993; Naylor 1998). The primary orientation tends towards the individual self rather than towards the significant other. Self-assertiveness, a high degree of self-reliance and independence are highly valued by Anglo-Americans (Chu 1985). The white middle-class Anglo-American concept of social self emphasises the ideal of development towards autonomy and the liberation of the self from external authority as a part of social growth (DeVos 1985: 178). The 'independent self-construal' (Markus and Kitayama 1991) which predominates in Anglo-American culture reflects the worldview in which "the person is defined by stable properties, separate from his or her social context". The individual's self is unique and independent.

Anglo-American face belongs exclusively to an individual who is independent of others and free to choose his/her optimal course of action. The individual's autonomy is a consequence of weak social, especially family, bonds. An individual's decisions and actions result from his/her being true to him/herself and to a rational way of thinking. Anglo-American face is "individualized" (Ervin-Tripp et al. 1995). Actions of one individual do not usually affect the face of any member of his/her family. Relative to other cultures, Anglo-Americans tend to take personal responsibility for their actions and it is only their face that can be threatened by these actions; any threat to the individual's face affects his/her face exclusively, not anyone else's. Anglo-American face, described by Morisaki and Gudykunst (1994: 57) as "independent face" (that is independent of any other person's face), is 'put on' by each participant and negotiated during social interaction. In fact, what is 'put on' is a mask-like face which is to be in line with the requirements of good social relations necessary for successful social interaction (for example, friendly, cheerful and happy).

In Polish culture, the primary orientation is to the significant others and to the relationship with them. Traditionally, the Polish concept of social self emphasizes the ideal of in-group interdependence and cooperation, although it is now undergoing changes connected with the societal shift from collectivism to individualism. Autonomy of the individual, self-reliance and independence have become highly valued especially among the younger generation of Poles. Thus, there is not one self-construal predominating in Polish culture. The interdependent self-construal predominates among the older generation and the less educated, while the independent self-construal predominates among the younger generation (who started their adult life during the last 20 years) and the educated (Bogdanowska-Jakubowska, 2010). Generally speaking, *the Polish self-construal*, like Polish culture, is 'in transition'; it reflects the view in which the person is created by his/her roles and relations with others as well as by 'stable properties, separate from his or her social context'. An individual's self can be either/partly unique and independent or/and interdependent and belonging. Members of the younger generation often fight an internal battle between the traditional Polish upbringing model, which requires close contact with the family, strong and long-lasting interdependence, and taking into consideration 'what others will say', and the new 'westernized'/'Americanized' model, according to which they are independent individuals who have the right to rid themselves of external authority and be 'unique'.

Polish face is based on the two competing self-construals existing simultaneously in current Polish culture. In this context, face can be described neither as purely independent nor as purely interdependent, it is rather 'face in transition'. Polish face is not 'individualised' to such an extent as Anglo-American face. The actions of one individual can still affect the face of other members of his/her family. Poles consider the actions of their family members as relevant to their own face. In other words, relative to other cultures, Poles tend to take responsibility for their own actions, but it is not only their face that can be threatened by these actions. Unlike Anglo-American mask-like face, which is often friendly and smiling, Polish face can be characterised as somewhat 'unhappy', although there are changes towards a more positive and optimistic self-image.

Here the two emic concepts, Anglo-American face and Polish *twarz* will be analysed in terms of their constituent elements. I will apply the cultural face model to real-life situations and present a number of authentic examples (taken from the Polish and American press and from observation of everyday interactions in Polish and American settings) which show the importance of certain face-sensitive attributes in the two cultures.

Moral face epitomizes what makes an individual human. Our moral ideals, such as justice, tolerance, freedom and rights, stem from our human concern with what is best for humanity. Morality is a code of conduct existing in every society. Polish and Anglo-American cultures have the same European roots, so integrity and honesty generally mean the same both for Poles and Anglo-Americans. Faithfulness to one's ideals and one's friends is of utmost importance in both cultures (see Examples 1 and 2).

Example 1

In 2008, Jarosław Kaczyński, the leader of the Law and Justice Party, accused Stefan Niesiołowski, the Deputy Speaker of the Sejm [Polish Parliament], a member of the Civic Platform Party, of having informed on his friends to the communist security services. Niesiołowski was one of the founders of the Ruch organization established in Łódź in 1964, which was the largest opposition group at the end of the Władysław Gomułka government. On 20 May 1970, Ruch organization activists, Niesiołowski included, were arrested the day before their planned arson of the Lenin Museum in Poronin. Referring to Niesiołowski's arrest on this occasion, Kaczyński said:

> *Stefan Niesiołowski sypał już na pierwszym przesłuchaniu. To haniebna sprawa.*
>
> (Stefan Niesiołowski informed [on other members of the Ruch organization] during the first interrogation. This is a disgrace.)

Niesiołowski commented on Kaczyński's statement:

> *To potwarz. Nienawiść rzuciła się Kaczyńskiemu na mózg.* (Czuchnowski and Wroński, 4 December 2008)
>
> (This is a slander. Hatred has made Kaczyński crazy.)

Informing on members of one's in-group is considered a highly immoral act whose performance definitely leads to a person's face loss; its moral aspect in particular. In this situation, however, no moral face loss is involved, as Niesiołowski did not commit the act of reporting on other Ruch activists. Kaczyński's false statement only represents a face threat. Although Kaczyński seems to commit himself to the truth of the presented proposition (he refers to a recently published book), his intention is not to draw on historical facts, but to damage Niesiołowski's good name and reputation as a man of moral integrity.

Thus, the perlocutionary effect of the act committed is that of slander. Niesiołowski's words uttered in self-defence explicitly define Kaczyński's intention. Reference to Kaczyński's impaired intellectual abilities can be interpreted as a case of defence by means of attack; Niesiołowski by attacking Kaczyński's prestige face defends his own moral face.

Example 2, taken from the Anglo-American context, also involves moral face.

Example 2

John McCain, who twice ran for president, presented himself as a person of high moral standards:

> *[McCain] reinvented himself as [...] a crusader for stricter ethics and campaign finance rules, a man of honor chastened by a brush with shame.* (Rutenberg et al., 21 February 2008)

Aware of the fact that both his political and private life is subject to public scrutiny, he tried to present an image of himself as internally consistent:

> *I would very much like to think that I have never been a man whose favor can be bought. [...] From my earliest youth, I would have considered such a reputation to be the most shameful ignominy imaginable. Yet that is exactly how millions of Americans viewed me for a time, a time that I will forever consider one of the worst experiences of my life.* (Rutenberg et al., 21 February 2008)

However, last year McCain's moral face was threatened twice. Firstly, by his own inconsiderate behaviour:

> *his friendship with Ms. Iseman, a lobbyist for telecommunications companies that had business before the commerce committee, which Mr. McCain once headed.* (Pérez-Peña, 20 February 2009)

Secondly, his moral face was threatened by the article, 'For McCain, Self-Confidence on Ethics Poses Its Own Risk', published in the *New York Times*:

> *The article said that in 1999, during a previous presidential run, some top McCain advisers were "convinced the relationship had become romantic", warned Ms. Iseman to steer clear of the senator, and confronted Mr. McCain about the matter.* (Pérez-Peña, 20 February 2009)

According to the article authors, McCain's advisers thought that his behaviour

> *threatened the story of redemption and rectitude that defined his political identity.*

To defend himself and maintain face, McCain, in a call to Bill Keller, the executive editor of *The New York Times*, made the following statement:

> *I have never betrayed the public trust by doing anything like that.*

In support of McCain, his presidential campaign issued the following statement:

> *It is a shame that The New York Times has lowered its standards to engage in a hit-and-run smear campaign. John McCain has a 24-year record of serving our country with honor and integrity.*

In both cultures, then, moral integrity is a very delicate issue. A threat to moral face always evokes strong emotions on the part of the person implicated and of his/her supporters and friends, and requires some action to counteract it.

In the case of prestige face, the differences between Anglo-American and Polish culture are not great either. One might expect that, as equality is one of the most important values for Anglo-Americans – and Poles are known for their obsession for titles and hypersensitivity to social status – the content of prestige face will differ in the two cultures. However, both cultures are rather conservative and hierarchical (Triandis 1995). What makes them different is that Poles often try to 'be like others' and look similar, stressing in-group solidarity, while Anglo-Americans tend to want to be different and to 'stand out'. The desire to be different (e.g. for one's knowledge, competence or social rank) is not alien to Poles, however. Any questioning of the person's right to social recognition for his/her talent, achievement or work is an attack on his/her prestige face (see Example 3).

Example 3

In December 2008, Bogdan Rymanowski, a television journalist (for the private channel TVN), was chosen as Journalist of the Year 2008. Piotr Pacewicz, a *Gazeta Wyborcza* journalist, published a commentary to this event, which he entitled:

> *Rymanowski – niedziennikarz roku.* (Pacewicz, 18 December 2008)
>
> (Rymanowski – non-journalist of the year.)

The subtitle read:

> *Nagradzajmy dziennikarzy, a nie arbitrów elegancji podczas kłótni w maglu.*
>
> (Let's give prizes to journalists, not arbiters of elegance during arguments in the laundry.)

In the article the author asks several questions:

> *Za co?! [...] Co takiego ważnego Bogdan Rymanowski ma do przekazania Polakom? Na czym się zna? Jakich wartości broni? Co ujawnia, czego byśmy nie wiedzieli?*
>
> (What for? [...] What, in particular, does Bogdan Rymanowski have to tell the Poles? What does he know? What values does he defend? What does he reveal that we would not otherwise know?)
>
> *Gdyby to były wybory 'Twarzy Roku' czy 'Ekranu 2008' – w porządku. Ale dziennikarz?*
>
> (If it were a contest for 'Face of the Year' or 'Screen of the Year 2008', alright. But journalist?)

In his attack on Rymanowski, Pacewicz even comments ironically upon the laureate's behaviour on receiving the title:

> *Bogdan Rymanowski – co było ujmujące! – stwierdził w środę, że to chyba nie jemu należy się ta nagroda. Rzeczywiście. I nie chodzi o Rymanowskiego jako takiego, lecz o profesję, którą uprawia. Nie określiłbym jej terminem dziennikarstwo.*
>
> (Bogdan Rymanowski – how charming! – stated on Wednesday that perhaps he did not deserve this award. Indeed. And it is not about Rymanowski as such, but about the profession that he practises. I would not call it journalism.)

As a reaction to Pacewicz's commentary, TVN 24 cancelled the programme 'Skaner polityczny', in which a *Gazeta Wyborcza* journalist was to take part. Another reaction was a commentary by Adam Pieczyński, the editor-in-chief of the channel TVN 24:

> *Może Durczok, Pochanke, Olejnik to po prostu pseudodziennikarze? Tak jak Rymanowski. Tylko sadzają tych gości i rozmawiają z nimi. Niczego nie tłumaczą, nie są tak dociekliwi, jak "Gazeta", nie są tak mądrzy jak "Gazeta", nie są tak profesjonalni jak "Gazeta". Tylko jeśli dziennikarze telewizyjni są tak straszni, tak żałośnie nieprofesjonalni, tak trywialnie pokazują rzeczywistość, więc jeśli taka właśnie jest prawda o telewizji – to dlaczego, do licha, tak chętnie oglądają ich widzowie?* (Pieczyński, 18 December 2008)

> (Perhaps Durczok, Pochanke, Olejnik are also simply pseudo-journalists like Rymanowski. They only give their guests a seat and talk to them. They do not explain anything, they are not as inquisitive as *Gazeta Wyborcza*, they are not as wise as *Gazeta*, they are not as professional as *Gazeta*. But if television journalists are so terrible, so miserably unprofessional, show reality in such a trivial way, if such is the truth about the television – why, for God's sake, are spectators so willing to watch them?)

Pacewicz's remarks are an example of an attack on prestige face. They are an attack on the individual face of Rymanowski as well as on the group face of television journalists. The cancellation of the programme and the response by the editor-in-chief of TVN 24 are aimed at defending the prestige face of the individual and of the group. In the first case, the strategy employed is 'an eye for an eye', consisting of retaliatory actions. In the commentary, Pieczyński expresses solidarity with the attacked: Rymanowski and all television journalists are denied professionalism by Pacewicz. He uses two face-saving strategies here, one consisting in comparison with the best (Rymanowski is put in the same line with leading journalists at TVN) and the argument-based-on-facts strategy, in which actual facts are used as arguments against a face threat.

In Anglo-American culture, a threat to prestige face also requires some action either on the part of the person involved or his/her supporters (see Example 4).

Example 4

In the article 'After Criticism, Paterson Cancels Trip to Davos' (*The New York Times*, 26 January 2009), Jeremy W. Peters describes the story of Governor David A. Paterson, who "seeking to contain some of the fallout over his administration's handling of the United States Senate appointment, said [...] that he had canceled a trip to the World Economic Forum in Davos, Switzerland". Mishandling of the problem damaged the prestige face of Paterson and his administration. To counteract the damage he took some redressive steps. He tried to distance himself from members of his administration who had been quoted anonymously as saying that "various problems with Caroline Kennedy sank her bid to become a senator". He unwillingly admitted that

> *[...] there've been leaks coming from my administration throughout this entire process of choosing a senator of contradictory types of information. Now as you know this is a pretty serious thing, and actually one that I would condemn.* (Peters, 26 January 2009)

In this way he expressed his disapproval of the incompetence of his administration. He also added that

> *I would love to know who is responsible. But at this point, I've been unable to determine that.*

Referring to his trip to the World Economic Forum, Paterson said:

> *I think I'll stay here. Perhaps it would be a better idea to go at another time, send a couple of assistants and stay right here with the leaders of the Legislature and work on the budget.*

The act of cancelling his trip to Davos is a reaction to the criticism of Paterson's administration and an act of redress. Although Paterson was not directly responsible for the leaks, he found himself responsible for the actions of members of his administration. His popularity suffered as a result of Ms. Kennedy's withdrawal from the selection process and the way his administration handled it. Summing up the whole situation, Paterson said:

> *You have ups and downs in public service, and you have to keep working. You have to keep trying. You have to keep doing your best. And if you conduct yourself ethically, I think over a period of time people see that.*

In the social dimension of face, the greatest differences between Polish and Anglo-American cultures can be observed in its relational component. They result from the disparate character of interpersonal and intergroup relations and different conceptualisations of self. These differences can be seen in the opening phase of a typical everyday conversation.

To a Polish bystander Anglo-Americans' social interaction may appear quite 'theatrical', and this also refers to greeting rituals. When two persons approach each other, the moment they make eye contact they often put on a broad friendly smile. They exchange greetings, often addressing each other by their first names/title + surname/professional title + surname. First names are used most commonly even in the case of wide social distance between interlocutors. The exchange of how-are-you type questions is the next necessary element of the ritual (Jakubowska 1999). The answers to the questions are positive, and as such they contribute to the 'good' self-image of the participants who have to look self-satisfied and 'successful'. Participating in this exchange, the persons show a ritual concern for each other (see Example 5). Greeting rituals, and their component elements – how-are-you type questions in particular – perform several functions. They have a phatic function, as they are used to establish or maintain social contact with the other. By showing willingness to do this, the speaker expresses concern for the other's solidarity face. He/she also performs greeting rituals for pragmatic reasons – to establish and maintain his/her own relational face.

Example 5

Sharon (Department Chair):	(smiling) *Good morning, Paula.*
Paula (Manager):	(smiling) *Good morning, Sharon. How are you?*
Sharon:	*Fine, thanks, and you?*
Paula:	*Oh, I'm all right, thank you.*
Sharon:	*Is there any mail for me?*
Paula:	*I have just left it in your pigeonhole.*
Sharon:	*Thanks.*

In a similar situation to the one presented in Example 5, Poles create their relational face in a different way. In Example 6, Polish interactants (work colleagues) tend to be less 'expressive' than many Anglo-Americans. The greeting ritual performed here consists of the same elements as the American greeting form. First, Ewa and Iwona exchange greetings proper. To show concern for the other's solidarity face and to help create her own relational face, Ewa asks a question that may be treated as a how-are-you type question (*Co u ciebie?*). What makes it different from the American how-are-you type question is that it usually implies some genuine concern for the other's situation. Iwona's answer to this question constitutes a norm in Polish culture: it includes more detailed information and is not trying to be as positive as possible; in fact, in this case it is a complaint. Iwona even tries to play down the positive fact that she is going for a weekend in the mountains.

Example 6

Ewa:	*Cześć!.* (Hi!)
Iwona:	*Cześć!* (Hi!)
Ewa:	*Co u ciebie?* (What's up?)
Iwona:	*Ach, nic ciekawego. Jestem okropnie zagoniona. Wiesz, koniec semestru, pełno prac mam do sprawdzenia. Jeszcze wyjeżdżamy na weekend w góry.* (Oh, nothing special. I'm terribly busy. You know, it's the end of the semester and I have loads of papers to read. And to top it all, we are going to the mountains for the weekend.)
Ewa:	*To świetnie!* (That's great!)
Iwona:	*Daj spokój! Nie wie w co ręce włożyć.* (Come on! I'm up to here in work.)

Examples 5 and 6 show how relational face is built from the start of everyday interaction. The greeting rituals by means of which members of the two cultures create their relational face do not differ much; however, differences in hierarchies of values in the two cultures translate into significant differences in face-sensitive attributes. In Anglo-American culture, these attributes are 'satisfied', 'happy', 'successful' and 'friendly', and they result from the American predilection for success and positive thinking. In Polish culture, a positive self-image is often based on complaint and negative thinking (see also Jakubowska 2007; Bogdanowska-Jakubowska, 2010).

The two types of face pertaining to the individual dimension are inherent in every individual, in every culture (O'Driscoll 1996). Members of the two cultures in question pay attention to both of them. What differs across cultures is the significance attached to solidarity face and autonomy face. Examples 7 and 8 present typical host–guest interaction sequences in Anglo-American and Polish cultures, respectively. The participants behave in accordance with culture-specific rules of politeness. In Example 7, Richard offers Sharon some spaghetti; however, he does not impose anything on her. He gives her freedom of action and choice. Sharon declines his offer. Richard verifies: 'Are you sure?'. Sharon confirms and gives a reason for her decision, which is accepted. American hosts tend to offer their guests once and expect sincere responses: 'No, thank you' generally means a sincere turning down of the offer.

Example 7

Richard:	*I'm just making myself spaghetti. Would you like some?*
Sharon:	*No, thanks.*
Richard:	*Are you sure?*
Sharon:	*Yes. I'm not hungry.*
Richard:	*OK.*

In a similar situation, the Polish host, Irena, imposes on her guest using the verb *musieć* ('must'). She does not give her interlocutor much choice. Such behaviour is sanctioned by the customs of Polish hospitality, which are based on the assumption that the host knows what is best for her guests. Her role, even obligation, is to make them eat and drink as much as possible. The guest's preferences do not count here. Although Danka turns down the offer and gives a reason for her decision, Irena does not stop trying to make her eat. Danka declines the offer twice and finally accepts it. This is a ritual that Polish guests follow: turning the offer down with *dziękuję* ('thank you') repeated several times, before finally accepting it. This ritual can be explained by timidity and lack of assertiveness, which are deeply rooted in the Polish culture (Jakubowska 2004).

Example 8

Irena:	*Zrobiłam pyszną sałatkę. Musisz spróbować.* (I have prepared a delicious salad. You must try it.)
Danka:	*Nie, dziękuję. Dopiero jadłam obiad.* (No, thank you. I have just had lunch.)
Irena:	*Może jednak dasz się skusić?* (Perhaps I can tempt you to it?)
Danka:	*Naprawdę dziękuję.* (No thanks, really.)
Irena:	*Chociaż spróbuj!* (At least taste it!)
Danka:	*To proszę. Ale nie dużo.* (I'll have it. But only a little.)

Examples 7 and 8 show the differences in the individual dimension of face in the two cultures. In Anglo-American culture, the maintenance of autonomy face, one's own as well as the other's face, is very important. Even concern for the other person's good does not allow the speaker to neglect his/her desire for distance, independence and individuation. In Polish culture, this desire is not so strong, and concern for the other person's automony face is of secondary importance in situations when other values prevail (for example, hospitality).

The discussion of the above examples shows the importance of certain face-sensitive attributes (morality, social position and interpersonal skills) in the overall image of self (face), and at the same time confirms the validity of the cultural face model. The data sources analysed in this chapter seem to show that there is no difference between public figures and ordinary people in the content of these aspects of face: there is one morality for all members of a given culture; and while a threat to one's social position is equally detrimental to all, its social consequences differ.

What makes the cultural face model different from other face models is that:

- It treats face both as a social and an individual phenomenon;
- The two-level characterization of face allows for the explanation of both cultural differences and similarities in its interpretation and management.

- Apart from 'traditional' components (morality and a social position), face also includes a relational component, which is the result of interaction with others;
- Solidarity face and autonomy face are perceived in terms of basic human desires, and as such constitute only one dimension of face.

Although it needs further elaboration, the model can be a good starting point for further analysis of the concept of face and its interpretation and management in different cultures.

References

Arundale, R.B. (2006) 'Face as Relational and Interactional: A Communication Framework for Research on Face, Facework, and Politeness', *Journal of Politeness Research*, 2, pp. 193–216.

Bargiela-Chiappini, F. (2003) 'Face and Politeness: New (Insights) for Old (Concepts)', *Journal of Pragmatics*, 35, pp. 1453–1469.

Bargiela-Chiappini, F. (2006) 'Face', in K. Brown (ed.), *Encyclopedia of Language and Linguistics*, Oxford, Elsevier, pp. 421–423.

Baumeister, R.F. (1982) 'A Self-Presentational View of Social Phenomena', *Psychological Bulletin*, 91/1, pp. 3–26.

Bogdanowska-Jakubowska, E. (2010) *Face: An Interdisciplinary Perspective*, Katowice, Wydawnictwo Uniwersytetu Śląskiego.

Brown, P., and Levinson, S.C. (1987) *Politeness: Some Universals in Language Usage*, Cambridge, Cambridge University Press.

Chu, G.C. (1985) 'The Changing Concept of Self in Contemporary China', in A.J. Marsella, G. DeVos and F.L.K. Hsu (eds), *Culture and Self: Asian and Western Perspectives*, New York and London, Tavistock, pp. 252–278.

Cooley, C.H. (1902) *Human Nature and the Social Order*, New York, Scribner's.

Cross, S.E. and Gore, J.S. (2003) 'Cultural Models of the Self', in M.R. Leary and J. Prince Tangney (eds), Handbook of Self and Identity, New York and London, The Guilford Press, pp. 536–564.

Czuchnowski, W., and Wroński, P. (2008) 'Kaczyński Książką IPN w Niesiołowskiego', *Gazeta Wyborcza*, 4 December.

DeVos, G. (1985) 'Dimensions of the Self in Japanese Culture', in A.J. Marsella, G. DeVos and F.L.K. Hsu (eds), *Culture and Self: Asian and Western Perspectives*, New York and London, Tavistock, pp. 142–184.

Durkheim, E. (2001 [1912]) *The Elementary Forms of Religious Life* (trans. C. Cosman), Oxford, Oxford University Press.

Earley, P.C. (1997) *Face, Harmony, and Social Structure*, New York and Oxford, Oxford University Press.

Ervin-Tripp, S., Nakamura, K., and Guo, J. (1995) 'Shifting Face from Asia to Europe', in M. Shibatani and S. Thompson (eds), *Essays in Semantics and Pragmatics in Honor of Charles J. Fillmore*, Amsterdam and Philadelphia, John Benjamins, pp. 43–71.

Goffman, E. (1967) *Interaction Ritual: Essays in Face-to-Face Behavior*, Chicago, Aldine.

Haugh, M. (2009) 'Face and Interaction', in F. Bargiela-Chiappini and M. Haugh (eds), *Face: Communication in Social Interaction*, London, Equinox, pp. 1–24.
Ho, D.Y.-F. (1994) 'Face Dynamics: From Conceptualization to Measurement', in S. Ting-Toomey (ed.), *The Challenge of Facework: Cross-Cultural and Interpersonal Issues*, Albany, State University of New York Press, pp. 269–286.
Holtgraves, T. (1992) 'The Linguistic Realization of Face Management: Implications for Language Production and Comprehension, Person Perception, and Cross-Cultural Communication', *Social Psychology Quarterly*, 55/2, pp. 141–159.
Hu, H.C. (1944) 'The Chinese Concepts of Face', *American Anthropologist* (n.s.), 46/1, Part 1, pp. 45–64.
Jakubowska, E. (1999) *Cross-Cultural Dimensions of Politeness in the Case of Polish and English*, Katowice, Wydawnictwo Uniwersytetu Śląskiego.
Jakubowska, E. (2004) 'Party Rituals in a Cross-Cultural Perspective', paper presented at the International Conference on Language, Politeness and Gender: 'The Pragmatic Roots', University of Helsinki, Helsinki.
Jakubowska, E. (2007) 'Cultural Transfer in the Presentation of Self', *Lingustica Silesiana*, 28, pp. 105–114.
James, W. (1890) *The Principles of Psychology*, New York, H. Holt.
Lim, T.-S. (1994) 'Facework and Interpersonal Relationships', in S. Ting-Toomey (ed.), *The Challenge of Facework*, Albany, State University of New York Press, pp. 209–230.
Mao, L.R. (1994) 'Beyond Politeness Theory: "Face" Revisited and Renewed', *Journal of Pragmatics*, 21, pp. 451–486.
Markus, H., and Kitayama, S. (1991) 'Culture and the Self: Implications for Cognition, Emotion, and Motivation', *Psychological Review*, 98, pp. 224–253.
Marsella, A.J. (1985) 'Culture, Self, and Mental Disorder', in A.J. Marsella, G. DeVos and F.L.K. Hsu (eds), *Culture and Self: Asian and Western Perspectives*, New York and London, Tavistock, pp. 281–307.
Mead, G.H. (1934) *Mind, Self, and Society*, Chicago, University of Chicago Press.
Naylor, L.L. (1998) *American Culture: Myth and Reality of a Culture of Diversity*, Westport and London, Bergin & Garvey.
O'Driscoll, J. (1996) 'About Face: A Defence and Elaboration of Universal Dualism', *Journal of Pragmatics*, 25, pp. 1–32.
Pacewicz, P. (2008) 'Niedziennikarz Roku', *Gazeta Wyborcza*, 18 December.
Penman, R. (1994) 'Facework in Communication: Conceptual and Moral Challenges', in S. Ting-Toomey (ed.), *The Challenge of Facework: Cross-Cultural and Interpersonal Issues*, Albany, State University of New York Press, pp. 15–45.
Pérez-Peña, R. (2009) 'Libel Suit against *The Times* Ends', *New York Times*, 20 February.
Peters, J.W. (2009) 'After Criticism, Paterson Cancels Trip to Davos', *New York Times*, 26 January.
Pieczyński, A. (2008) 'Seans Zazdrości Piotra Pacewicza', 18 December, available at: www.Tvn24.pl.
Ruhi, S., and Işik-Güler, H. (2007) 'Conceptualizing Face and Relational Work in (Im)politeness: Revelations from Politeness Lexemes and Idioms in Turkish', *Journal of Pragmatics*, 39, pp. 681–711.
Rutenberg, J., Thompson, M.W., Kirpatrick, D.D., and Labaton, S. (2008) 'For McCain, Self-Confidence on Ethics Poses Its Own Risk', *New York Times*, 21 February.

Schlenker, B.R. (2003) 'Self-Presentation', in M.R. Leary and J. Prince Tangney (eds), *Handbook of Self and Identity*, New York and London, Guilford Press, pp. 492–518.
Showers, C.J., and Zeigler-Hill, V. (2003) 'Organization of Self-Knowledge: Features, Functions, and Flexibility', in M.R. Leary and J. Prince Tangney (eds), *Handbook of Self and Identity*, New York and London, Guilford Press, pp. 47–67.
Singelis, T.M., and Brown W.J. (1995) 'Culture, Self, and Collectivist Communication: Linking Culture to Individual Behavior', *Human Communication Research*, 21/3, pp. 354–389.
Spencer-Oatey, H. (2005) '(Im)politeness, Face and Perceptions of Rapport: Unpackaging Their Bases and Interrelationships', *Journal of Politeness Research*, 1, pp. 95–119.
Spencer-Oatey, H. (2007) 'Theories of Identity and the Analysis of Face', *Journal of Pragmatics*, 3, pp. 639–656.
Spindler, G., and Spindler, L. (1993) *The American Cultural Dialogue and Its Transmission*, Bristol, Falmer Press.
Terkourafi, M. (2007) 'Toward a Universal Notion of Face for a Universal Notion of Cooperation', in I. Kecskes and L.R. Horn (eds), *Explorations in Pragmatics: Linguistic, Cognitive and Intercultural Aspects*, Berlin and New York, Mouton de Gruyter, pp. 313–344.
Ting-Toomey, S., and Kurogi, A. (1998) 'Facework Competence in Intercultural Conflict: An Updated Face-Negotiation Theory', *International Journal of Intercultural Relations*, 22/2, pp. 187–225.
Triandis, H.C. (1995) *Individualism and Collectivism*, Boulder, Westview Press.
Triandis, H.C., Brislin, R., and Hui, C.H. (1988) 'Cross-Cultural Training across the Individualism-Collectivism Divide', *International Journal of Intercultural Relations*, 12, pp. 269–289.

Epilogue

Sandra Harris

1. Politeness and culture

Both 'politeness' and 'culture', the focal points of this volume, are multidisciplinary and multifaceted concepts which have, in the past, generated a huge amount of literature and come with a very considerable amount of intellectual, and perhaps equally important, emotional baggage. Both have proved surprisingly resistant to canonical definition and have largely shuffled off their historical associations with 'refinement', 'high art' and 'polite society', that is, Matthew Arnold's nineteenth-century definition of 'culture' as "the acquainting ourselves with the best that has been known and said in the world, and thus with the history of the human spirit" (Preface to the 1873 edition of *Literature and Dogma*). Yet both remain as crucially important concepts as ever, which reach well beyond the large number of academic disciplines that make use of them (perhaps particularly culture). Indeed, in his seminal book on *Contesting Culture*, Baumann (1996: 9) argues that

> no idea is as fundamental to an anthropological understanding of social life as the concept of culture. At the same time, no anthropological term has spread into public parlance and political discourse as this word has done over the past twenty years.

To a lesser extent, the same might be said of politeness, which has seen not only a burgeoning of research since the publication of Brown and Levinson's work (1978, 1987) but has also been the subject of more general public concern (see, for example, *The Economist*, 19 December 2009), at least in the UK and North America.

The chapters in this volume represent attempts to explore the conjunction between politeness and culture in different ways, with different emphases, and perhaps most importantly, through a diverse number of different cultures and languages, many of which have had very little written about them. Goddard (2010) has recently suggested that there are at least four meanings of 'culture' as it is currently interpreted, but rather than offering precise definitions of these, he points out that they share some key conceptual components, namely the idea of a collectivity of people living in a place and/or doing things together; the idea that these people behave and think in distinctive ways and have distinctive values; and the idea that these people's distinctive ways of behaving, thinking and evaluating have been inherited or transmitted from their predecessors. Central to his perspective of culture is the nature of that collectivity, whether what is involved is a 'way of life' or, more selectively, a way of doing things in a particular occupational or activity-based context (Goddard 2010: 95). Matsumoto (2006) makes a particularly useful distinction between 'cultural practices', which refer to the 'doing of culture', and 'cultural worldviews', which involve belief systems about a particular culture and refer primarily to 'thinking and talking about culture'.

Thus, some chapters in *Politeness Across Cultures* (Sifianou, Bogdanowska-Jakubowska, Gu, Brown) examine the conjunction of politeness and culture primarily through looking at culture as a manifestation of national and/or linguistic identity, while others focus on activity-based or occupational cultures (Mullany, Kampf and Blum-Kulka). Watanabe explores how the fact that business colleagues belong to different linguistic and national cultures (Japanese and Australian) makes it possible (necessary) to create a particular kind of work/activity culture within a specific business and Rusieshvili looks at how a national cultural identity such as Georgian influences the use of address forms which signal the in-group and out-group status of participants in certain professional work situations (medical, academic). Several writers (Grainger, Ogiermann and Suszczyńska) address politeness in intercultural contexts, and both of the writers in Part I of the volume consider the relationship between 'politeness' and 'face' as a particular issue.

2. Future developments and research in politeness across cultures

This is a diverse volume, and its very diversity is a significant part of its strength. Examining cultures and languages which have attracted relatively little attention in the recent burgeoning in the field of politeness research is both exciting and illuminating. *Politeness Across Cultures* has made a significant beginning, and a move away from the dominance of English language and English speaking contexts is, in my view, one of the most obvious ways forward for research in politeness across cultures and should certainly be encouraged. However, there are perhaps several other less obvious candidates for the future development of the field which this book brings to light.

Firstly, there is a need for more work in politeness research which investigates the role of ideologies in the construction of politeness and for research which takes into consideration the need for researchers to take seriously the existence of 'alternative' cultural meanings in what have been previously regarded as stable national standard languages. The work of Lucien Brown (Chapter 6) calls explicitly for this change and is particularly insightful in dealing with Korean honorifics and the 'revealed', 'ignored' and 'suppressed' aspects of Korean culture and politeness. Brown points out that Korea has always maintained a "high congruity between speech community and nation" (p. 110) but that representation of a unified language and culture comes with obvious contradictions, given the lack of contact which has been accentuated by opposing political systems, ideologies and language policies since Korea was divided into two countries in 1948. The aspirations of both South and North Korea to promote ideals of homogenous populations speaking a standard language do not, according to Brown, correlate with linguistic reality (ibid.). Brown demonstrates in his chapter how the use of honorifics in both present-day Koreas illustrates the existence of 'suppressed' and 'ignored' patterns which are particularly interesting. They also represent, he argues, significant 'alternative' cultural meanings which have implications for politeness theory. Brown ends with a plea for further research into Korean honorifics and "the way that these forms are used amongst different social groups, speakers of dialects and Korean populations overseas to provide a more detailed picture of how their usage is involved in the struggle for politeness" (p. 124). Such a study would not only tell us a great deal about the form and use of Korean honorifics but also provide a model for future work on the nature of 'alternative' cultural meanings in relationship to theories of politeness more generally.

In a related chapter but one with a significantly different approach and use of data, Ogiermann and Suszczynska (Chapter 10) also consider how political and social changes influence the perception of politeness in Poland and Hungary, both before and after the fall of the Iron Curtain in 1989. Like Brown, Ogiermann and Suszcznska stress the importance of "the complex political and social changes these countries have been undergoing in the past century", including "an imposition of a collectivist mentality and the assumed values of the 'proletariat'" (p. 196). In addition,

> political oppression and permanent shortages of basic goods led to new power constellations affecting public face-to-face communication,

> particularly in service encounters and in interactions between representatives of state institutions and citizens. (p. 196)

Their data includes primarily 19 'episodic interviews' with a selection of Poles and Hungarians who lived through and remember the 'communist times'. Though the use of such 'episodic interviews' as data has obvious methodological difficulties and limitations, Ogiermann and Suszczynska maintain convincingly that they

> helped to access not only aspects of (im)politeness discussed in theories of politeness but also those that have been largely overlooked. Our analysis of the influence of economic factors on interactional styles seems to validate the parallel between money and politeness drawn by Werkhofer (1992). (p. 213)

Like Brown, they call for further work on how more broadly based socio-political contexts act to "redefine cultural values" and have a significant "impact on politeness-related concepts and behaviour" (ibid.). Eastern Europe, which since the end of World War II has, arguably, undergone even greater political, ideological and social changes than Western Europe, has been the subject of relatively little research in either intra- or intercultural politeness, and studies are still comparatively rare. Although the small number of participants and over-dependence on memory perhaps call for some caution in interpreting their results and drawing firm conclusions (as they themselves concede), Ogiermann and Suszczyńska, like Brown, are right to point to the relative neglect of political, historical and economic features in "previous theorising about politeness" (ibid.) and the clear need for further research.

Secondly, it is significant that this volume begins with a section of two chapters that are centrally focussed on 'face', a theoretical concept which, particularly since the publication of Brown and Levinson's (1987) work which attempted (among other things) to identify politeness universals in language usage, has dominated politeness theory, including more recent theoretical work on impoliteness. Although many current theorists suggest a return to Goffman's original work as a more fruitful and broadly based way forward than Brown and Levinson (see O'Driscoll, this volume; Bargiela-Chiappini 2003; Bousfield 2008), *perhaps it is time that the dominance of face-based models to explain the relationship between politeness and culture should be subject to more critical scrutiny in future work*. O'Driscoll considers the relationship between face and politeness explicitly, maintaining that "it is one of mutual hyponymy, not a causal one" (p. 22). He goes on to argue that the conception of politeness is culture-specific and that of face is cultural-neutral, the latter thus being the best candidate for a "second-order notion" (p. 23). Although this is certainly an arguable point and O'Driscoll puts forward a compelling case, the fact that the writers in this volume put forward a number of versions of face might make it seem questionable whether it is possible for any important analytical concept to be culturally neutral. Certainly, the chapters in this volume are diverse in their individual interpretations and applications of face (see Bogdanowska-Jakubowska, this volume, for a particularly complex model, stemming from the "concept of multiple selves": p. 241) and there is a continuing debate throughout the book as to whether people have face only when they are interacting, as O'Driscoll maintains or that face is, crucially and necessarily, also "a property of the individual" (Bogdanowsky-Jakubowska, p. 239) and essentially the same as self-image or even multiple selves.

Sifianou in her chapter on face and politeness agrees with O'Driscoll that "the concepts of face and facework are undoubtedly broader than that of politeness" (p. 49) but also explores in an interesting way the problems of translating the conceptualisation of 'face' in Greek and its related metaphorical expressions into English. She too argues that face "is not simply an image co-constructed in specific encounters" but in Greek, at least, "face is understood as an individual's property which may be modified in interaction" (ibid.). She also suggests that the concept of face in Greek seems to be a broader one than in English and that Greek has several terms for 'face', which serve related functions, centring primarily around crucial notions of honour and dignity and concludes that, unlike English, "face expressions in Greek are restricted to informal uses of language" (ibid.). What these examples seem to suggest is the difficulty of adopting face as the primary second-order notion in relationship to politeness in very different cultures and to raise the issue as to whether any such concept can truly be culturally neutral.

Finally, what is perhaps needed most urgently is an even more critical engagement with culture and its intersection with politeness, an increasingly sharply defined awareness not only of the complexities but the usefulness of both concepts as well as their conjunction. Mullany (Chapter 4), for example, uses as data "a series of [video-recorded] interactions between groups of men working on Canadian ice-roads as seasonal truck drivers", and demonstrates "how the interplay between im/politeness, gender and workplace culture can be observed through a communities of practice approach" (p. 62). Although the setting is Canadian, once again a context which is probably under-researched, her analysis highlights how the truckers use humour, along with expletives, as a strategic politeness and impoliteness device through which their gender and professional (rather than their national) cultural identities are enacted in a workplace situation. Mullany demonstrates how research which is explicitly focused on an occupational group engaged in a particular type of activity can be illuminating in terms of the conjunction of politeness and culture. Although her participants are primarily 'doing culture' according to Matsumoto's definition, they are at the same time engaged in constructing a more broadly based masculine gender identity, which must have a significant influence on their cultural 'worldview'.

Grainger's work on indirectness in Zimbabwean English (Chapter 9) also maintains a high level of critical engagement in taking an intercultural approach which is focused explicitly on 'indirectness'. She demonstrates clearly that because the latter "relies heavily on speakers' shared understanding of the situation for its communicative value, participants' perceptions of what is polite behaviour become crucial" (p. 172), necessitating an analytical methodology that combines both first- and second-order politeness. Grainger also, insightfully, sees the need to problematise the notion of 'culture'. She goes on to explain that "in cross-cultural and intercultural studies of politeness there can be a tendency to assume that language, nationality and culture are coterminous with one another and that they have homogeneous behaviours and practices" (p. 179), an assumption that clearly involves the risks which Brown also highlights, i.e. of overlooking crucial aspects of variation and ignoring contested norms. Yet, as Grainger argues, "if we do not attempt to talk about intercultural communication, how will we broach some of the problems of negative stereotyping and misunderstanding that can arise from ignorance and intolerance of difference?" (ibid.); an important question to which Grainger provides at least a tentative answer in her chapter based on encounters between herself and English speaking Zimbabweans in Sheffield.

Although as she says, "we need to be cautious, therefore, about what conclusions we draw about interactions between people of different nationalities", she is at the same time "convinced that people's interactional behaviour *is* connected to their experiences as members of various groups, including ethnic and national ones, and that this membership can at least in part explain common communication phenomena across people who share the same group memberships" (ibid.).

She concludes by aptly cautioning that

> where the participants do not share the same interpretation frameworks misunderstanding or misattribution of intention may result. There is great potential for the recipient of 'indirectness' to misinterpret it as vagueness, weakness or rudeness and ultimately for the deterioration of intercultural relations. (p. 189)

This is a significant conclusion and one that has practical as well as theoretical implications. By engaging with culture through a process of explicitly 'problematising' it, Grainger has managed to devise an analytical approach which is both thoughtful and illuminating.

I began by contending that both 'culture' and 'politeness' have long been resistant to canonical definition, and it seems to me that several of the chapters in this volume have provided evidence for Baumann's contention, with regard to culture at least, that "definitions…are not judged by their truth value but by their usefulness" (1996: 11), nor should they be. Indeed, Stolzenberg (2001) goes further to suggest that "it is precisely because of its lack of precision that culture remains a useful concept for both anthropologists and those outside the field". Perhaps both 'culture' and 'politeness' appear to be terms for which the 'disjunction of meanings' (Borofsky 2001: 433) they contain become something positive and useful and enduring. Once again, Stolzenberg goes further, suggesting that culture's most crucial role is to be "a placeholder for a set of inquiries" (2001: 444). This is not the same as saying that we should use the term *culture* unthinkingly or without definition in the context in which it is being applied – quite the reverse. Perhaps engaging critically with politeness research is also to view what is now more commonly cited as *im/politeness*, like *culture,* most usefully as 'a placeholder for a set of inquiries', fruitful and revealing as many of these have often proved to be in the past. With the shift in emphasis away from predictable norms of 'politeness behaviour' within stable language communities and towards the variable, argumentative and discursive in interactive encounters, politeness too has become a contested concept both theoretically and methodologically. Like Stolzenberg's version of culture, perhaps the time has come when "rather than seeking the concept's underlying essence or reality, we should view it as a conceptual tool that can be applied in different ways for different ends with different effectiveness" (Stolzenberg 2001: 433). This is what the best work in this volume has already achieved alongside the setting out of a challenging and exciting agenda for research in the future.

References

Bargiela-Chiappini, F. (2003) 'Face and Politeness: New (Insights) for (Old) Concepts', *Journal of Pragmatics*, 35, pp. 1452–1469.

Baumann, G. (1996) *Contesting Culture: Discourses of Identity in Multi-Ethnic London*, Cambridge, Cambridge University Press.

Borofsky, R. (2001) 'Introduction', in 'WHEN: A Conversation about Culture', *American Anthropologist*, 103/2, pp. 432–435.

Bousfield, D. (2008) *Impoliteness in Interaction*, Amsterdam and Philadelphia, John Benjamins.

Brown, P., and Levinson, S. (1978) 'Universals in Language Usage: Politeness Phenomena', in E.N. Goody (ed.), *Questions and Politeness*, Cambridge, Cambridge University Press, pp. 56–311.

Brown, P., and Levinson, S. (1987) *Politeness: Some Universals in Language Usage*, Cambridge, Cambridge University Press.

The Economist (2009) 'Hi there!', 19 December, pp. 115–117.

Goddard, C. (2010) 'Culture', in L. Cummings (ed.), *The Pragmatics Encyclopedia*, London, Routledge, pp. 95–97.

Matsumoto, D. (2006) 'Culture and Cultural World Views: Do Verbal Descriptions about Culture Reflect Anything Other Than Verbal Descriptions of Culture?', *Culture & Psychology*, 12/1, pp. 33–62.

Stolzenberg, N.M. (2001) 'What We Talk About When We Talk About Culture', in 'WHEN: A Conversation about Culture', *American Anthropologist*, 103/2, pp. 442–444.

Werkhofer, K. (1992) 'Traditional and Modern Views: The Social Constitution and the Power of Politeness', in R. Watts, S. Ide and K. Ehlich (eds), *Politeness in Language: Studies in Its History, Theory and Practice*, Berlin, Mouton de Gruyter, pp. 155–199.

Index of Names

Adams, K.L., 2, 12
Akdogan, P., 152, 168
Al Batal, M., 174, 178, 179, 192
Antaki, C., 92, 103
Arndt, H., 195, 214
Arundale, R.B., 18, 32, 34–36, 38, 43, 44, 48, 56, 195, 213, 216, 219, 234, 238, 239, 242, 243, 255
Avni, H., 88, 103

Babiniotis, D., 49, 56
Baek, E., 115, 125
Baker, P., 62, 67, 82
Baratz, S., 37, 41
Bargiela-Chiappini, F., 4, 12, 32, 38, 42, 43, 48, 56, 81, 217, 234, 237, 238, 240, 255, 261, 265
Baumann, G., 258, 264, 265
Baumeister, R.F., 239, 255
Bax, M., 2, 12
Baxter, J., 61, 62, 82
Bayraktaroğlu, A., 46, 55, 56
Bence, L., 195, 196, 213
Berger, T., 197, 213
Blondheim, M., 87, 91, 103
Blum-Kulka, S., 7, 9, 85–91, 93, 97, 102–105, 176, 177, 180, 190, 191, 198, 213, 259
Bodganoswka-Jakubowska, E., *see* Jakubowska
Bonn, M., 190, 191
Borofsky, R., 264, 265
Bousfield, D., 4, 12, 63, 75, 77, 78, 82, 83, 151, 167, 261, 265
Bowe, H., 173, 191
Bowers, J.W., 37, 40, 47, 57
Braun, F., 153, 167
Bravo, D., 37, 38, 47, 48, 56
Brislin, R., 239, 257
Brown, L. 7, 10, 121, 125, 259–261, 263
Brown, P., 3, 4, 7, 10, 13, 20–22, 28, 31, 33, 36–38, 42–44, 46–49, 54–56, 64, 65, 82, 130–133, 135, 146, 149–151, 167, 173–175, 177, 178, 183, 185, 186, 189, 191, 195, 213, 216, 234, 240, 243, 255, 258, 261, 265
Brown, R., 152, 167
Brown, W.J., 240, 257
Brückner, A., 197, 213
Bull, P., 87, 95, 96, 104
Butler, J., 67, 82
Byon, A., 125
Byrne, B., 197, 213

Caffi, C., 91, 104
Cameron, D., 62, 82
Carlson, T.B., 219, 234
Chen, L.z., 134, 148
Chen, R., 130, 131, 147
Chick, K., 180, 181, 191
Chilton, P., 87, 104
Cho, E., 112, 118, 125
Choi, S.H., 34, 40
Chŏng, C., 113, 126
Christie, C., 176, 177, 191
Chu, G.C., 240, 244, 255
Clark, H.H., 219, 234
Clyne, M., 182, 191
Coates, J., 62, 67, 68, 72, 82
Cobb-Moore, C., 90, 104
Connell, R., 62, 67, 82
Cook, H., 10, 13, 121, 125
Cooley, C.H., 239, 255
Corner, J., 102, 104
Corsaro, W.A., 88, 101, 104
Coulmas, F., 110, 125
Cromdal, J., 88, 104
Crozet, C., 220, 235
Culpeper, J., 11, 13, 22, 25, 39, 63–66, 77, 79, 82, 83, 151, 167, 172, 191
Czuchnowski, W., 246, 255

Danby, S., 90, 104
Danet, B., 87, 88, 103
Davies, B.L., 25, 39, 40

Davies, E., 171, 192
de Kadt, E., 32, 39, 46, 56, 152, 167, 179–181, 190, 191
DeVos, G., 244, 255
Domonkosi, Á., 195, 197, 213
Duan, J., 134, 135, 147
Durkheim, E., 243, 255

Earley, P.C., 240, 242, 255
Eckert, P., 62, 65, 83
Economidou-Kogetsidis, M., 25, 39
Eelen, G., 3, 4, 13, 22, 39, 43, 56, 86, 104, 108, 125, 150, 151, 167, 194–197, 214
Ehlich, K., 22, 41, 43, 58, 108, 127, 194, 214
El Bakary, W., 174, 178, 179, 192
Elliott, J., 87, 95, 96, 104
Endler, J.A., 2, 13
Ervin-Tripp, S., 49, 52, 55, 56, 217, 221, 235, 244, 255
Eun, J., 121, 125

Fairbank, J.K., 128, 147
Farrel, A., 90, 104
Ferenčik, M., 25, 39
Fitzsimons, A., 67, 83
Flick, U., 198, 214
Ford, M., 152, 167
Fraser, B., 216, 235
Fu, W., 50, 51, 55, 57

Galasiński, D., 204, 214
Gao, G., 34, 39
Garfinkel, H., 97, 103, 104
Gerson, R., 87, 88, 103
Geyer, N., 5, 13
Gilman, A., 152, 167
Goddard, A., 25, 39, 40
Goddard, C., 258, 259, 265
Goffman, E., 8, 13, 17–19, 21, 22, 24–30, 32, 33, 35, 36, 38, 39, 42–46, 48, 49, 51, 56, 66, 83, 86, 92, 97, 104, 133, 137, 138, 147, 216, 217, 235, 237, 238, 240, 242, 243, 255, 261
Goodenough, W., 152, 167
Gou, C.y., 129, 135, 147
Grainger, K., 6, 8, 10, 11, 179, 180, 182, 185, 191, 259, 263, 264
Gramsci, A., 67, 83
Grice, P., 2, 13, 38, 39, 43, 75, 132, 134, 135, 137, 146, 147, 185, 186, 191
Gu, Y., 3, 10, 128–148, 259
Gumperz, J., 171, 181, 182, 186, 191
Guo, J., 49, 52, 55, 56, 217, 221, 235, 244, 255

Hacohen, G., 87, 91, 103
Hadfield, H., 34, 37, 39
Hahn, J.-W., 34, 37, 39
Hamo, M., 85, 88, 102, 103, 104
Hankiss, E., 196, 214
Harris, S., 8, 82, 83, 150, 151, 167
Haugh, M., 23, 25, 35, 39, 40, 46, 48–50, 52, 55–57, 64, 83, 172, 191, 194, 195, 214, 217–219, 221, 227, 229, 233–235, 238, 255
Hayashi, S., 6, 13
Held, G., 108, 125
Herzfeld, M., 50, 54, 57
Hickey, L., 6, 13
Hill, B., 28, 39
Hinze, C., 49, 57, 217, 219, 233, 235
Hirschon, R., 46, 48, 50, 57
Ho, Y.-F.D., 45, 46, 50, 51, 55, 57, 216, 235, 238, 241, 242, 256
Hodder, I., 1, 13
Holliday, A.R., 179, 191
Holmes, J., 61, 70, 72, 80, 83, 229, 230, 235
Holtgraves, T., 173, 176, 178–180, 191
House, J., 176, 177, 180, 191
Hu, H.C., 238, 256
Huang, S.p., 134, 135, 147
Huck-Taglicht, D., 88, 103
Hui, C.H., 239, 257
Huszcza, R., 195, 214
Hwang, J., 107, 111, 114, 115, 125
Hymes, D., 29, 35, 39

Ide, S., 3, 6, 13, 14, 22, 28, 39, 41, 43, 57, 58, 108, 116, 125, 127, 148, 235
Ige, B.O., 180, 191
Ikuta, S., 28, 39
Irvine, J., 108, 112, 114, 115, 125
Işik-Güler, H., 23, 40, 50, 55, 58, 240, 256

Ishikawa, A., 153, 167
Iuzuka, H., 153, 167

Jakubowska, E., 7, 8, 12, 18, 45, 46, 195, 215, 241, 245, 251, 253–256, 259, 262
James, W., 241, 256
Janney, R., 195, 214
Jay, T., 75, 83
Jiang, T., 129, 134, 135, 147
Jin, Z.k., 129, 134, 135, 147
Johnson, D., 87, 105
Johnson. E.G., 174, 176–178, 192
Jupp, T., 171, 192

Kádár, D.Z., 2, 4–6, 11, 13, 14, 25, 35, 39, 131, 132, 147, 172, 179, 191, 192
Kamei, Y., 152, 167
Kampf, Z., 7, 9, 85–89, 93, 95, 99, 100, 103, 104, 259
Kamwangamulu, N., 190, 192
Kasanga, L.A., 180, 181, 192
Kasper, G., 176, 177, 180, 191
Katriel, T., 87, 94, 101, 104
Kawasaki, A., 28, 39
Kerbrat-Orecchioni, K., 5, 13
Kerswill, P., 82, 83
Kienpointner, M., 108, 125
Kiesling, S.F., 174, 176–178, 192
Kikvidze, Z., 153, 167
Kim, A.H., 10, 13
Kim, D., 112, 118, 125
Kim, Hee-jung, 117, 126
Kim, Hi-jean, 118, 119, 125
Kim, J., 116, 120, 126
Kim, S., 111, 126
Kim, Y., 118, 125
Kim-Renaud, Y., 118–121, 126
Kimmerling, B., 100, 104
King, R., 110, 124, 126
Kirkpatrick, D.D., 247, 256
Kiss, J., 195, 214
Kitayama, S. 240, 243, 244, 256
Kontra, M., 195, 214
Koo, J., 114, 115, 126
Koutlaki, S.A., 23, 46, 48, 57
Koutsantoni, D., 25, 39, 54, 55, 57
Koyama, W., 108, 110, 112, 126
Kriaras, E., 49, 57
Kurogi, A., 48, 58, 242, 257

Labaton, S., 247, 256
Lakoff, R. T., 1–3, 6, 13, 14, 87, 104
Lee, C., 118, 120, 122, 126
Lee, H., 114, 126
Lee, I., 112, 115, 124, 126
Lee, J., 118, 120, 126
Lee, K., 113, 124, 126
Lee-Wong, S.M., 152, 167
Leech, G., 2, 14, 130–132, 134, 135, 145–147, 173, 174, 176, 177, 192
Lévi-Strauss, C., 1, 14
Levinson, S. C., 3, 4, 7, 10, 13, 20–22, 28, 29, 31, 33, 36–39, 42–44, 46–49, 54–56, 64, 65, 82, 130–133, 135, 146, 149–151, 167, 173–175, 177, 178, 183, 185, 186, 189, 191, 195, 213, 216, 234, 240, 243, 255, 258, 261, 265
Li, J.w., 132, 147
Li, W., 131, 148
Li, Y., 131, 148
Liao, C.-c., 132, 133, 148
Liddicoat, A., 220, 235
Lim, D., 120, 126
Lim, T., 111, 126
Lim, T.-S., 23, 33, 34, 37, 39, 40, 47, 52, 57
Limberg, H., 63, 83
Lo Bianco, J., 220, 235
Locher, M., 4, 12, 14, 22, 24, 40, 43, 48, 57, 82, 83, 172, 182, 192
Lubecka, A., 195, 196, 214

Makino, S., 152, 167
Mao, L.M.R., 37, 40, 43, 46, 49, 57, 216, 217, 235, 237, 238, 243, 256
Marcjanik, M., 194, 196, 214
Markus, H.R., 117, 126
Marquez-Reiter, R., 25, 40
Marsella, A.J., 240, 256
Martin, K., 173, 191
Matsumoto, D., 259, 263, 265
Matsumoto, Y., 43, 46, 57, 217, 235
McConnell-Ginet, S., 62, 65, 83
Mead, G.H., 239, 241, 256

Merrison, A.J., 25, 39
Miller, E.F., 85, 105
Mills, S., 2, 4–6, 9, 13, 14, 22, 40, 64–66, 79, 81–83, 86, 105, 150, 151, 153, 167, 172, 179, 180, 182, 185, 192 191, 192, 194, 214
Milroy, L., 69, 83
Minami, F., 6, 13
Minya, K., 195, 214
Miyaki, M., 153, 167
Mor, E., 93, 105
Mullany, L., 6, 7, 9, 61, 65, 68, 83, 259, 262, 263
Myers, G., 25, 40

Nagao, A., 153, 167
Nakamura, K., 49, 52, 55, 56, 217, 221, 235, 244, 255
Nam, S., 113, 126
Naylor, L.L., 244, 256
Nelson, G., 174, 178, 179, 192
Ng, S.M., 50, 51, 55, 57
Nikolaishvili, M., 154, 167
Nogata, T., 153, 167
Nwoye, O.G., 3, 14, 32, 40, 43, 46, 57, 180, 192
Nyomárkay, I., 195, 214

O'Driscoll, J., 7, 8, 23, 28, 29, 33–37, 40, 43–45, 47, 48, 53, 55, 57, 172, 192, 216, 235, 237, 243, 253, 256, 261, 262
Ogiermann, E., 6–8, 11, 178, 192, 195, 214, 259–261
Ogino, T., 28, 39
Okamoto, S., 123, 126, 153, 167

Pacewicz, P., 248–250, 256
Palmer, D., 87, 95, 96, 104
Pan, Y., 133, 148, 151, 167
Park, T., 118, 125
Patterson, T.E., 85, 105
Pels, D., 102, 104
Penman, R., 240, 256
Perez de Ayala, S., 100, 105
Pérez-Peña, R., 247, 256
Peters, J.W., 250, 256
Pieczyński, A., 249, 250, 256
Pinker, S., 174–178, 183, 189, 192
Pizziconi, B., 10, 14, 25, 40

Ramsey, S.R., 112, 115, 124, 126
Raven, B.H., 234, 235
Reményi, A.Á., 195, 214
Roberts, C., 171, 179, 192
Ronowicz, E., 202, 215
Rotschild, J., 196, 215
Ruhi, Ş., 23, 40, 50, 55, 58, 240, 256
Rukhadze, N., 149, 152, 153, 166, 168
Rutenberg, J., 247, 256

Sarangi, S., 179, 192
Scannell, P., 136, 146, 148
Schlenker, B.R., 239, 257
Schnurr, S., 61, 65, 68, 83, 84
Schwartz, S.H., 218, 219, 222, 223, 227, 229, 230, 234, 235
Scollon, R., 49, 58, 149, 152, 153, 166, 168
Scollon, S.W., 49, 58, 149, 152, 153, 166, 168
Sells, P., 116, 120, 126
Sheldon, A., 87, 105
Shin, H., 124, 126
Showers, C.J., 241, 257
Shu, D.f., 130, 148
Sibanda, M., 179, 180, 182, 185, 191
Sifianou, M., 7, 8, 23, 25, 32, 34, 38, 40, 54, 58, 259, 262
Silverstein, M., 108, 109, 126, 174, 176, 192
Simmel, G., 86, 101, 105
Simonyi, Z., 197, 215
Singelis, T.M., 240, 257
Smith, T., 29, 40
Snow, C.E., 86, 103
Soh, J., 119, 126
Sohn, H., 107, 111, 114, 127
Spencer-Oatey, H., 25, 28, 37, 40, 41, 45, 46, 48, 58, 64–66, 81, 82, 84, 216–219, 221, 223, 235, 236, 238–240, 242, 257
Sperber, D., 176, 192
Spindler, G., 244, 257
Spindler, L., 244, 257
Stalpers, J., 92, 105

Stewart, J., 135, 148
Stewart, M., 6, 13
Stolzenberg, N.M., 264, 265
Strauss, S., 121, 125
Stubbe, M., 61, 70, 83
Sukle, R., 152, 168
Sunaoshi, Y., 216, 236
Suszczyńska, M., 6–8, 11, 195, 215, 259–261
Szili, K., 195, 215

Takiura, M., 220, 236
Tannen, D., 95, 105, 171, 173, 174, 176, 178, 179, 190–193
Terkourafi, M., 4, 14, 23, 25, 36, 41, 44, 46, 48, 55, 58, 150, 168, 195, 212, 215, 243, 257
Thomas, J., 29, 41, 173, 176–178, 187, 193
Thompson, B.J., 86, 95, 96, 102, 105
Thompson, M.W., 247, 256
Ting-Toomey, S., 35, 37, 41, 45, 47, 48, 58, 242, 257
Tótfalusi, I., 197, 215
Tracy, K., 28, 37, 41
Triandafyllidis, M., 49, 55, 58
Triandis, H.C., 54, 58, 239, 248, 257
Tutu, D., 190, 192

Ukosakul, M., 23, 34, 41, 48, 58

Vassiliou, V., 54, 58
Verschueren, J., 216, 236

Walker, G., 10, 14, 107, 109, 127
Walker, L., 87, 95, 96, 104
Wallace, K., 61, 62, 82
Wang, H., 124, 127
Wang, Hong, 130, 148
Wang, J.h., 134, 148
Wang, X.j., 129, 148
Watanabe, Y., 6, 8, 11, 45, 221, 235, 259
Watts, R.J., 1, 3, 4, 14, 22, 24, 40–43, 48, 53, 55, 57, 58, 82, 83, 86, 105, 108, 127, 135–137, 148, 150, 151, 168, 172, 182, 192, 194, 197, 198, 200, 212, 215
Weizman, E., 97, 105
Wenger, E., 7, 14, 65, 84
Werkhofer, K.D., 43, 45, 58, 213, 215, 261, 265
Wetherell, M., 92, 103
Wetzel, P., 110, 127
Wichmann, A., 63, 77, 83, 151, 167
Wierzbicka, A., 174–177, 179, 193, 195, 215
Wilson, D., 176, 192
Wilson, J.J., 25, 40
Wingfield, N.M., 196, 215
Winter, A., 2, 12
Wittgenstein, L., 137, 148
Wolfson, N., 29, 41
Wroński, P., 246, 255

Xing, S.j., 134, 148

Yabuuchi, A., 217, 236
Yang, D.h., 134, 148
Yeon, J., 110, 124, 127
Yeung, L.N.-T., 179, 193
Yoo, S., 118, 127
Yoon, K., 107, 112, 115, 117, 127
Yu, K., 111, 127
Yun, S., 124, 127

Zadunaisky-Ehrlich, S., 88–90, 103, 105
Zeigler-Hill, V., 241, 257
Zgółkowie, H., 195, 215
Zgółkowie, T., 195, 215
Zhong, J.w., 134, 148
Zhu, W.f., 131, 148

Index of Subjects

address forms, 152–153
  in Georgian, 153, 165
  in Hungarian, 196, 205, 207–208
  in Polish, 196, 203
apologies, 93
  in children's interaction, 93
  in political discourse, 98

collectivism, 244–245
communities of practice, 65, 86
conflict, 88, 101
  avoidance, 2–3
  and children, 88
  management, 89
conversation analysis, 217, 222
Cooperative Principle, 2, 3, 38, 132
corporate roles, 221, 223
culture, 35
  and children's interaction, 94
  conformity, 117
  definitions of, 196, 220
    (and problems with), 179
  Georgian, 151
  Israeli, 87
  and politeness in Korea, 123
  as 'third place', 220
  tripartite model of, 107, 109
  workplace culture, 65

discernment, 28, 29, 108, 230
distance (social)
  and autonomy face, 243
  and conflict avoidance, 2
  in Georgian, 146, 156, 165
  in Hungarian, 197, 212
  in Polish, 196, 199, 203–204, 254
  and terms of address, 251
diversity, 7, 8, 10, 142, 259
documentary media data, 63

emotion
  and cognition, 242
  and confrontation, 101, 248
  and face, 48, 50
  and masculinity, 67, 79
  and politeness, 146, 195, 199, 258
  public emotions, 52
  style, 93
ethnography, 181, 217

face
  African, 185
  autonomy face, 243
  in Belgian culture, 29
  cultural face model, 241
  and dignity, 50
  in dislocated communication, 27
  in English collocations, 30
  in Goffman, 24
    v. reputation, 25
    v. self-image, 25
  in Greek, 50
  group face, 32
  and honour, 48ff
  as image of self, 240
  in Israel, 87
  Japanese (*kao*), 227
  Korean (*cheymyoň*), 111
  longitudinal aspects of, 44
  in multiparty interaction, 234
  pan-situational, 242
  Polish concept of, 245
  and politeness, 22, 53
  and politicians, 95, 102
  as relational, 32
  and reputation, 25
  face sacrifice, 221
  situation-specific, 242
  and sociality rights, 66
  solidarity face, 243, 252–253, 255
  and speech acts, 29
  as wants, 33, 47
friendship
  in Hungary, 211
  in Israel, 89, 90, 93, 94, 101, 102

gender performativity, 67

hegemonic masculinity, 62
  and swearing, 80
hierarchy, 12, 99, 114, 115, 131, 143, 209, 229, 240, 242, 243
honorifics
  egalitarian use of, 117
  in Georgian, 158
  Korean, 110–112
  neo-Confucian ideology, 115
  non-normative use of, 118
  North Korea v South Korea, 117
  over-honorification, 120
humour, 68–70
  banter, 72–73, 80
  and expletives, 67, 80

impoliteness, 53, 64, 262–263
  In Chinese, 139
  definition of, 64, 79
  expletives, 67–68, 263
  Hungarian terms for, 207
  insults, 96
  Polish terms for, 201
  Swearing, 80
indirectness, 173ff
  African, 180
  in intercultural communication, 171
  off-record, 184, 188
  and politeness, 177ff
  and second-order politeness, 189
individualism, 46, 244, 245
in-group/out-group, 149
  in Georgia, 151–152, 164–165
  in Poland, 246
  in professional settings, 156
intercultural sociolinguistics, 182
interviews, 122, 155, 180, 197–198, 212

language city, 137

metaphor
  and 'face', 8, 27, 30, 37, 38, 42, 50, 54, 262
  and politics, 85, 86, 101

norms/normative, 2, 3, 5–7, 9, 10, 12, 23, 33, 35, 46, 51–53, 65, 67, 80, 94, 101, 102, 107, 109–120, 122, 123, 134, 141, 149, 150, 153, 155, 163, 165, 179, 185, 195, 198, 216, 218–220, 234, 240, 242, 243, 252, 263, 264

politeness
  in Chinese, *limao* (*li*), 129, 135
    liyi, 134
    self-denigration/other elevation, 130, 132
  deference, 112
  discursive approaches to, 5, 6, 14, 64, 67
  first-order politeness, 22
    and indirectness, 189
  in Hungarian, 196
  in Korean (*chaudae*) (*kongson*), 111
  lay (understanding of politeness), 4, 5, 10, 11, 42, 54, 55, 108, 111, 117, 120, 123, 195–197, 199, 212
  Leech's maxims, 130
  as lived experience, 146
  in Polish, 197, 203
  as relational, 139
  non-verbal, 136
  postmodernist approach to, 136
  respect, 114
  second-order politeness, 172
    and indirectness, 189
  tripartite experiential characterization of, 139
  wakimae, 106
power, 67, 80
  and address forms, 150
  in communist Poland, 202
  in communist Hungary, 209
  and humour, 68
  in institutional contexts, 151
  and Korean honorifics, 123
  in political contexts, 96
  in pretend play, 92
  as a value construct, 218

rapport management, 65
  and humour, 70
refusals, 91–92, 99

self, 240, 254
  American concept of, 244
  Chinese concept of, 131
  creation of, (in Goffman), 238
  as multiple selves, 241
  Polish concept of, 244–245
  self-presentation, 239
  and southern African 'face', 185
sociality
  in children, 88, 92
    rights, 66
      in workplace interaction, 78
      see also rapport management
  and im/politeness, 86
solidarity, 9, 68, 69, 72, 80, 94, 98,
    101, 122, 131, 152, 153, 158,
    162, 163, 210, 230, 248, 250
  see also 'solidarity face'

'third place', 220
third parties (role of), 219, 230

value constructs (Schwartz's), 218
  and face, 227, 230